Monika Reif and Justyna A. Robinson (Eds.)
Cognitive Perspectives on Bilingualism

Trends in Applied Linguistics

Edited by
Ulrike Jessner
Claire Kramsch

Volume 17

Cognitive Perspectives on Bilingualism

Edited by
Monika Reif and Justyna A. Robinson

DE GRUYTER
MOUTON

ISBN 978-1-5015-1632-0
e-ISBN (PDF) 978-1-61451-419-0
e-ISBN (EPUB) 978-1-5015-0040-4
ISSN 1868-6362

Library of Congress Cataloging-in-Publication Data
A CIP catalog record for this book has been applied for at the Library of Congress.

Bibliographic information published by the Deutsche Nationalbibliothek
The Deutsche Nationalbibliothek lists this publication in the Deutsche Nationalbibliografie;
detailed bibliographic data are available on the Internet at http://dnb.dnb.de.

© 2016 Walter de Gruyter Inc., Boston/Berlin
This volume is text- and page- identical with the hardback published in 2016.
Cover image: Roswitha Schacht/morguefile.com
Typesetting: RoyalStandard, Hong Kong
Printing and binding: CPI books GmbH, Leck
♾ Printed on acid-free paper
Printed in Germany

www.degruyter.com

Table of contents

V **Concluding remarks**

Acknowledgements

The growing need for research in bilingualism is being motivated by academic and professional interests as well as the public debates which seek a greater understanding of linguistic implications of multilingual social situations. In response to that need, the idea for the present volume was formed. Concrete plans for this collection of research grew out of thought-provoking discussions at the 35th International LAUD Symposium on "Cognitive Psycholinguistics: Bilingualism, Cognition and Communication", which was held in March 2012 at the University of Koblenz-Landau. With support from de Gruyter editors we cooperated with established and emerging scholars in the field to bring forward cutting-edge research which tackles the phenomenon of bilingualism from various perspectives. The outcome of these efforts is the present volume entitled *Cognitive Approaches to Bilingualism*. We would like to take this opportunity to thank all the contributors to this volume for producing impressive scholarly work and for conscientiously responding to revisions and other requests. Furthermore we are grateful to all external reviewers for helping us achieve a high quality publication. This book would not have happened without the continuous support of Lara Wysong from de Gruyter and Birgit Sievert, who first initiated our cooperation with the publisher. We would also like to thank our colleagues and families for giving us the support and time that allowed us to bring the book to completion. In this vein, special thanks go to Martin Pütz, the main organizer of the biannual LAUD Symposia, who sparked our interest in cognitive aspects of bilingualism and provided a platform that enabled us to get in contact with leading researchers in the field.

The Editors
Monika Reif & Justyna A. Robinson

Contributors

Catrin Bellay
Centre de Recherche sur les Identités Nationales et l'Interculturalité
Université de Nantes
Faculté des Langues et Cultures Etrangères
Chemin de la Censive du Tertre
44312 Nantes
France
Email: catrin.bellay@orange.fr

HuiPing Chan
University of Groningen
Chemin de Rionza 5
Renens
Switzerland
Email: huipingchan1981@gmail.com

Kees de Bot
University of Groningen
Oude Kijk in 't Jatstraat 26
9712 EK Groningen
The Netherlands
Email: c.l.j.de.bot@gmail.com

Antje Endesfelder Quick
Max Planck Institute for Evolutionary Anthropology
Department of Developmental and Comparative Psychology
Deutscher Platz 6
04103 Leipzig
Germany
AND
University of Leipzig
GWZ – English Department
Beethovenstraße 15
04107 Leipzig
Germany
Email: antje.quick@eva.mpg.de

Nikolay Hakimov
University of Freiburg
German Department
Platz der Universität 3
79098 Freiburg
Germany
Email: Nikolay.Hakimov@posteo.de

István Kecskés
Professor of Linguistics and Communication
School of Education
State University of New York
Albany
USA
Email: ikecskes@albany.edu

Elena Lieven
The ESRC International Centre for Language and Communicative
Development (LuCiD)
School of Psychological Sciences
Coupland 1
University of Manchester
Manchester M139PL
United Kingdom
Email: elena.lieven@manchester.ac.uk

Wander Lowie
University of Groningen
Oude Kijk in 't Jatstraat 26
9712 EK Groningen
The Netherlands
Email: W.M.Lowie@rug.nl

Pieter Muysken
Radboud University
Centre for Language Studies
Department of Linguistics
Erasmusplein 1
6525 HT Nijmegen
The Netherlands
Email: p.muysken@let.ru.nl

Monika Reif
Universität Koblenz-Landau
Fach Anglistik
Fortstrasse 7
76829 Landau
Germany
Email: reif@uni-landau.de

Justyna A. Robinson
School of English
Arts B
University of Sussex
Falmer, Brighton BN1 9QN
United Kingdom
Email: justyna.robinson@sussex.ac.uk

Michael Tomasello
Max Planck Institute for Evolutionary Anthropology
Department of Developmental and Comparative Psychology
Deutscher Platz 6
04103 Leipzig
Germany
Email: tomas@eva.mpg.de

Philipp Wasserscheidt
Humboldt-Universität zu Berlin
Institut für Slawistik
Unter den Linden 6
10099 Berlin
Germany
Email: philipp.wasserscheidt@hu-berlin.de

I Introductory remarks

Monika Reif and Justyna A. Robinson
Introduction

While the study of bilingualism goes back to ancient times (cf. Lewis 1977) and a myriad of empirical explorations have sought to investigate the language development and behavior of bilingual users, the emergence of new (interdisciplinary) theories and methodologies requires a constant reinterpretation of findings and revision of study designs. Since the late 1980s, cognition-oriented and constructionist approaches to language (e.g. Langacker's Cognitive Grammar, Goldberg's Construction Grammar, Croft's Radical Construction Grammar) have shifted the focus from structural analyses to studies and theories of the bilingual mind. At the same time, the increasing use of computer-assisted, longitudinal bilingual corpora, as well as advances on the methodology front in the cognitive neurosciences and in psycholinguistics, have opened up new doors to the bilingual mind. In a context where a range of bilingual phenomena are encountered, for many speakers on a daily basis, there is a great need for theoretical, empirical and methodological frameworks to be regularly revised, updated and challenged.

By bringing together scholars from various disciplines, including cognitive linguistics, psycholinguistics, (bilingual) language acquisition research and anthropology, the current volume aims at gaining a greater understanding of the phenomenon of bilingualism. In the theory-oriented contributions to the present volume, the focus lies on areas of bilingual competence (e.g. the development of pragmatic knowledge in bilinguals) that have only been touched upon in the research to date, as well as more recent theoretical models of language (e.g. Construction Grammar) in the light of which bilingual speech phenomena such as code-mixing may need to be reinterpreted. The empirical studies contained in this volume unanimously endorse a usage-based perspective on language, taking into account probabilistic input values as a potentially crucial factor influencing bilingual language development and use.

In this book we conceive of bilingualism as encompassing a range of phenomena where two or more linguistic codes interact in creating linguistic outputs. Although in most cases bilingualism will be used to refer to a typical 'one speaker, two languages' situation, we also use the shorthand of bilingualism to refer to multilingualism and phenomena such as code-mixing and code-switching. The problem of defining bilingualism has been extensively discussed in the literature, and depending on the criteria employed (e.g. age of onset; levels of proficiency in pronunciation, morpho-syntax and lexis; degree of competence in the four language skills of speaking, writing, listening and reading; context of acquisition; frequency of exposure and use in various domains) varying definitions have been suggested. While the popular perception of bilingualism pictures bilinguals as individuals with a native-like competence in both their languages (compare also Bloomfield's (1933) maximalist view), other approaches are extreme in the other direction by proposing that anyone with a minimal L2 competence in one of the four skills may be regarded as bilingual (cf. Macnamara 1967 for a minimalist perspective). For the purpose of this volume, we assume a rather "open" notion of bilingualism which does not stipulate any definite cutoff points (but continua) and therefore also includes the sequential acquisition of a second language in childhood/early adolescence in the category of bilingual language development. We see bilingualism as a dynamic process that has a mutual impact on both languages involved and is heavily influenced by the linguistic and social environment of the speaker. In this latter respect, our view incorporates Mohanty's (1994: 13) definition, who posits that "bilingual persons [...] are those with an ability to meet the communicative demands of the self and the society in their normal functioning in two or more languages in their interaction with the other speakers of any or all of these languages". While the discussion of cognitive processes and effects of bilingualism lies at the heart of this volume, it is important not to lose sight of the pragmatic and socio-cultural dimensions.

The present volume brings together theoretical considerations and empirical findings on patterns observable in bilingual language development and production. In the theory-oriented contributions, largely neglected language levels (i.e. pragmatics) in bilingualism research are discussed, as well as recent theoretical frameworks (i.e. Construction Grammar) which may necessitate a reinterpretation of the bilingual data collected so far. In the empirical studies, bilingual phenomena such as code choice and code mixing/switching are analysed from a usage-based perspective, hence taking into account input frequencies and (syntactic) primes as potential factors influencing bilingual language production and development. It is shown that frequency of exposure to certain linguistic constructions may have an impact on switch placement in code-mixed utterances, and may also shape the lexical acquisition process in bilingual language learners. Furthermore, the immediate co-text surrounding a particular speech act may serve as a trigger for code choices, an aspect that is investigated with the help of bilingual corpora and experimental priming paradigms.

The present volume contains three thematic strands which are bookended with an extended introductory chapter and a concluding commentary. **Part I, *Introductory remarks***, offers an overview of recent developments and future directions in the linguistic study of individual bilingualism (also termed *bilinguality*; cf. Hamers and Blanc 2000), mainly from the research perspective of usage-based and cognitively-oriented approaches. **Robinson** and **Reif** critically discuss key topics as well as methodological advances in the field. Particular room is given to the bilingual phenomenon of code-mixing/code-switching, since a usage-based account may shed new light on (previous) findings related to code choice. All in all, Robinson and Reif endorse the furthering of interdisciplinary approaches to bilingual language use and users.

Part II, *Theoretical considerations in bilingualism research*, reflects two recent developments in theory building, i.e. the integration of the pragmatic level into investigations of bilingual language knowledge and use, and the reinterpretation of bilingual language data from the perspective of current linguistic frameworks such as Cognitive Linguistics and Construction Grammar. The first paper in this section offers theoretical perspectives on a rather neglected area in the field of bilingualism, i.e. the development of pragmatic knowledge in bilinguals. **István Kecskés** in his contribution **"Bilingual pragmatic competence"** focuses on analyzing how the emerging new language with its own developing socio-cultural foundation affects the existing L1-governed knowledge and pragmatic competence of adult sequential bilinguals. Kecskés demonstrates that there is a difference between the development of pragmatic competence in L1 and the development of bilingual pragmatic competence. While the former is controlled mainly by the socio-cultural environment, the latter is mostly motivated by individual will. In the L1 context, language development and social development go hand in hand as subconscious, automatic and instinctive processes in which the individual consciousness and willingness to acquire social skills and knowledge play a limited role. These processes depend mainly on the exposure to and nature of the socio-cultural environment of the individual. However, bilingual pragmatic competence develops differently. The process is affected by individual control, consciousness and willingness to modify existing skills and behavior patterns. In other words, bilinguals control what they find acceptable from the norms and conventions of the L2 (and occasionally L1); they control which particular social skills to acquire and which to ignore. One of the key consequences of this view is that the language socialization process in subsequent languages may not take place through osmosis. Kecskés shows that contrary to previous research, bilingual conceptual socialization relies predominantly on the learners' investment in language rather than just on extended social networks.

Kecskés' paper provides a range of examples in support of this 'hands-on' view of bilingual pragmatic competence. However, Kecskés argues that the individual control of the pragmatic socialization is most clearly demonstrated in the use of situation-bound utterances, such as English *have a good one* or Turkish *gülü gülü oturun* 'stay laughingly'. These formulaic expressions represent cultural models and ways of thinking of members of a particular speech community.

Thus, since the use of formulaic expressions is group identifying, pragmatic competence is directly tied to and developed through the use of such formulas.

Philipp Wasserscheidt in his paper **"Construction grammar and code-mixing"** also offers a more theoretical take on bilingual phenomena. He suggests that constructionist approaches to grammar (e.g. Goldberg 1995, 2006; Croft 2001) possess some promising qualities to account for typical occurrences in bilingual language production, such as code-mixing and loan translations. His argumentation mainly focuses on the following three characteristics. Firstly, construction grammar aims at covering all levels of language within one consistent model and using primarily one theoretical notion, that is, *constructions*. It abandons the principled distinction between, for example, lexis and grammar, viewing language as a network of constructions of varying degrees of complexity and abstraction instead. Therefore, it seems well suited to provide explanations for highly complex phenomena such as code-mixing, where all language levels and a wide variety of features may be involved. Secondly, since constructions are defined as socially conventionalized and individually entrenched form-meaning pairings (or units), accounts of switch triggers and switch placement in code-mixed utterances may also make reference to the conceptual-semantic pole and the phonological pole of a construction, not just its formal structure. Thus, differing semantic loads of constructions may serve as a motivation for bilingual speakers to choose one construction over another one, and phonologically similar constructions may act as a switch trigger in bilingual language production (see Wasserscheidt's example *I have to bring my Ukrainian passport so mnoj*, where the inter-lingual homophone *passport* may have tempted the speaker to switch codes).

This essentially leads to a reformulation of the Matrix Language Frame Model (cf. Myers-Scotton 1993 for the original version), insofar as not languages, but constructions are assumed to serve as a matrix frame in Wasserscheidt's model. Wasserscheidt (this volume) proposes that "the phonologically specified elements of a construction [. . .] form some kind of matrix that can be filled with elements from any language". Furthermore, he hypothesizes that constructions need to be processed and produced as holistic units in language use. Corpus examples containing loan translations (e.g. the Dutch-Turkish expression *piano oynamak*) are analyzed within this context, resulting in the claim that in loan translations, bilinguals use a construction from language A but translate part of the signifiers into language B; the constructional meaning is thus left intact. Thirdly, in line with Hakimov's probabilistic approach to switch placement (see this volume), Wasserscheidt provides evidence for the position that code-mixing is essentially a statistical phenomenon. This claim is based on the usage-oriented nature of constructionist approaches, which hold that any language can be captured solely by virtue of frequency-based descriptions of the linguistic means a speech community employs. In consequence, conventionalized practices of code-mixing in a particular bilingual community may even be described in their own right, and it is rendered impossible for us to make universal *a priori* predictions about concrete structural realizations of code-mixed utterances.

After considering theoretical aspects of bilingualism, the papers in the following two parts shift the focus towards the exploration bilingualism on the ground. **Part III, *Input-related cognitive effects in code-mixing***, analyses data containing mixed output in order to tackle two important questions. First, what role does input frequency play in bilingual language representation and use, and second, to what extent is linguistic information integrated across languages, which may in turn have an effect on language choice in the bilingual output.

With the rise of usage-based approaches to language acquisition and language use, research on bilingual language production has also started to take into account probabilistic information as a potential factor influencing bilingual speakers' choice between competing structures. Frequency and recency effects can be studied, e.g. through the analysis of bilingual corpora or by means of experimental priming studies. The purpose of **Nikolay Hakimov's** contribution **"Effects of frequency and word repetition on switch-placement"** is to account for patterns of insertional code-mixing in German-Russian bilinguals by considering co-occurrence frequencies and word repetition as predictors of switch placement. All of the analyzed data have been derived from a corpus of German-Russian bilingual speech recorded in various Russian-speaking communities across Germany. The participants of the study belong to the intermediate generation of Russian-German late repatriates. Prepositional phrases (PP) were chosen as the target phenomenon under investigation because PPs have widely been reported to be among the most commonly affected elements in code-mixing. Since the switch may occur either at the phrase boundary, e.g. a German PP inserted into a Russian clause, or within the phrase, e.g. a German noun phrase embedded into a Russian PP, the question arises as to which factors determine switch placement in which contexts.

In Hakimov's present study, the following aspects are hypothesized to influence switch placement. Firstly, the frequency of the PP, i.e. of the specific preposition– noun phrase combination, in native language use is considered. Along the lines of the unit hypothesis (Backus 2003), it can be argued that frequent morpheme combinations have become entrenched as units in the bilingual's mental lexicon and are therefore also produced as holistic chunks, repelling a switch between the preposition and the noun phrase and instead resulting in switch placement at the boundary to adjacent syntactic elements. With low-frequency combinations, by contrast, a switch seems more probable within the prepositional phrase. Secondly, the general frequency of usage of individual nouns occurring in the examined PPs may have an impact on switch placement because high frequency nouns can trigger prepositions typically accompanying them and can thus block phrase-internal switches. Lastly, in conjunction with the effect of repetition priming, a particular lexical realization of the PP is assumed to be more likely if the preceding discourse contains identical lexical material.

For the statistical analyses, Hakimov takes his own German-Russian bilingual corpus as a starting point to select the set of PPs to be investigated, to calculate co-occurrence frequencies (i.e. the strengths of association between particular nouns and prepositions) and to examine possible lexical priming effects. However, in order to retrieve representative frequency values for individual nouns as well as preposition–noun combinations in native language use, one needs to rely on larger monolingual corpora, which is why these data are extracted from the deWaC, a 1.6 billion word corpus constructed from the web. Hakimov's results provide evidence that "an interplay of usage and processing factors is capable of predicting switch placement in the context of the prepositional phrase in Russian-German code-mixing" (this volume). While the strongest predictor of switch placement appears to be a prior occurrence of the preposition in question, serving as a prime, the two other hypotheses can also be supported: Co-occurrence frequencies for prepositions and noun phrases as well as usage frequencies of individual nouns are shown to affect switch placement (phrase-internal vs. phrase boundary switches).

Much research on bilingualism has also addressed the question of the extent to which grammatical information is integrated across languages. While the separate syntax account holds that bilinguals have separate representations for each language, the shared syntax account assumes that those constructions or rules which are identical or at least similar in both languages are only represented once (cf., for example, Hartsuiker, Pickering and Veltkamp 2004; McDonough and Trofimovich 2011). Cross-linguistic syntactic priming is a relatively recent technique in bilingualism research and has been applied to explore how bilinguals process and represent syntactic information. Syntactic priming refers to "the tendency for speakers to produce a particular syntactic structure (as opposed to an equally acceptable structure) after recent exposure to that structure" (McDonough and Trofimovich 2011: 98). That is, the syntactic structure of the initial prime is believed to facilitate subsequent production of the same syntactic structure due to residual activation (ibid.: 98). In their study on **"Mixed NPs in German-English and German-Russian bilingual children"**, **Antje Endesfelder Quick, Elena Lieven** and **Michael Tomasello** investigate cross-language activation and (shared) mental representations in young children aged 3;6 to 5;6. Also using a cross-linguistic syntactic priming paradigm, their aim is to find out if structural as well as functional similarities and differences between the languages of the bilingual participants correlate with positive/ negative priming effects, which may provide evidence for or against the above-mentioned syntax representation models. While the separate syntax account would not expect cross-linguistic priming to occur since activation of linguistic information in one language is not assumed to affect subsequent output in the other language, the shared syntax account would predict cross-linguistic priming for any related syntactic constructions. Endesfelder Quick et al. focus on the grammatical phenomenon of noun phrases in German, English and Russian, since these show systematic cross-linguistic overlaps and differences in their form and function: German noun phrases typically consist of a determiner and a noun, and grammatical gender is marked on the determiner. English noun phrases display the same determiner-noun structure, but are not marked for grammatical gender at all. Russian does not have any definite/indefinite determiners, but has gender marking, whereby grammatical gender is indicated on the noun itself. In their priming experiment, Endesfelder Quick et al. attempt to elicit mixed noun phrases from German-English and German-Russian bilingual children with the help of monolingual interlocutors. In various games, the bilingual participants are supposed to label novel objects while interacting with different (monolingual) conversation partners. The results show that German-English bilinguals produce significantly more mixed noun phrases than German-Russian bilinguals, suggesting that similarity in grammatical structure may facilitate mixing and that the grammatical systems interact in language production, possibly due to shared representations. Two further factors that are taken into account refer to the age of the participants and their preferred language strategies at home. Here, the findings suggest that older children as well as children who have been reported to use code-mixing in the home are more likely to provide answers and also to answer in the primed language.

In **Part IV**, *Input sources in bilingual language development*, contributions focus on answering the question as to what extent input from sources outside the commonly investigated interactions, such as parent–child communication and classroom conversations, influences bilingual children's and learners' output. Child-targeted material (e.g. nursery rhymes, songs, children's stories), as well as technology-mediated input/communication (e.g. via smartphones, internet sources, social media) are considered as potential factors shaping the acquisition/learning process of bilinguals. Both contributions in this section present results from longitudinal studies involving four cases of child bilingualism (Bellay) and four cases of early L2 learning (Chan, Lowie and de Bot).

Catrin Bellay in her contribution discusses **"Musical, audio-visual, poetic, and narrative input: A longitudinal case study of French-English bilingual**

first language acquisition". She shows that children treat the linguistic material they acquire from nursery rhymes, songs, stories and children's television as part of their linguistic repertoire, and readily quote it and deploy it in regular conversation. Bellay carefully analyses data taken from a longitudinal observation of four French-English bilingual siblings living in France. The English language input for these children has mainly come from their mother and a collection of English DVDs, read aloud stories and nursery rhymes that were provided by the mother of the children. Bellay proposes a set of criteria to support intuitive judgements that a particular item of child language production is an instance of use of linguistic material from a nursery rhyme, storybook, or children's film/television programme. Thus, the analysis of data revolves around examples of productive use of four kinds of phrases from the input (i.e. verbatim quote, verbatim borrowing, verbatim repetition, and adapted reuse) and three types of responses to the ongoing communicative situation (i.e. response to the wording of the preceding utterance(s), response to the conversational context, response to the thematic context). For example, Bellay analyzes the use of a child's thematic response "It's pouring?" to a mother's directive "Put your hood up. It's raining" as a type of verbatim borrowing from a common nursery rhyme ("It's raining, it's pouring, the old man is snoring..."). For some examples, Bellay also makes suggestions about the possible linguistic and pragmatic knowledge developed by the children through exposure to the source item, and discusses the way the children have applied that knowledge to the interaction in which the example occurred. The bilingual context of this study also provides insights into the development of natural translation competence in these simultaneous bilinguals, and its application to the specific skill of oral narrative translation.

"**Input outside the classroom and vocabulary development: A dynamic perspective**" is a paper co-authored by **HuiPing Chan**, **Wander Lowie** and **Kees de Bot**. Although learners have had access to second language usage via the internet, smartphones, and computers for a while, the role that such 'external' language input outside the classroom plays in second language acquisition has hardly been given due consideration. In this context, the authors focus on investigating whether the quality of written language samples (operationalized in terms of lexical sophistication) of English language learners changes depending on the amount of their exposure to input outside the classroom. The data for this study comes from the analysis of fifty-six written productions of four low-proficient Taiwanese beginning learners of English who received differing degrees of quantitative input over five months. These speakers were asked to keep a log of their English language exposure outside the classroom. Thus, they wrote about online news read on Breaking News English, free online movies watched in English with Chinese subtitles on Tube+, the latest English music videos watched on YouTube, English songs they listened to on iTunes, and Facebook conversations in English. The authors used a logistic model to explicitly investigate the three dynamically interacting factors that shaped the process of the lexical development, i.e. initial value, learning rate, and carrying capacity. Their results, focusing on the process rather than the product of vocabulary learning, demonstrate that each learner's vocabulary learning process was variably dependent on input outside the classroom.

This study shows that learners, with input outside the classroom, kept themselves in an English context and benefited from having more opportunities for using English. With pure incidental English input in the form of movies and online reading, the increase of lexical sophistication was approximately 500 words in five months. Although this longitudinal study has collected data on a relatively short-term time scale, it provides a new understanding of the dynamics of actual vocabulary development.

In **Part V**, *Concluding remarks*, **Pieter Muysken** critically reflects upon the diversity of topics, language pairs, theoretical approaches and methodologies by which current studies of bilingualism are characterized and provides an outlook, including a list of desiderata, for future research. Before discussing the main points raised in this paper, we would like to draw attention to the way Muysken regrouped the papers in the present volume (in contrast to our grouping) for the sake of illustrating similarities and differences between the various approaches. This slightly deviating classification, which uses criteria such as simultaneous vs. sequential bilingualism or corpus-based vs. theoretical approaches, nicely shows that different perspectives on the same bilingual phenomena (and studies) are feasible. A multi-dimensional and diverse view on bilingual data is an aspect that should be continuously enhanced in the research of bilingualism, as is also argued by Robinson and Reif (this volume), who comment that the most fruitful ways forward in bilingualism research is precisely the incorporation of multiple perspectives in bilingual epistemologies.

However, next to all the positive aspects that multidisciplinarity and methodological diversity bring with them, there is always also a risk of terminological confusion and concomitant definitional inexactitude. According to Muysken, one major point for improvement in bilingualism research pertains to the terminological jungle which has grown over the years and which has – at least to some extent – led to obscurity (and in turn conceptual vagueness) in the field. Muysken conducts a contrastive analysis of the terminology used in the contributions to this volume, thereby showing how varied the vocabulary can be. According to Muysken, the main danger deriving from this diversity lies in an insufficient integration of different research paradigms (cf. also Robinson and

Reif, this volume). However, the final part of Muysken's commentary focuses on cross-study similarities and recent trends, particularly stressing the usage-based nature and cognitive orientation of the papers included here – a tendency that can also be observed in other publications of the past decade (e.g. Schwieter's *Cambridge Handbook of Bilingual Processing* (2015), Grosjean and Li's *The Psycholinguistics of Bilingualism* (2013), Pavlenko's *Thinking and Speaking in Two Languages* (2011), Kecskés and Albertazzi's *Cognitive Aspects of Bilingualism* (2007), and Kroll and De Groot's *Handbook of Bilingualism: Psycholinguistic Approaches* (2009), to name just a few). Thus, the present volume reflects current developments in (cognitive and usage-based) bilingualism research, while at the same time identifying some of the challenges, if not even weaknesses, that still persist in the field. In this vein, we hope that the volume brings us, i.e. the academic community, professionals, members of the general public, closer to a greater understanding of the meaning and consequences of this fascinating part of human communication.

References

Backus, Ad. 2008. Data banks and corpora. In Li Wei & Melissa G. Moyer (eds.), *The Blackwell guide to research methods in bilingualism and multilingualism*, 232–248. Malden, MA: Blackwell.

Bloomfield, Leonard. 1933. *Language*. New York: Henry Holt.

Croft, William. 2001. *Radical Construction Grammar: Syntactic theory in typological perspective*. Oxford: Oxford University Press.

Goldberg, Adele. 2006. *Constructions at work: The nature of generalization in language*. Oxford: Oxford University Press.

Goldberg, Adele. 1995. *Constructions: A construction grammar approach to argument structure*. Chicago: University of Chicago Press.

Grosjean, Francois & Ping Li. 2013. *The psycholinguistics of bilingualism*. Malden, MA & Oxford: Wiley-Blackwell.

Hamers, Josiane F. & Michel H. A. Blanc. 2000. *Bilinguality and bilingualism*. Cambridge: Cambridge University Press.

Hartsuiker, Robert J., Martin Pickering & Eline Veltkamp. 2004. Is syntax separate or shared between languages? Cross-linguistic syntactic priming in Spanish-English bilinguals. *Psychological Science* 15(6). 409–414.

Kecskés, István & Liliana Albertazzi (eds.). 2007. *Cognitive aspects of bilingualism*. Dordrecht: Springer.

Kroll, Judith F. & Annette M. B. De Groot (eds.). 2009. *Handbook of bilingualism: Psycholinguistic approaches*. Oxford: Oxford University Press.

Lewis, E. Glyn. 1977. Bilingualism and bilingual education: The ancient world of the renaissance. In Bernard Spolsky & Robert L. Cooper (eds.), *Frontiers of bilingual education*, 22–93. Rowley, MA: Newbury House.

Macnamara, John. 1967. The Bilingual's Linguistic Performance. A Psychological Overview. *Journal of Social Issues* 23(2). 58–77.

McDonough, Kim & Pavel Trofimovich. 2011. Expanding the scope of priming research. In Pavel Trofimovich & Kim McDonough (eds.), *Applying priming methods to L2 learning, teaching and research*, 241–250. Amsterdam: John Benjamins.

Mohanty, Ajit K. 1994. *Bilingualism in a multilingual society: Psychosocial and pedagogical implications.* Mysore: Central Institute of Indian Languages.

Myers-Scotton, Carol. 1993. *Duelling languages: Grammatical structure in codeswitching.* Oxford: Oxford University Press.

Pavlenko, Aneta (ed.). 2011. *Thinking and speaking in two languages.* Bristol, Buffalo & Toronto: Multilingual Matters.

Robinson, Justyna A. & Monika Reif. 2016. Understanding bilingualism: Trends, challenges and perspectives. In: Monika Reif & Justyna A. Robinson (eds.), *Cognitive approaches to bilingualism*, 15–36. Berlin/Boston: de Gruyter.

Schwieter, John W. 2015. *The Cambridge Handbook of bilingual processing.* Cambridge: Cambridge University Press.

Justyna A. Robinson and Monika Reif

Understanding bilingualism: Trends, challenges and perspectives

Abstract: This chapter presents a critical overview of the main theoretical and methodological approaches that have been pursued in bilingualism research. Particular attention is paid to paradigms which investigate bilingual speech from a usage-based and cognitive-linguistic perspective. Although such studies are relatively recent, we argue that they offer vast explanatory potential with regard to contact phenomena such as code-mixing/switching and with regard to the neural representation of a bilingual's two (or more) languages in the brain. This is especially evident in cases where the cognitive approach incorporates socio-cultural epistemological frameworks. The chapter concludes by proposing that our understanding of bilingualism can be best enhanced by integrating a more interdisciplinary perspective into bilingual research designs.

Keywords: methods in bilingualism research, cognitive sociolinguistics, usage-based perspectives, code-mixing, code-switching

1 Recent topics in individual bilingualism

The past two decades have witnessed a growing interest in aspects of individual bilingualism and multilingualism, both at an academic and a personal level. Various reasons have been suggested for this unprecedented increase in research and publications. One obvious explanation is undoubtedly the realization that the knowledge and use of more than one language is far more widespread than previously thought. In the literature on bilingualism, it has been repeatedly stressed that over half of the world's population is bilingual. While unfortunately no exact figures seem to exist, guesstimates based on data from *Ethnologue* set the value at between 50% and 70% (see Francois Grosjean's post "Chasing Down Those 65%" on the *Psychology Today* blog "Life as a bilingual"). Thus, bilingualism affects the majority of people worldwide and can be found in all age groups, in all levels of society, and in most countries (Grosjean 2013). Even in predominantly monolingual countries, individual bilingualism is becoming more and more prevalent, mainly because parents and educators aim to create an enriching language environment for their children, often in order to improve their professional prospects.

However, the ongoing fascination with topics of bilingualism is also owed to the insight that observations of bilingual language development and use may serve as a window to understanding the way that language-specific and domain-general cognition interact in the neural processes involved in language representation and control. With the rise of cognitively oriented approaches to language, such as Cognitive Linguistics and Construction Grammar (for an overview see, for example, Geeraerts 2006; Evans and Green 2006; Evans, Bergen and Zinken 2007; Langacker 2008; Goldberg 2006), the focus within bilingualism research has likewise shifted from structural and functional analyses to questions of cognitive processing, development and representation. At the present stage, there are obviously more questions than answers regarding the exact mechanisms involved in bilingual processing. Nevertheless, a number of models have been suggested to describe the processes involved in bilingual word recognition (e.g. the BIA+ model by Dijkstra and van Heuven 2002), lexical selection mechanisms in bilingual language production (e.g. Costa et al. 2000; Costa et al. 2006; De Bot 2004; Pavlenko 2009b), and the representation of syntactic information in bilinguals (compare the shared vs. separate syntax accounts; Hartsuiker, Pickering and Veltkamp 2004), to name just a few. One desideratum for further research is, of course, the collection and evaluation of more empirical data to validate existing models, or, if necessary, to create new ones.

Furthermore, a considerable number of empirical studies have been conducted to investigate potential positive effects of bilingual upbringing and education on metalinguistic and non-linguistic cognitive abilities, such as metalinguistic awareness, communicative competence, executive control, or divergent thinking (e.g. Bialystok and Barac 2012; Kharkhurin 2007; Kovács 2007). While for a considerable period of time – approximately up to the 1960s – the dominant belief among academics was that bilingualism may have detrimental effects on a person's intelligence and on the full-fledged development of both languages in question, recent research paints a far more optimistic picture. After many of the methodological deficiencies of earlier studies had been identified and corrected, the "period of additive effects" commenced, investigating possible cognitive advantages of bilingualism over monolingualism (Baker 2006: 144–150). This "cognitive" trend is also reflected in the thematic specification of recently published handbooks and collective volumes, most notably Grosjean and Li's *The Psycholinguistics of Bilingualism* (2013), Kecskés and Albertazzi's *Cognitive Aspects of Bilingualism* (2007), and Kroll and De Groot's *Handbook of Bilingualism: Psycholinguistic Approaches* (2009). Nevertheless, a substantial amount of further research is needed to thoroughly explore the specific interrelations between bilinguality and general cognition. For instance, while bilinguals are commonly assumed to possess enhanced creative thinking skills, Hommel et al.'s (2011) findings suggest that "bilingualism should not be related to 'creativity' as a unitary concept but, rather, to the specific processes and mechanisms that underlie creativity". That is, we need to be careful when it comes to the presumption of direct links between bilingualism and other cognitive functions. Athanasopoulos (2011), for instance, in his discussion of various empirical studies investigating the relationship between linguistic categories and non-linguistic cognition in the bilingual mind, addresses a multitude of factors that need to be controlled for.

Since approaches such as Cognitive Linguistics or Construction Grammar claim to adhere to the so-called "Cognitive Commitment", i.e. the "view that principles of linguistic structure should reflect what is known about human cognition from the other cognitive and brain sciences" (Evans 2007: 4–5), it is not surprising that cognitively inspired approaches to bilingualism frequently are interdisciplinary in nature. This openness to and cooperation with other disciplines has also led to the consequence that bilingualism research today is characterized by a remarkable methodological diversity, enabling a wider range of perspectives on bilingual phenomena. Given the complex network of factors involved in, for example, code-alternation practices such as switching and borrowing (e.g. Gardner-Chloros 2009; Coulmas 2005; Auer 1995), this interdisciplinarity is a welcome development since it would be impossible to fully capture the dynamics of bilingualism from a single theoretical or methodological angle. Not only have traditional psycho- and sociolinguistic designs (e.g. of naturalistic observation studies or laboratory experiments) become progressively refined over the years, but new methods and technologies typically used in neighboring fields have also found their way into bilingualism research. For instance, neuroimaging techniques have been borrowed from the medical and neurosciences to find out more about the cerebral representation of languages in polyglots (for a review of the functional imaging literature on bilingualism see Abutalebi, Cappa and Perani 2001; for a critical comment see Ch. 6 in Paradis 2004). Eye tracking technology, commonly used in psychology, or magnetic resonance imaging has been employed to measure eye movement during the online comprehension and production of linguistic input/output in order to draw conclusions about attention, reference/lexical representation, and sentence parsing (cf. the studies by Marian, Spivey and Hirsch 2003; van Heuver et al. 2010). In code-switching experiments, new kinds of priming methods have been employed to investigate not only lexico-semantic, but also syntactic choices of bilinguals. Endesfelder Quick, Lieven and Tomasello (this volume), for instance, use cross-linguistic syntactic priming to investigate cross-language activation and (shared) mental representations in young bilinguals. As its name suggests, syntactic priming refers to priming effects that arise from the activation of structural representations or procedures even if there is no (or not much) lexical overlap between the prime and the target (cf., for example, Snedeker and Thothathiri 2008;

Trofimovich and McDonough 2011). For a comprehensive overview of research methods in bilingualism and multilingualism, see Wei and Moyer 2008.

Another central characteristic of cognitively oriented approaches is their usage-based, emergentist perspective on language development and use. In this view, language learning involves the "associative learning of representations that reflect the probabilities of occurrence of form-function mappings" (Ellis 2012: 9) based on the learners' analysis of the distributional characteristics of the input they have been exposed to. It is this idea which has sparked a renewed wave of research on the role of input in bilingual language development. On the one hand, linguists have been interested in the more general question as to what extent variation in the quantity and quality of input in each language affects the rate at which the respective language is learned. On the other hand, comparisons have been drawn between monolinguals and bilinguals, because it is generally assumed that children growing up bilingually are exposed to quantitatively less input than their monolingual peers (cf. Paradis and Genesee 1996). Such comparisons might provide some evidence as to how much input is necessary for acquisition to take place, and ideally also as to additional factors and processes involved in lexical (and conceptual) development, especially when it comes to the incorporation of partially overlapping elements into the bilingual's mental lexicon. Three of the contributions in this volume are concerned with the role of input in bilingual language development and production. While the majority of studies investigating frequency effects in early bilinguals narrow their focus to the main input sources of parents, other siblings and peers, Bellay (this volume) presents evidence that children treat the linguistic material they acquire from musical, audio-visual, poetic and narrative input (MAPNI) also as part of their linguistic repertoire and readily deploy it in their own output. In a similar vein, Chan, Lowie and de Bot (this volume), when analyzing the impact of the quantity and quality of language input on the lexical development of sequential bilinguals, move away from typical input sources in the classroom (e.g. teachers, textbooks) to multimedia contexts outside the classroom in which students regularly encounter the L2. They argue that classroom-external activities, such as reading online news or communicating via social media platforms in the L2, may well influence bilingual learners' degree of lexical sophistication. While these two longitudinal studies consider retention effects based on the actual input contained in the linguistic experience of their participants, Hakimov (this volume) relies on generalizations from native speaker corpora instead. The assumption underlying his investigation of switch placement in code-mixed utterances is that bilingual language choices (just like monolingual language production) are influenced by word frequencies, probabilistic relations between adjacent elements, and the likelihood of morpho-syntactic structures with which a certain item occurs. In other words, the more frequently we come across a certain word or compositional sequence in our input, the more cognitively entrenched it becomes over time and the more easily it can be accessed in language production (cf., for example, Blumenthal-Dramé 2012; Bybee 2007; Langacker 2000).

As we already mentioned above, parents and educators today wish to raise their children in the best possible linguistic environment. This "trend" can be ascribed to the multilingual workforce demands brought about by globalization. Due to the integration of economies, cultures and policy-making around the world, the rapid increase in migration and international mobility, and the development of modern technologies, businesses and institutions have become more and more interconnected. Cooperation and communication across national boundaries do of course require multilingual and intercultural competencies on the part of the interlocutors, which is why people's personal interest in bilingual language acquisition has risen over the years. Even parents who do not speak a global language such as English natively may consider imitating a bilingual or multilingual environment (so-called *artificial bilingualism*; Kielhöfer and Jonekeit 1983) in order to improve their children's employment opportunities in the long run. This development has triggered the publication of a series of guides and handbooks targeted at bilingual families and teachers containing recommendations of strategies for effective bilingual language socialization and education (e.g. Baker 2014; Barron-Hauwaert 2004; De Houwer 2009).

Along with this aim to be prepared for a multilingual working environment came a growing interest in intercultural aspects of bilingualism. In order to use language in culturally and socially appropriate ways, bilinguals and second language learners need to develop sociopragmatic competence. Kecskés (this volume) suggests that while for the first language(s), linguistic and socio-cultural development are inextricably intertwined and happen subconsciously, in sequential bilingualism sociopragmatic competence needs to be motivated by the speakers' individual will to modify existing conceptual structures and discourse practices in accordance with the conventions of the target language culture. He uses the term *conceptual socialization* to refer to "the transformation of the conceptual system [of the sequential bilingual] which undergoes characteristic changes to fit the functional needs of the new language and culture" (Kecskés 2002: 11). The development of bilingual sociopragmatic competence can be regarded as a somewhat neglected area in both bilingualism and pragmatics research, and empirical studies are still rare (with the exception of, for example, the dissertation project by Kaya [2012], who examined the bilingual pragmatic competence of Turkish-German bilinguals with a focus on the speech act of apologizing).

Pavlenko (2011: 5) has found that according to the bilinguals' autobiographic accounts in her corpus, "it is only when speakers move to the country where the language is spoken that this language begins to exert influence on their thinking". This observation partly fits in with Grosjean's (2014: 7) claim that "just as one can be bicultural without being bilingual, and bilingual without being bicultural, [...] one must leave open the possibility that the development of each component of the bicultural bilingual person may take place at different times, even if, for many, the two often go hand in hand". Thus, bilinguals living in mono- or bicultural communities or circumstances constitute excellent test cases for hypotheses related to theories of linguistic relativity, i.e. of the language-thought/thinking relationship. While the debate surrounding the so-called Sapir-Whorf-Hypothesis (as well as neo-Whorfian approaches) has historically taken place against the background of language in the singular, more recent models (e.g. Robinson and Ellis' [2008] idea of "L2 Re-thinking for Speaking" as an extension of Slobin's [1996] "Thinking for Speaking" hypothesis) and studies (e.g. the research contained in Pavlenko [2011]) also take into account bilingual and L2 contexts. The role of typological differences in L2 restructuring processes, the interplay between linguistic diversity and language universals, as well as methodological issues in the study of linguistic relativity are also thoroughly discussed in Filipović and Pütz (2014).

2 Methodological advances in bilingualism research

"From the start of a project, a researcher should be constantly evaluating the link between the theoretical framework, the research questions, the methods for data collection, the analysis as well as the best way to present and argue for the results" (Moyer 2008: 25). Due to the high complexity of the phenomenon of bilingualism and the multitude of angles from which bilingual language acquisition, representation and use can be investigated, it is practically impossible to provide a comprehensive overview of all the theoretical positions, data types and methods that have been of relevance in bilingualism research to date. Therefore, we limit our discussion to the main research traditions of the field, with a particular focus on those methods applied in the contributions to this volume.

Depending on the research perspective and the field of interest, studies may either tackle structural-linguistic, cognitive-psychological or social-behavioral aspects of bilingualism, or a combination thereof. Quite naturally, each discipline brings with it its own research practices and instruments. For instance, while psycholinguists tend to conduct experimental studies displaying different types of laboratory designs and paradigms, sociolinguists traditionally rely on natural speech recordings, interviews and questionnaires as data collection techniques. At the same time, we also need to keep in mind that a discussion of methods in bilingualism research should go hand in hand with a discussion of innovations in child language research, since the study of bilingual first language acquisition (or simultaneous bilingualism) takes up a considerable portion of bilingualism research (cf. also De Houwer 1998: 251).

Structural aspects of bilingualism can best be observed in the everyday language use of speakers who regularly move between two or more languages. In this case, "[a] linguistic form constitutes a datum that becomes the object of linguistic analysis" (Moyer 2008: 19). With the advancement of corpus linguistics, and especially with the emergence of bilingual speech corpora, corpus data have become a valuable source of information in bilingualism research. For one thing, bilingual corpora usually contain (semi) spontaneous speech recorded in naturalistic settings. Compared to data produced by experimental or quasi-experimental designs, corpus data thus tend to be more representative of actual, authentic language use. Moreover, they are less prone to misrepresentations than, for example, self-report data derived from interviews or questionnaires, which have been found to sometimes project (either deliberately or unconsciously) skewed images. Nevertheless, we need to keep in mind that in annotated corpora, the categories and labels chosen by the compiler during the tagging process are always influenced by a particular theoretical framework as well as the terminology associated with it (cf. Backus 2008: 233). As McEnery et al. (2006: 10) state, "[a] truly corpus-driven approach [...] would require something such as someone who has never received any education related to language use and therefore is free from preconceived theory". In terms of objectivity, this does of course mean that the analysis and interpretation of the corpus data are somewhat influenced by preexisting ideas and expectations about certain linguistic categories and bilingual phenomena. A further consequence is that researchers who adhere to a different paradigm may encounter difficulties when trying to "read" and use the respective corpus.

With regard to bilingual language use, Backus (2008: 234) has identified two main research questions that a bilingual corpus can help analyze: "(1) the use of lexical material from two or more languages (code-switching) and (2) the use of structural (e.g. grammatical, phonological, semantic) features not found in or typical of the speech of monolingual speakers of the languages, and perhaps taken from the other language (interference)". For contact phenomena such as code-mixing and code-switching, additional annotations can frequently be found in bilingual corpora, like, for instance, the type of switching (according to a particular model), the kind of element inserted (word/word class, chunk/length and type of chunk), the presence versus absence of syntactic integration, or the switch point (Backus 2008: 242). However, as Backus deplores, the majority of bilingual speech corpora do not meet all the requirements for a professional corpus due to a lack of time and funding on part of the researchers, who in many cases are PhD students. Often such corpora contain data that were collected for one specific research project on one particular language pair and have only been rudimentarily annotated. With the exception of larger compilations such as *CHILDES Biling* or the *Hamburg Adult Bilingual Language (HABLA)* corpus, bilingual corpora further tend to be quite small and relatively difficult to access for other researchers (Backus 2008: 233).

Hakimov in his contribution to this volume works with two different kinds of corpora. The first corpus displays many of the characteristics listed by Backus. It is a corpus on one particular language pair, i.e. Russian-German bilingual speech recorded in Russian-speaking communities across Germany, and it contains approximately 28 hours of spontaneous speech and informal group interviews. Since the focus of Hakimov's study is on switch placement in the context of prepositional phrases, the corpus analysis takes into account those features relevant to the research question at hand, i.e. type of switching (insertion versus alternation; Muysken 2000) and exact switch point, asymmetry between the two languages (matrix versus embedded language; Myers-Scotton 1993a), as well as phrase complexity. By contrast, the second corpus, which is consulted as a reference resource for word and co-occurrence frequencies in monolingual German speech, can be classified as a very large, general-purpose native speaker corpus. *deWaC* comprises over a billion words and is currently the largest publicly documented resource for the German language. It was built by web crawling and contains basic linguistic annotation such as part-of-speech tagging and lemmatization (cf. Baroni et al. 2008: 1). One obvious desideratum for the future development of bilingual speech corpora is pointed out by Backus (2008: 234), who says that people in the field of bilingualism research should "join forces and link various separate data collections into a bigger database. This may be feasible in the long run for some of the well-studied contact situations, such as Spanish in the US, Punjabi or Bengali in the UK, Turkish in northwestern Europe, or Arabic-French contact".

Cognitive linguists and psycholinguists are predominantly less concerned with structural aspects of bilingualism and more interested in the cognitive representation of bilingual language knowledge, as well as the online processes involved in bilingual language comprehension and production (cf. also Wei 2008: 9). Over the past ten years or so, there has been a notable increase in the amount of studies that take a cognitive or psycholinguistic approach to bilingualism, and with the development of neuroimaging techniques such as Event-Related Potential (ERP) or functional Magnetic Resonance Imaging (fMRI), modern and non-invasive ways have been created to study the neural architecture of the bilingual brain (for an overview on both electromagnetic and hemodynamic approaches, see Abultalebi and Della Rosa 2008, and Kovelmann 2012). Neuroimaging techniques are supposed to provide measures of brain activity, i.e. to identify which areas of the brain are activated during a particular language task. Evidence from neuroimaging studies for or against parallel activation may thus bring us one step closer to answering the question of whether and how the lexical and syntactic systems of the different languages in a bilingual interact with each other. One major problem that remains, though, is that the researcher needs to determine which of the activated brain areas subserves which component of the task that is being performed by the bilingual subject, since language tasks are commonly associated with activity in several cortical regions (Paradis 2004). This means that, to some degree, the results of such studies rely on inferencing and interpretation on the part of the researcher.

A further instrument that has gained increasing popularity in the study of real-time speech processing is the eye tracking device. Eye trackers monitor the movements of the subjects' eyes while they are reading or listening to a text. In bilingualism research eye trackers are mainly used to investigate if exposure to a lexical item from one language may lead to a parallel activation of words in both languages (cf. Kroll et al. 2008: 112). Recent interest in this procedure can be attributed to the methodological advancements that have been made in the field, as well as to the fact that eye tracking studies can also easily be conducted with younger bilinguals. "It is now possible for instance to record children's eye movements as they carry out relatively natural tasks involving language, such as following spoken instructions, inspecting images that are being described, and even engaging in a spoken conversation with interlocutors" (Trueswell 2012: 177).

One of the most popular and traditional methods applied in the psycholinguistic research of bilingualism is priming. "The term 'priming' has been used to refer to a wide range of phenomena in which exposure to a certain type of material increases people's ability to mentally access that material in their subsequent behavior" (Vasilyeva et al. 2012: 163). A great deal of priming research to date has focused on lexico-semantics in order to find out more about the networks in a (bilingual) speaker's mental lexicon, i.e. about how the lexical units of the languages are activated, stored, processed and retrieved. Findings from semantic priming studies suggest that semantically related words are somehow linked in the minds of language users, and that bilinguals organize the meanings of words in their two languages in an interdependent manner

(Trofimovich and McDonough 2011: 7–8). While Hakimov (this volume) in his study of frequency and word repetition effects on switch placement in German-Russian bilingual speech also examines potential lexical priming effects, Endes-felder Quick et al. (this volume) use a different priming procedure, i.e. cross-linguistic syntactic priming.

Syntactic priming can be considered a relatively recent methodology in bilingualism research which has mainly been utilized to examine structural priming effects in (bilingual) language production. An increasing amount of observational and experimental evidence suggests that language users tend to choose a particular syntactic pattern for their utterance over an equally appropriate alternative pattern if the first pattern already appeared in the previous stretch of discourse. This tendency towards local syntactic consistency further seems to be largely inde-pendent of lexical content, since the prime sentences and the target sentences in the respective studies did not show any lexical overlap. That is, the partici-pants would extract the syntactic structure from the prime and reuse it in their utterance with different lexical items (cf., for example, Bock 1986; Pickering and Branigan 1999; Pickering and Ferreira 2008; Trofimovich and McDonough 2011; Vasilyeva et al. 2012). With regard to (bilingual) language development, two key questions can be addressed with the help of structural priming techniques: The first question concerns the nature of syntactic representations in children versus adults. Usage-based approaches like the one by Tomasello (2003) assume that early syntactic constructions are specific to individual lexical items and only gradually become more abstract and independent of lexical content. By testing language users of different age groups, it should thus be possible to determine at what stage lexically independent syntactic representations emerge (cf. Vasilyeva 2012: 165). Obviously, this question is of relevance to both monolingual and bilingual language development.

The second point solely concerns bilingual speakers, because here the rela-tion between syntactic representations across two (or more) languages is explored. Cross-linguistic syntactic priming studies aim to investigate the potential inter-action between the syntactic structures of a bilingual's languages, as well as the impact of L2 proficiency on the development and strength of shared syntactic representations. Results from studies on the use of the passive versus active voice by Spanish-English bilingual children (Vasilyeva et al. 2010) and adults (Hartsuiker et al. 2004) provide evidence for the integration of syntactic repre-sentations in bilinguals and thus for the shared syntax account. Vasilyeva et al. (2008) further found that syntactic priming may be unidirectional, which hints at an asymmetry between the bilinguals' two languages. While most of the cross-linguistic syntactic priming studies concentrate on constructions that are identical or at least very similar in the bilinguals' languages, Bernolet et al.

(2007) also investigated if there are any priming effects across languages with deviant word order patterns. Their target structures were Dutch, English and German relative clauses and they found priming effects between Dutch and German, which both have verb-final relative clauses, but no priming effects between Dutch and English, which differ in their relative clause word order. As McDonough and Trofimovich (2011) rightly observe, one obvious desideratum in bilingualism research is the systematic examination of cross-linguistic syntactic priming with constructions that are realized differently in the bilinguals' two or more languages.

In contrast to cognitive linguists and psycholinguists, who focus on bilingualism as a feature of individuals, sociolinguists conceive of bilingualism as a societal and socially constructed phenomenon and treat bilingual speakers as "social actors" who constantly negotiate and communicate identities through their linguistic choices (Wei 2008: 13). The research questions investigated by sociolinguists hence differ in essence from the ones outlined above, which concomitantly impacts on the types of data generated and the kinds of methods applied.

Sociolinguists are primarily interested in locating and exploring social meaning that is communicated via a choice of a particular linguistic construction. Thus, sociolinguistic work carried out in multilingual contexts seeks to understand the meaning that lies behind the use of various combinations of two or more languages or codes, phenomena referred to as code-switching and code-mixing. In order to achieve such aims, variation in structural properties of these contact phenomena (described in detail in Section 4) is mapped on situational or metaphorical (when the participant's setting is the same) contexts of speech production. Exploration of language alternations in a range of contexts, such as topic, passive knowledge, attitudes to and perceived status of codes/languages, has been most frequently carried out in early sociolinguistic studies of code-switching (Gumperz 1970; Blom and Gumperz 1972; Fishman 1965; Romaine 1986).

The analysis of code-switching and mixing from the perspective of Conversation Analysis also allows us to gain insights into the ways in which bilingual speakers manage social relations and the strategies speakers employ to organize a piece of discourse. For instance, Auer shows how Italian-German alternations can be studied "by taking into account grammatical restrictions where necessary" and relating them "to larger scale sociolinguistic statements" (Auer 1988: 209). One of the most widely applied models aiming to explain social motivations for code-switching in interactions is offered by Myers-Scotton (1993b). This framework is based on the idea that in conversational encounters bilinguals choose between using marked or unmarked linguistic alternations. This choice of a linguistic alternation indexes a particular set of so-called rights and obligations and this carries associated social benefits and costs. There is also a large strand of sociolinguistic research in bilingualism that has focused on gaining a better understanding of the identity of bilingual speakers (Heller 1982; Hoffman 1991).

A range of applied sociolinguistic studies of bilingualism have a macro-sociolinguistic character and focus on groups of bilinguals, such as students, minority groups, and whole nations. These studies aim to assess the consequences of bilingualism and relevant language policies in everyday contexts, especially in education and in matters important for the organization of communities. A range of these studies focus on exploring power relations that emerge through bilingual use in formal contexts. These often lead to insights into issues of minority language maintenance, language revival, and language decay. Another group of sociolinguistic studies focuses on pedagogical and psycholinguistic consequences of bilingual situations. Such studies investigate bilingual speech in classroom contexts and look into issues of learners' performance or of assessment strategies, just to name a few (cf. Baker 2006). A growing body of research goes on to incorporate a psycholinguistic element into the socio-pedagogical studies by exploring bilingual attitudes or bilingual self-perception (Grosjean and Li 2013).

3 Focus on contact phenomena: Code-switching and code-mixing

Code-switching, i.e. the alternating use of two (or more) languages by a bilingual speaker (Bullock and Toribio 2009: 2), has undoubtedly dominated the field of bilingualism research over the last decades. Hamers and Blanc (1989: 148) argue that code-switching is "one of the most common and original strategies used between bilinguals themselves". The code-switching behavior of bilinguals has been studied by linguists from various disciplines and for various reasons. On the one hand, it may be used as an indicator of a bilingual speaker's proficiency level. As Poplack (1980) has shown, proficient bilinguals tend to engage more frequently in intra-sentential code-switching, which requires a high level of morpho-syntactic skill, while non-fluent bilinguals favor the "safer" option of emblematic or tag-switching. Thus, the number and type of constituents being switched may reflect different degrees of bilingual ability. At the same time, the structural analysis of code-switched utterances can reveal patterns at the conceptual-semantic, morpho-syntactic and phonological levels of both languages involved. Speakers' choices regarding switch placement (e.g. phrase-internal switches vs. switches at phrase boundaries), as well as the extent to which the two languages are "merged" at the word level, may offer valuable clues as to the units with which both monolingual and bilingual language users operate. As Bullock and Toribio (2009: 14) stress, "it has been demonstrated that CS [code-switching] does not constitute a distinct or third grammar; instead, CS forms emerge from and conform to the constraints of both language systems".

Depending on switch placement and the length and internal complexity of the alternating elements, different types of code-switching have been assumed. One of the most prominent classification schemes has been put forward by Muysken (2000), who proposes the three categories of alternation, insertion and congruent lexicalization. In alternation, a whole string of constituents is switched and the individual fragments retain their original structure and internal complexity. Due to the lack of syntactic integration, the two languages remain relatively separate, which is represented in a schema of non-nested "A ... B ... A" sequences. Emblematic or tag-switching, i.e. the insertion of a formulaic expression from Language B, constitutes one particular case of alternation in Muysken's model (cf. Muysken 2000: 96–99). An example of alternation would be the following excerpt from a French-Alsatian telephone conversation that took place in Strasbourg:

> Ce gars était lá l'autre jour UN DANN HAT ER EBBS GEMACHT, HET G'SAAT ... et puis tout d'un coup ça a fait clic et effectivement ça a remarché. [This guy was here the other day AND THEN HE DID SOMETHING, HE SAID ... and then all of a sudden it went click and it did work again.] (Gardner-Chloros 1991: 98)

Insertions, on the other hand, involve single constituents (e.g. words, frequent word combinations, fixed expressions) from Language B that are implemented into a nested "aba" structure, as in the following Spanish-English example:

> Yo anduve IN A STATE OF SHOCK pa dos días. [I walked IN A STATE OF SHOCK for two days.] (Pfaff 1979: 297)

A crucial characteristic of insertions is that the switched elements tend to be content rather than function words. They sometimes even display morphological integration (cf. Muysken 2000: 63–64), as can be seen in the example of French-English code-switching below, where the English verb *pick up* is inflected with the French infinitival suffix {er}:

> Tu peux ME PICK UP-er? [Can you pick me up?] (Gardner-Chloros 2009: 97)

A last switch type suggested by Muysken (2000) is congruent lexicalization, which requires that the languages involved are structurally related. Lexical items from Language A and Language B are more or less randomly inserted into a (fully or partially) shared grammatical framework. The following Spanish-English example illustrates quite nicely how words and phrases from both languages are interwoven with each other because the syntactic patterns allow for it;

> Bueno, IN OTHER WORDS, el FLIGHT que sale de Chicago AROUND THREE O'CLOCK. [Good, IN OTHER WORDS, the FLIGHT that leaves Chicago AROUND THREE O'CLOCK.] (Pfaff 1976: 250)

When looking at Muysken's (2000) and various other classification schemes that have been adopted, one very basic question arises, namely, what the linguistic constituents or units actually are that bilingual speakers select for production. The term *code-switching*, as well as labels such as 'Language A' and 'Language B', might suggest that we are dealing with transitions from one code or language to another. This view has already been challenged by Kecskés (2009: 7), who holds that when it comes to bilingual language users' choices "it is not languages that compete for selection, but words". In a similar vein, Wasserscheidt (this volume) makes a theoretical, albeit sample-based, attempt to develop a constructionist approach to code-switching. Following the theoretical frameworks by Goldberg (Construction Grammar; 1995, 2006), Croft (Radical Construction Grammar; 2001) and Langacker (Usage-based approach; 2005, 2009), Wasserscheidt claims that "constructions are the only linguistic elements that have to be taken into account when talking about storage and processing of language" (this volume, 67). Constructions can be defined as socially conventionalized and individually learned form-meaning/function pairings that may display various degrees of specificity and internal complexity. Constructionist approaches seem to have high explanatory potential with respect to code-switching data since they take into account all levels of language (including the conceptual-semantic level) and work with only a single theoretical construct, i.e. 'constructions' (ibid.).

When investigating code-switching patterns, the structural features of these patterns have frequently been explained in terms of constraints. As Muysken (1997: 363) notes, for alternation the best candidate at present is Poplack's (1980) equivalence constraint, which states that the switch occurs between constituents that are ordered in the same way in both languages, thus ensuring the linear coherence of the syntactic structure and simultaneously avoiding lexico-semantic redundancy. Insertion can best be accounted for by means of Myers-Scotton's (1993a) Matrix Language Frame (MLF) model, according to which one of the participating languages dominates in the sense that it supplies the morpho-syntactic frame as well as the majority of the function words for the bilingual sentence. While these models of constraints primarily focus on the formal-structural side of language, more recent cognitive and usage-oriented approaches to code-switching show an increased interest in the cognitive processes that are in operation during speech production in bilinguals, and in what ways these processes may affect output patterns. In these accounts, structural compatibility (and concomitant constraints) is considered as only one factor of many that may influence the shape of code-switched utterances. Further aspects taken into account include the degree of cognitive entrenchment of competing units in Language A and Language B, as well as potential (lexical and syntactic) priming effects from the previous discourse (cf. also Hakimov, this volume).

Code-switching data have also been claimed to afford inferences about the neural representations of the two languages in bilinguals as well as the neuro-cognitive mechanisms involved in language processing. Various neuroimaging studies (e.g. Mechelli et al. 2004; Reiterer et al. 2005a, 2005b) have found that certain areas of the bilingual brain differ from the monolingual brain in terms of size and structure. These differences seem to be more pronounced in bilingual speakers with an early age of onset and/or a high proficiency level in both languages, suggesting that extensive experience with an additional language results in structural reorganization of particular brain regions. Further factors that may have an impact on the differential patterns of brain activity when comparing monolinguals to bilinguals include the typological relationship between the languages involved as well as the task types (e.g. comprehension vs. production) and language levels (e.g. morpho-syntax vs. phonology) targeted in the respective experiments (cf. Kutas, Moreno and Wicha 2009). As Kutas et al. (ibid.: 293) conclude, "there is no simple answer to the question of whether the neural representations of the two languages in a bilingual are or are not the same. Neuropsychological data and intraoperative electrocortical stimulation mapping data in bilinguals suggest that the brain regions serving L1 and L2 are not identical, although there may be substantial overlap." This idea of partial overlap in neural representations is also reflected in current models of the bilingual lexicon, such as Pavlenko's Modified Hierarchical Model. Here, the conceptual representations underlying Language A and Language B "may be fully shared, partially overlapping or fully language-specific" (Pavlenko 2009a: 146).

The question as to which degree syntactic structures are integrated across the two languages in a bilingual has also been investigated with the help of code-switching data derived either from psycholinguistic experiments or from naturalistic speech corpora. Hartsuiker, Pickering and Veltkamp (2004), Vasileva et al. (2010) and Endesfelder Quick, Lieven and Tomasello (this volume), among others, have employed cross-linguistic syntactic priming paradigms for different target structures (e.g. active vs. passive voice) to find evidence for or against the shared vs. separate syntax accounts. Code-switching lends itself relatively well as an indicator insofar as the effective production of one language by a bilingual hypothetically relies on the inhibition of the currently unused language and on attentional/executive control mechanisms (cf. Kutas, Moreno and Wicha 2009: 299). It has also been assumed that due to the fact that bilinguals are constantly "selecting words and structures from the active language, exerting inhibitory control over the currently inactive language, and switching between languages" (ibid.: 290), they are at an advantage in tasks involving attentional/executive control (cf. the studies on various components of executive control by Bialystok and her colleagues at the Cognitive Development Lab at York University, Toronto, Canada). The bilingual mind is also dicussed by Filipović and Pütz (2014).

4 Outlook

In the previous sections we outlined the key theoretical and methodological strands that have been pursued in bilingualism research. The wealth and diversity of these studies do justice to the multiplicity of social and cognitive contexts in which bilingual speech can be observed. Nevertheless, the complexity of bilingual interaction still poses many challenges which require ongoing investigations.

Having evaluated a wide range of perspectives from which bilingualism can be explored, we argue that studies that are open to interdisciplinary views on bilingual phenomena are best suited to address current and future challenges in the field. One such perspective is offered by socio-cognitive research, which aims to explore the way in which cognitive mechanism of language use happen on the ground. The task now before us is to further the interdisciplinary explorations of the multi-faceted language use by bi-/multilinguals through "creating a novel context for the study of language" (Filipović and Pütz 2014: 6; cf. also Muysken, this volume) that takes into account socio-pragmatic, psychological as well as cognitive aspects.

References

Abutalebi, Jubin, Stefano F. Cappa & Daniela Perani. 2001. The bilingual brain as revealed by functional neuroimaging. *Bilingualism: Language and Cognition* 4. 179–190.

Abutalebi, Jubin & Pasquale A. Della Rosa. 2008. Imaging technologies. In Li Wei & Melissa G. Moyer (eds.), *The Blackwell guide to research methods in bilingualism and multilingualism*, 132–157. Malden, MA: Blackwell.

Athanasopoulos, Panos. 2011. Cognitive restructuring in bilingualism. In Aneta Pavlenko (ed.), *Thinking and speaking in two languages*, 29–65. Bristol, Buffalo & Toronto: Multilingual Matters.

Auer, Peter. 1988. A conversation analytic approach to code-switching and transfer. In Monika Heller (ed.), *Codeswitching: Anthropological and sociolinguistic perspectives*, 187–213. Berlin: Mouton de Gruyter.

Auer, Peter. 1995. The pragmatics of code-switching: A sequential approach. In Lesley Milroy & Pieter Muysken (eds.), *One speaker, two languages: Cross-disciplinary perspectives on code-switching*, 115–135. Cambridge: Cambridge University Press.

Backus, Ad. 2008. Data banks and corpora. In Li Wei & Melissa G. Moyer (eds.), *The Blackwell guide to research methods in bilingualism and multilingualism*, 232–248. Malden, MA: Blackwell.

Baker, Colin. 2014. *A parents' and teachers' guide to bilingualism*. Clevedon: Multilingual Matters.

Baker, Colin. 2006. *Foundations of bilingual education and bilingualism*. Clevedon: Multilingual Matters.

Baroni, Marco, Silvia Bernardini, Adriano Ferraresi & Eros Zanchetta. 2008. The WaCky Wide Web: A collection of very large linguistically processed web-crawled corpora. Kluwer Academic Publishers.

Barron-Hauwaert, Suzanne. 2004. *Language strategies for bilingual families: The one-parent – one-language approach*. Clevedon: Multilingual Matters.

Bellay, Catrin. 2016. Musical, audio-visual, poetic, and narrative input: A longitudinal case-study of French-English bilingual first language acquisition. In Monika Reif & Justyna A. Robinson (eds.), *Cognitive approaches to bilingualism*, 149–182. Berlin/Boston: de Gruyter.

Bernolet, Sarah, Robert J. Hartsuiker & Martin Pickering. 2007. Shared syntactic representations in bilinguals: Evidence for the role of word-order repetition. *Journal of Experimental Psychology: Learning, Memory, and Cognition* 33(5). 931–949.

Blom, Jan-Petter & John J. Gumperz. 1972. Social meaning in linguistic structures: Code switching in northern Norway. In John J. Gumperz & Dell Hymes (eds.), *Directions in sociolinguistics*. New York: Holt, Rinehart & Winston.

Blumenthal-Dramé, Alice. 2012. *Entrenchment in usage-based theories: What corpus data do and do not reveal about the mind*. Berlin/New York: De Gruyter Mouton.

Bullock, Barbara E. & Alemeida J. Toribio. 2009. Themes in the study of code-switching. In Barbara E. Bullock & Almeida J. Toribio (eds.), *The Cambridge handbook of linguistic code-switching*, 1–18. Cambridge: Cambridge University Press.

Bybee, Joan. 2007. *Frequency of use and the organization of language*. Oxford: Oxford University Press.

Chan, HuiPing, Wander Lowie & Kees de Bot. 2016. Input outside the classroom and vocabulary development: A dynamic perspective. In Monika Reif & Justyna A. Robinson (eds.), *Cognitive approaches to bilingualism*, 183–204. Berlin/Boston: de Gruyter.

Costa, Albert, Àngels Colomé & Alfonso Caramazza. 2000. Lexical access in speech production: The bilingual case. *Psicológica* 21(2). 403–437.

Costa, Albert, Wido La Heij & Eduardo Navarrete. 2006. The dynamics of bilingual lexical access. *Bilingualism: Language and Cognition* 9(2). 137–151.

Coulmas, Florian. 2005. *Sociolinguistics: The study of speakers' choices*. Cambridge: Cambridge University Press.

Croft, William. 2001. *Radical Construction Grammar: Syntactic theory in typological perspective*. Oxford: Oxford University Press.

De Bot, Kees. 2004. The multilingual lexicon: Modelling selection and control. *International Journal of Multilingualism* 1(1). 17–32.

De Houwer, Annick. 2009. *An introduction to bilingual development*. Clevedon: Multilingual Matters.

De Houwer, Annick. 1998. By way of introduction: Methods in studies of bilingual first language acquisition. *The International Journal of Bilingualism* 2(3). 249–263.

Dijkstra, Ton & Walter J. B. van Heuven. 2002. The architecture of the bilingual word recognition system: From identification to decision. *Bilingualism: Language and Cognition* 5. 175–197.

Ellis, Nick C. 2012. Frequency-based accounts of second language acquisition. In Stefan Th. Gries & Dagmar S. Divjak (eds.), *Frequency effects in language learning and processing*, 7–33. Berlin: Walter de Gruyter.

Endesfelder Quick, Antje, Elena Lieven & Michael Tomasello. 2016. Mixed NPs in German-English and German-Russian bilingual children. In Monika Reif & Justyna A. Robinson (eds.), *Cognitive approaches to bilingualism*, 127–146. Berlin/Boston: de Gruyter.

Evans, Vyvyan. 2007. The cognitive linguistics enterprise: An overview. In Vyvyan Evans, Benjamin Bergen & Jörg Zinken (eds.), *The cognitive linguistics reader*, 2–36. London & Oakville: Equinox.

Evans, Vyvyan, Benjamin Bergen & Jörg Zinken (eds.). 2007. *The cognitive linguistics reader*. London & Oakville: Equinox.

Evans, Vyvyan & Melanie Green. 2006. *Cognitive linguistics: An introduction*. Edinburgh: Edinburgh University Press.

Filipović, Luna & Martin Pütz (eds.). 2014. *Multilingual cognition and language use: Processing and typological perspectives*. Amsterdam: John Benjamins.

Fishman, Joshua A. 1965. 'Who speaks what language to whom and when?' *La Linguistique* 2. 67–88. (Reprinted in Li Wei (ed.), 2000, *The bilingualism reader*, 89–106. London & New York: Routledge.)

Gardner-Chloros, Penelope. 2009. *Code-switching*. Cambridge: Cambridge University Press.

Gardner-Chloros, Penelope. 1991. *Language selection and switching in Strasbourg*. Oxford: Oxford University Press.

Geeraerts, Dirk (ed.). 2006. *Cognitive linguistics: Basic readings*. Berlin: Walter de Gruyter.

Goldberg, Adele. 2006. *Constructions at work: The nature of generalization in language*. Oxford: Oxford University Press.

Goldberg, Adele. 1995. *Constructions: A construction grammar approach to argument structure*. Chicago: University of Chicago Press.

Grosjean, Francois. 2014. Bicultural bilinguals. *International Journal of Bilingualism*. 1–15. Published online before print April 1, 2014, doi: 10.1177/1367006914526297

Grosjean, Francois. 2013. Bilingualism: A short introduction. In Francois Grosjean & Ping Li (eds.), *The psycholinguistics of bilingualism*, 5–26. Malden, MA: Blackwell.

Grosjean, Francois & Ping Li. 2013. *The psycholinguistics of bilingualism*. Malden, MA & Oxford: Wiley-Blackwell.

Grüter, Theres & Johanne Paradis (eds.). 2014. *Input and experience in bilingual development*. Amsterdam: John Benjamins.

Gumperz, John J. 1970. Verbal strategies and multilingual communication. In James E. Atlatis (ed.), *Georgetown round table on language and linguistics*, 129–147. Washington, DC: Georgetown University Press.

Hakimov, Nikolay. 2016. Effects of frequency and word repetition on switch placement. In Monika Reif & Justyna A. Robinson (eds.), *Cognitive approaches to bilingualism*, 91–126. Berlin/Boston: de Gruyter.

Hamers, Josiane. F. & Michel A. Blanc. 1989. *Bilinguality and bilingualism*. Cambridge: Cambridge University Press.

Hartsuiker, Robert J., Martin Pickering & Eline Veltkamp. 2004. Is syntax separate or shared between languages? Cross-linguistic syntactic priming in Spanish-English bilinguals. *Psychological Science* 15(6). 409–414.

Heller, Monica. 2000. Bilingualism and identity in the post-modern world. *Estudios de Sociolingüística* 1(2). 9–24.

Hoffman, Charlotte. 1991. *Introduction to bilingualism*. New York: Longman.

Hommel, Bernhard, Lorenza S. Colzato, Rico Fischer & Ingrid K. Christoffels. 2011. Bilingualism and creativity: Benefits in convergent thinking come with losses in divergent thinking. *Frontiers in Psychology* 2. Published online 10 November 2011: http://www.ncbi.nlm.nih.gov/pmc/articles/PMC3212749/.

Kaya, C. Tanya. 2012. *Bilingual pragmatic competence: Turkish-German bilinguals' apologising strategies*. University of Duisburg-Essen, PhD thesis.

Kecskés, István. 2016. Bilingual pragmatic competence. In Monika Reif & Justyna A. Robinson (eds.), *Cognitive approaches to bilingualism*, 39–64. Berlin/Boston: de Gruyter.

Kecskés, István. 2009. Dual and multilanguage systems. *International Journal of Multilingualism*. 1–19. Published online before print October, 14 2009.doi: 10.1080/14790710903288313

Kecskés, István & Liliana Albertazzi (eds.). 2007. *Cognitive aspects of bilingualism*. Dordrecht: Springer.

Kharkhurin, Anatoliy V. 2007. The role of cross-linguistic and cross-cultural experiences in bilinguals' divergent thinking. In István Kecskés & Liliana Albertazzi (eds.), *Cognitive aspects of bilingualism*, 175–210. Dordrecht: Springer.

Kielhöfer, Bernd & Sylvie Jonekeit. 1983. *Zweisprachige Kindererziehung*. Tübingen: Stauffenberg.

Kovács, Agnes M. 2007. Beyond language: Childhood bilingualism enhances high-level cognitive functions. In István Kecskés & Liliana Albertazzi (eds.), *Cognitive aspects of bilingualism*, 301–323. Dordrecht: Springer.

Kovelmann, Ioulia. 2012. Neuroimaging methods. In Erika Hoff (ed.), *Research methods in child language. A practical guide*, 43–59. Malden, MA: Blackwell.

Kroll, Judith F. & Annette M. B. de Groot (eds.). 2009. *Handbook of bilingualism. Psycholinguistic approaches*. Oxford: Oxford University Press.

Kroll, Judith F., Chip Gerfen & Paola E. Dussias. 2008. Laboratory designs and paradigms: Words, sounds, and sentences. In: Li Wei & Melissa Moyer (eds.), *The Blackwell guide to research methods in bilingualism and multilingualism*, 108–131. Malden, MA: Blackwell.

Kutas, Marta, Eva Moreno & Nicole Wicha. 2009. Code-switching and the brain. In Barbara E. Bullock & Almeida J. Toribio (eds.), *The Cambridge handbook of linguistic code-switching*, 289–306. Cambridge: Cambridge University Press.

Langacker, Ronald. 2008. *Cognitive grammar: A basic introduction*. Oxford & New York: Oxford University Press.

Langacker, Ronald. 2000. A dynamic usage-based model. In Michael Barlow & Suzanne Kemmer (eds.), *Usage-based models of language*, 1–63. Stanford: CSLI Publications.

Marian, Viorica, Michael Spivey & Joy Hirsch. 2003. Shared and separate systems in bilingual language processing: Converging evidence from eyetracking and brain imaging. *Brain and Language* 86. 70–82.

McDonough, Kim & Pavel Trofimovich. 2011. Expanding the scope of priming research. In Pavel Trofimovich & Kim McDonough (eds.), *Applying priming methods to L2 learning, teaching and research*, 241–250. Amsterdam: John Benjamins.

McEnery, Tony, Richard Xiao & Yukio Tono. 2006. *Corpus-based language studies: An advanced resource book*. New York/London: Routledge.

Mechelli, Andrea, Jenny T. Crinion, Uta Noppeney, John O'Doherty, John Ashburner, Richard S. Frackowniak & Cathy J. Price. 2004. Structural plasticity in the bilingual brain: Proficiency in a second language and age at acquisition affect grey-matter density. *Nature* 431. 757.

Moyer, Melissa G. 2008. Research as practice: Linking theory, method, and data. In Li Wei & Melissa G. Moyer (eds.), *The Blackwell guide to research methods in bilingualism and multilingualism*, 18–32. Malden, MA: Blackwell.

Muysken, Pieter. 2016. Fine tuning cross-linguistic interaction: The nuts and bolts. In Monika Reif & Justyna A. Robinson (eds.), *Cognitive approaches to bilingualism*, 207–214. Berlin/ Boston: de Gruyter.

Muysken, Pieter. 2000. *Bilingual speech: A typology of code-mixing*. Cambridge: Cambridge University Press.

Muysken, Pieter. 1997. Code-switching processes: Alternation, insertion, congruent lexicalization. In Martin Pütz (ed.), *Language choices: Conditions, constraints, and consequences*, 361–380. Amsterdam & Philadelphia: John Benjamins.

Myers-Scotton, Carol. 1993a. *Duelling languages: Grammatical structure in codeswitching*. Oxford: Oxford University Press.

Myers-Scotton, Carol. 1993b. *Social motivations for codeswitching: Evidence from Africa*. Oxford: Oxford University Press (Clarendon Press).

Paradis, Johanne & Fred Genesee. 1996. Syntactic acquisition in bilingual children. *Studies in Second Language Acquisition* 18(1). 1–25.

Paradis, Michel. 2004. *A neurolinguistic theory of bilingualism*. Amsterdam & Philadelphia: John Benjamins.

Pavlenko, Aneta. 2011. Introduction: Bilingualism and thought in the 20th century. In Aneta Pavlenko (ed.), *Thinking and speaking in two languages*, 1–28. Bristol, Buffalo & Toronto: Multilingual Matters.

Pavlenko, Aneta. 2009a. Conceptual representation in the bilingual lexicon and second language vocabulary learning. In Aneta Pavlenko (ed.), *The bilingual mental lexicon: Interdisciplinary approaches*, 125–160. Bristol, Buffalo & Toronto: Multilingual Matters.

Pavlenko, Aneta. (ed.). 2009b. *The bilingual mental lexicon: Interdisciplinary approaches*. Bristol, Buffalo & Toronto: Multilingual Matters.

Pfaff, Carol. 1979. Constraints on language-mixing: Intrasentential code-switching and borrowing in Spanish/English. *Language* 55(2). 291–318.

Pfaff, Carol. 1976. Functional and syntactic constraints on syntactic variation in code-mixing. In Sanford B. Steever, Carol A. Walker & Salikoko S. Mufwene (eds.), *Papers from the parasession on diachronic syntax*, 248–259. Chicago: Chicago Linguistic Society.

Pickering, Martin. J. & Holly P. Branigan. 1999. Syntactic priming in language production. *Trends in Cognitive Sciences* 3(4). 136–141.

Pickering, Martin. J. & Victor S. Ferreira. 2008. Structural priming: A critical review. *Psychological Bulletin* 134. 427–459.

Poplack, Shana. 1980. Sometimes I'll start a sentence in Spanish y termino en español. *Linguistics* 18. 581–618.

Reif, Monika & Justyna A. Robinson (eds.). 2016. *Cognitive approaches to bilingualism*. Berlin/ Boston: de Gruyter.

Reiterer, Susanne, Michael L. Berger, Claudia Hemmelmann & Peter Rappelsberger. 2005a. Decreased EEG coherence between prefrontal electrodes: A correlate of high language proficiency? *Experimental Brain Research* 163(1). 109–113.

Reiterer, Susanne, Michael L. Berger, Claudia Hemmelmann & Peter Rappelsberger. 2005b. Characteristic functional networks in high- versus low-proficiency second language speakers detected also during native language processing: An explorative EEG coherence study in 6 frequency bands. *Cognitive Brain Research* 25(2). 566–578.

Robinson, Peter & Nick C. Ellis. 2008. Conclusion: Cognitive linguistics, second language acquisition and L2 instruction – issues for research. In Peter Robinson & Nick C. Ellis (eds.), *Handbook of cognitive linguistics and second language acquisition*, 489–545. New York: Routledge.

Romaine, Suzanne. 1986. The syntax and semantics of the code-mixed compound verb in Panjabi/English bilingual discourse. In Deborah Tannen & James E. Alatis (eds.), *Languages and linguistics: The interdependence of theory, data, and application*, 35–50. Washington, D.C.: Georgetown University Press.

Slobin, Dan I. 1996. From 'thought and language' to 'thinking for speaking'. In John Gumperz & Steven Levinson (eds.), *Rethinking linguistic relativity*, 70–96. Cambridge: Cambridge University Press.

Snedeker, Jesse & Malathi Thothathiri. 2008. What lurks beneath: Syntactic priming during language comprehension in preschoolers (and adults). In Irina Sekerina, Eva M. Fernández & Harald Clahsen (eds.), *Developmental psycholinguistics. On-line methods in children's language processing*, 137–168. Amsterdam: John Benjamins.

Tomasello, Michael. 2003. *Constructing a language: A usage-based theory of language acquisition*. Cambridge, Massachusetts: Harvard University Press.

Trofimovich, Pavel & Kim McDonough. 2011. Using priming methods to study L2 learning and teaching. In Pavel Trofimovich & Kim McDonough (eds.), *Applying priming methods to L2 learning, teaching and research*, 3–20. Amsterdam: John Benjamins.

Trueswell, John C. 2012. Studying language processing using eye movements. In Erika Hoff (ed.), *Research methods in child language: A practical guide*, 177–189. Malden, MA: Blackwell.

van Heuven, Walter J. B & Ton Dijkstra. 2010. Language comprehension in the bilingual brain: fMRI and ERP support for psycholinguistic models. *Brain Research Reviews* 64(1). 104–122.

Vasilyeva, Marina, Heidi Waterfall & Ligia Gómez. 2012. Using priming procedures with children. In Erika Hoff (ed.), *Research methods in child language: A practical guide*, 162–175. Malden, MA: Blackwell.

Vasilyeva, Marina, Heidi Waterfall, Perla B Gámez, Ligia Gómez, Edmond Bowers & Priya Shimpi. 2010. Cross-linguistic syntactic priming in bilingual children. *Journal of Child Language* 37(5). 1047–1064.

Wasserscheidt, Philipp. 2016. Construction Grammar and code-mixing. In Monika Reif & Justyna A. Robinson (eds.), *Cognitive approaches to bilingualism*, 65–88. Berlin/Boston: de Gruyter.

Wei, Li. 2008. Research perspectives on bilingualism and multilingualism. In Li Wei & Melissa G. Moyer (eds.), *The Blackwell guide to research methods in bilingualism and multilingualism*, 3–17. Malden, MA: Blackwell.

Wei, Li & Melissa. G. Moyer. 2008. *The Blackwell guide to research methods in bilingualism and multilingualism*. Malden, MA: Blackwell.

II Theoretical considerations in bilingualism research

István Kecskés
Bilingual pragmatic competence

Abstract: This paper discusses bilingual pragmatic competence, which has been a somewhat neglected area in the fields of both bilingualism and pragmatics. Because of the monolingual perspective pragmatic competence has never been a primary issue in linguistic/philosophical pragmatics or other subfields of pragmatics, with the exception of interlanguage pragmatics.

The paper focuses on discussing how the emerging new language with its own developing socio-cultural foundation affects the existing L1-governed knowledge and pragmatic competence of adult sequential bilinguals. These bilinguals already have an L1-governed pragmatic competence in place, which will be adjusted to accommodate the socio-cultural requirements of the new language(s). I argue that there is a difference between the development of pragmatic competence in L1 and the development of bilingual pragmatic competence. While the former is controlled mainly by the socio-cultural environment the latter is mostly motivated by individual will. In L1, language development and social development go hand in hand as a subconscious, automatic and instinctive process in which the individual consciousness and willingness to acquire social skills and knowledge play a limited role. The process depends mainly on exposure to and the nature of the socio-cultural environment. Bilingual pragmatic competence develops differently. The process is affected by individual control, consciousness and willingness to modify existing skills and behavior patterns and to acquire particular social skills and ignore others.

Keywords: conceptual socialization, sociopragmatics, dynamic continuum, situation-bound utterances, bidirectional pragmatic influence

1 Introduction

This paper aims to discuss bi- and multilingual pragmatic competence, which has been a somewhat neglected area in the field of bilingualism. There are, of course, many articles about bilingual language use, but it has scarcely been discussed what role pragmatic competence plays in the linguistic behavior of bilinguals. Pragmatics research has not paid much attention to the issue either. Because of the monolingual focus pragmatic competence has never been a primary issue in the agenda of linguistic/philosophical pragmatics or other subfields of pragmatics, with the exception of interlanguage pragmatics. This lack of attention may also be explained by the fact that linguistics proper has never really focused on pragmatic competence. Chomsky (1978: 224) introduced a distinction between "grammatical competence", which is related to form and meaning, and "pragmatic competence", which involves "knowledge of conditions and manner of appropriate use, in conformity with various purposes". Appropriateness of use is expressed in terms of the relations between intentions and purposes and between linguistic means, of certain forms and meanings, within linguistic institutional settings (Kasher 1991). However, Chomsky did not take any interest in this pragmatic competence and considered the separation of linguistic competence from pragmatic competence to be indispensable for practical reasons, for the ability to explore and discover the pure, formal properties of the genetically pre-programmed linguistic system.

This paper has a relatively limited scope. It focuses mainly on discussing how the emerging new language with its own developing socio-cultural foundation affects the existing L1-governed knowledge and pragmatic competence of *adult sequential bilinguals*. It is assumed that these bilinguals already have an L1-governed pragmatic competence in place, which will be adjusted to accommodate the socio-cultural requirements of the new language(s). I will argue that *there is a basic difference between the development of pragmatic competence in L1 and the development of bilingual pragmatic competence.* While the former is controlled mainly by the socio-cultural environment, the latter is mostly motivated by individual will. In the L1, language development and social development go hand in hand as a subconscious, automatic and instinctive process in which the individual consciousness and willingness to acquire social skills and knowledge play a limited role. The whole process depends mainly on exposure to and the nature of the socio-cultural environment. However, bilingual pragmatic competence develops differently. The process is affected by individual control, consciousness and willingness to modify existing skills and behavior patterns and to acquire particular social skills while ignoring others.

2 What is pragmatic competence?

There is no doubt about the fact that besides grammatical competence there exists pragmatic competence attached to the L1, which keeps being modified with the exposure to and/or addition of other languages and cultures. Grammatical competence is about correctness while pragmatic competence is more about appropriateness. Grammar contains facts and rules about the given language system that must be followed (at least to some extent), otherwise the language is unrecognizable. This is something that can systematically be acquired by the language learner. However, pragmatic rules (language use rules) are different. Not following them may cause misinterpretation of linguistic behavior. If grammar is bad, the utterance may not convey the right message or any message, while if pragmatics is bad, the utterance will usually convey the wrong message. This is how Crystal (1997: 240) defines pragmatic ability: "The study of language from the point of view of users, especially of the choices they make, the constraints they encounter in using language in social interaction and the effects their use of language has on other participants in the act of communication." Yorio's (1980) example of a North American shop attendant's saying "What can I do for you?" versus "What do you want?", the former being a routine formula while the latter being a grammatically and semantically accurate question, highlights how the latter could be inappropriate and even impolite at the pragmatic and sociolinguistic levels due to the preferences of the speech community. Rules of language use function like suggestions, recommendations by the members of a speech community, which are based on norms, behavioral patterns, conventions and standards of that community. So the language user has more leverage there than in the case of grammatical rules.

Pragmatic competence in the L1 is the result of language socialization. As said above, language and social development in the L1 go hand in hand and are inseparable. However, this is not exactly the case in L2 and subsequent languages. The socio-pragmatic norms concerning appropriateness developed through L1 are very influential and difficult to change. Sometimes L2 norms and patterns need conscious acts by the language learner to accept and/or acquire them. Bilinguals may see things in L2 through their L1 socio-cultural mindset. Thomas (1983) indicated that if we should try to force non-native speakers (NNS) to conform to native speaker (NS) norms, it would be nearly the same as NSs' ideological control over NNSs or cultural imposition on NNSs by NSs' socially hegemonic strata. Some recent studies have pointed out that NNSs may have some kind of resistance toward the use of NS norms and speech conventions to maintain their own identity, and so they may commit pragmatic negative transfer "on purpose" (e.g. Al-Issa 2003; Fujiwara 2004; Siegal 1996). Siegal (1996) discussed the case of a female Western learner of Japanese who felt affective resistance to a Japanese norm, because Japanese female language appeared too humble to her. According to Siegal (1996), these findings mean real difficulty for researchers because frequently it is impossible to establish whether some inappropriate or misleading language use results from the NNSs' affective resistance to the NS practice or whether it is just a lack of native-like pragmatic competence.

Willingness, motivation and ability of bilinguals to assume and use L2 (or sub-sequent language) socio-cultural beliefs and norms seem to play a decisive role in multilingual development and language use. An advanced L2 speaker cannot be expected "simply to abandon his/her own cultural world" (Barro et al. 1993: 56). Adamson (1988) pointed out that NNSs are often reluctant to accept and share the values, beliefs, and presuppositions of an L2 community even if they have been living there for a long period of time and can speak the language quite well. The influence of culture on communication patterns is so strong that even if the conceptual socialization process in L2 is very advanced and the individual has high proficiency and excellent skills in the L2, his/her interaction with NSs is severely blocked by the limits imposed by cultural factors. According to Lu (2001), the influence of the traditional Chinese culture is so far-reaching and persistent that even second- or third-generation Americans of Chinese descendants are unable to fully ignore it although their English proficiency is on a par with that of native English speakers. Many of these people do not speak Chinese and totally depend on English as the tool of thinking and communication. "Nevertheless, their speech acts are still in the shadow of culturally governed modes of thinking, talking and behaving" (Lu 2001: 216).

3 Pragmatic competence in a second language

As mentioned in the introduction, research in pragmatic competence has been a very important part of interlanguage pragmatics. In that paradigm, pragmatic competence is usually defined as the ability to produce and comprehend utterances (discourse) that is adequate to the socio-cultural context in which interaction takes place (e.g. Rose and Kasper 2001; Thomas 1983). According to Barron's definition (2001), who has researched study abroad programs in L2, "[P]ragmatic competence (...) is understood as the knowledge of the linguistic resources available in a given language for realising particular illocutions, knowledge of the sequential aspects of speech acts, and finally, knowledge of the appropriate contextual use of the particular language's linguistic resources".

Based on the research of Leech (1983) and Thomas (1983), two aspects of pragmatic competence have been distinguished. The pragmalinguistic aspect refers to the resources for conveying communicative acts and relational or interpersonal meanings. These resources include pragmatic strategies such as directness and indirectness, routines, and a great variety of linguistic forms which can intensify or soften communicative acts. For one example, compare these two versions of a request:

(1) Waiter to the customer:
     – Come with me, please. I'll show you to your table.

(2) Mary to her husband:
     – Why don't you come with me? I'll show you something.

In both cases, the speaker chooses from among a great variety of available pragmalinguistic resources of the English language which can function as a request. However, each of these two expressions indexes a very different attitude and social relationship. This is where the sociopragmatic aspect comes in and becomes important in speech analysis. It is not enough, for instance, to know that "you bet" can be a response to "thank you". The speaker also needs to know when it is an appropriate response. For instance:

(3) At the end of the plenary talk the chair of the session turns to the plenary speaker and says:
     – Professor Green, thank you for this thought-provoking presentation.
     – You bet / No problem / Thanks / My pleasure / Not at all.
     "You bet" is definitely not the right response in this situation. Neither is "no problem".

Leech (1983: 10) defined sociopragmatics as "the sociological interface of pragmatics". He referred to the social perceptions underlying participants' interpretation and performance of their communicative action. Speech communities differ in their assessment of speakers' and hearers' social distance and social power, their rights and obligations, and the degree of imposition involved in particular communicative acts (Rose and Kasper 2001). According to Thomas (1983), while pragmalinguistics is, in a sense, akin to grammar in that it consists of linguistic forms and their respective functions, sociopragmatics is about appropriate social behavior. In many cases adult bilinguals do not have many problems with pragmalinguistics. They know several linguistic ways to express a particular social function. What they have trouble with is sociopragmatics. Which of the available form(s) is/are appropriate in the given situation? (see example 3). Bilingual speakers must be aware of the consequences of making pragmatic choices.

Bialystok (1993: 54) argued that bilingual "adults make pragmatic errors, not only because they do not understand forms and structures, or because they do not have sufficient vocabulary to express their intentions, but because they choose incorrectly". Although Bialystok identifies the cause of "incorrect choices" in adult learners' lacking the ability to control attentional resources, another explanation may be that learners' sociopragmatic knowledge is not yet developed enough for them to make contextually appropriate choices of strategies and linguistic forms.

The difference between pragmalinguistic and sociopragmatic factors is especially important in intercultural communication, where bilinguals usually have more access to pragmalinguistics than to sociopragmatics, especially if they have acquired the target language in the classroom. This presupposes that bilinguals in their L2 usually have greater pragmalinguistic skills than sociopragmatic knowledge. How pragmatic competence correlates with language proficiency is not yet known. However, what is known is the fact that while NSs of a language are privileged by access to a range of linguistic devices from which they can draw, NNSs are less so. The few studies that focused on the effect of L2 proficiency on pragmatic competence development have often presented different findings (Bardovi-Harlig 1999; Maeshiba, Yoshinaga, Kasper and Ross 1996). Language proficiency is, of course, a crucial factor, but not the only factor involved. It has been argued that learners of high grammatical proficiency will not necessarily show concomitant pragmatic skills. Bardovi-Harlig (1999) argued that grammatical competence and pragmatic competence are independent of each other though a lack of grammatical competence in a particular area may cause a particular utterance to be less effective. According to another view (e.g. Barron 2001), grammatical competence is the prerequisite of pragmatic competence, but Barron argued that these two aspects are interrelated, and the way they correlate with each other is not linear, but rather complex. More research is needed to investigate this complicated issue because the impact of low level pragmatic competence may lead to serious consequences, especially in native speaker – non-native speaker communication. Platt (1989) pointed out that when somebody speaks very little of the target language, s/he is usually considered to be an 'outsider', so pragmatic mistakes do not generate any problems. However, when a NNS speaks English fluently, NSs tend to consider the person to be part of the speech community and interpret his/her behavior according to the socio-cultural rules of that community. So the tendency is to consider a misconstructed utterance to have been deliberate rather than just an error. In lingua franca communication this issue is even more complex, as we will see later.

4 How does the pragmatic competence of bilinguals develop and change?

The development of pragmatic competence is basically a part of language socialization both in L1, L2 and Lx. However, there are basic differences between how L1 socialization contributes to bilingual pragmatic competence and how L2 (and subsequent languages) socialization does that. Linguistic and socio-cultural knowledge are constructed through each other. This interplay between language acquisition and socialization was described by Ochs (1996: 407) as follows: "[T]he acquisition of language and the acquisition of social and cultural competence are not developmentally independent processes, nor is one process a developmental prerequisite of the other. Rather, the two processes are inter-twined from the moment a human being enters society." Leung (2001: 2) empha-sized that language socialization basically deals with how novices "become competent members of their community by taking on the appropriate beliefs, feelings and behaviors, and the role of language in this process".

Focusing on second language development, some studies (e.g. Blum-Kulka 1997; Li 2008) spoke about pragmatic socialization rather than language social-ization. Pragmatic socialization is defined by Blum-Kulka (1997: 3) as "the ways in which children are socialized to use language in socially and culturally appropriate ways". Research that has been done within the framework of prag-matic socialization reflects a more social, contextual, and cultural orientation in comparison with cognitive or psychological approaches to first- and second-language pragmatics (Ochs 1986; Schieffelin and Ochs 1986). Pragmatic develop-ment through language socialization depends mostly on the degree of active and purposeful involvement in interactions. Language socialization relies on two processes, i.e. a) socialization through the use of language, referring to "interac-tional sequences in which novices are directed to use language in specific ways", and b) socialization to use the language, referring to "the use of lan-guage to encode and create cultural meaning" (Poole 1994: 594). This view emphasizes the importance of language use to develop socio-cultural behavior (appropriateness), and on the other hand it underlines the role of social pro-cesses in developing individual language skills (correctness). The appropriate use of language within a speech community depends on conventions, norms, beliefs, expectations, and knowing the preferred ways of saying things and the preferred ways of organizing thoughts (Kecskés 2007). People can get to learn all these only if they go through the socialization process with the other members of the speech community. Pragmatic socialization is a life-long process (e.g. Duff 2003; Schieffelin and Ochs 1986) as people enter new socio-cultural con-texts and take up new roles in society.

4.1 Conceptual socialization of bilinguals

The language socialization paradigm, built mainly on the works of Ochs and Schieffelin, has had a strong ethnographic orientation and paid close attention

to contextual dynamics of language behavior and human agency in L1. Following the traditions of language socialization research, interlanguage pragmatics has aimed to identify deviations from native speakers' norms (Kasper 2001) and emphasized the dynamism and ever-lasting change of the individual's pragmatic competence that is modified under the new socio-cultural environments, situations, and challenges. Bilingual pragmatics, which is the focus of this paper, takes into account the results of language socialization research both in L1 and L2. However, its concerns are slightly different from those of interlanguage pragmatics. The main issue for bilingual pragmatics concerning pragmatic socialization can be summarized as follows: *How will the existing, L1-based pragmatic competence change under the influence of the newly emerging language, and how will the new strategies, behavioral patterns and socio-cultural knowledge blend and/or interact with the existing ones?* These questions presuppose that
- *change* primarily means the modification of an existing system;
- the process is dynamic with its ups and downs;
- there is a bidirectional influence between languages and cultures;
- subjectivity plays a leading role in what new elements are accepted and incorporated into the existing system.

In order to describe how language socialization takes place in L2 and subsequent languages, Kecskés (2002: 199) proposed the term *conceptual socialization*, which he defined as "the transformation of the conceptual system which undergoes characteristic changes to fit the functional needs of the new language and culture". *During the process of conceptual socialization the L1-dominated conceptual base of a bilingual is being gradually restructured, making space for and engaging with the new knowledge and information coming through the second language channel* (e.g. Kecskés 2002; Ortactepe 2012). This leads to the development of a conscious awareness of how another culture is different from one's own culture, the ability to reflect upon this difference in language production, and the development of an identity that is the reflection of the dual culture. The term "conceptual socialization" has been used to distinguish the process of socialization in L2 or Lx from "language socialization" (cf. Mitchell and Myles 1998; Ochs 1988; Willett 1995), which has its roots in anthropological linguistics. With the use of this term I wanted to underline that changes are primarily conceptual and are reflected in the functioning of the dual language system.

Ochs' and Schieffelin's work has focused on L1 development. They did not pay much attention to L2 socialization. There are only a restricted number of studies that extend the paradigm to second language acquisition (e.g. Platt 1989; Willett 1995). Willett (1995), for instance, conducted a longitudinal study with young classroom learners of ESL in an elementary school with an international intake. Based on her results she argued that language socialization is a complex process in which participants construct and evaluate shared understandings through negotiation. This process leads to changes not only in their identity but also in social practices. Ortactepe (2012) conducted a longitudinal, mixed-method study that relied on the assumption that international students as newcomers to the American culture experience bilingual development through conceptual socialization, which enables them to gain pragmatic competence in the target language through exposure to the target language and culture. By collecting qualitative and quantitative data three times over a year, the study examined the linguistic and social development of Turkish bilingual students as a result of their conceptual socialization in the U.S. Socio-cultural and linguistic features of the language socialization process were analyzed together to emphasize the interplay between them in shaping the social and linguistic behavior of the subjects. Ortaztepe provided evidence that L2 learners' conceptual socialization relies predominantly – contrary to what previous research says – on learners' investment in language rather than only on extended social networks.

4.2 Differences between conceptual socialization and language socialization

Conceptual socialization broadens the scope of the paradigm of language socialization, which has its main focus on language developmental issues. Conceptual socialization has a multilingual perspective and differs from language socialization in that it emphasizes the primacy of mental processes in the symbiosis of language and culture, and aims at explaining the bidirectional influence of the two or more languages. The process of conceptual socialization is strongly tied to the emergence of the common underlying conceptual base that is responsible for the operation of two or more language channels (Kecskés 2010; Kecskés and Papp 2000). The child acquiring his/her first language lives in the culture that is responsible for the development of the encyclopedic knowledge base, social skills, image system, and concepts which give meaning to all linguistic signs that are used in the given language. This is not exactly the case if the target language is acquired as a second or foreign language. The main differences between L1 language socialization and conceptual socialization can be summarized as follows.

4.2.1 Partial consciousness of the process

L1 language socialization is basically a subconscious, and partly automatic, process through which the child gradually integrates into his/her environment and speech community both linguistically and socially. However, in the L2 much more consciousness is involved in the process in which age is a decisive variable. Several researchers have noted that bilinguals make deliberate, conscious choices about pragmatic strategies and/or features of the target language. Taguchi (2011: 303) claimed that when learners' L1 and L2 cultures do not operate under the same values and norms, or when learners do not agree with L2 norms, linguistic forms that encode target norms are not easily acquired. Research has indicated that not all language learners wish to behave pragmatically just like native speakers of the target language (e.g. Li 1998; Siegal 1996). Li (1998) reported that Chinese immigrant women sometimes resisted more expert peers' pragmatic socialization based on their personal values and cultural beliefs. The important thing here is that bilinguals may know target language norms and expectations but do not wish to act accordingly. In intercultural communication (especially in the lingua franca), this fact may support rather than hamper the smoothness of the communicative process. The too frequent use of "thank you", "I am sorry", "have a nice day" type of expressions may be annoying for non-native speakers.

4.2.2 Age and attitude of bilinguals

The later the L2 is introduced, the more bilinguals rely on their L1-dominated conceptual system, and the more they are resistant to any pragmatic change that is not in line with their L1-related value system and norms. Ochs (1988: 14) claimed about L1 socialization that "not only are language practices organized by the world views, they also create world views for the language users carrying out these practices". For second/foreign language users the crucial question is whether those existing world views will be modified to any extent under the influence of the new language and culture, and how this new blend (if any) will affect language production in both languages. Gee (1999: 63) argued that the situated and local nature of meaning is largely invisible to us. It is easy for us to miss the specificity and localness of our own practices and think that we have general, abstract, even universal meanings. We come to think, when we have learned no other languages, that 'standing' is just standing, 'eating' is just eating, 'over there' is just over there. In fact, the situated, social and cultural nature of meaning often becomes visible to us only when we confront language-at-work in languages and cultures far distant from our own. This "confrontation" often occurs at the level of fixed expressions, as will be discussed below.

4.2.3 Direct or indirect access to the target culture and environment

In L1, language and social development are intertwined because people have direct access to the socio-cultural environment that shapes their norms, values, conventions, and beliefs. This is not the case in L2. Bilinguals usually have limited access to the L2 culture and environment. Even if they live in the target language environment, it cannot be certain that they have full access to it because of personal or external reasons. In L2 pragmatic socialization is more about discourse practices as related to linguistic expressions than how these practices relate to cultural patterns, norms, and beliefs. Language learners may have direct access to the L2 linguistic materials they need but not to the socio-cultural background knowledge that gives sense to the particular linguistic expressions in the L2.

4.3 How do the pragmalinguistic and sociopragmatic dimensions relate to the skill side and the content side of conceptual socialization?

I found it important to make a distinction between the skill side and the content side of conceptual socialization (Kecskés 2002). They are two sides of one and the same phenomenon. Changes in both sides are qualitative rather than quantitative. The skill side means that conceptual socialization is reflected in the actual language skills of the learner, i.e. structural well-formedness, language manipulation, sentence-structuring, lexical quality, and formulaic language use. It should be emphasized that the skill side of L2 conceptual socialization is not the same as the pragmalinguistic factors that were discussed above. Primarily, pragmalinguistic factors refer to the knowledge of pragmatic expressions, phrases, and utterances that can be used in a particular situation. They refer to some kind of pragmatic "repertoire" which the learners should know in order to choose the appropriate one according to the situation at hand. Language learners with low proficiency often do not know what expression to use in a particular situation and they say something influenced by their L1. The following example of pragmalinguistic failure is taken from Richards and Sukwiwat (1983: 116), and makes reference to a situation in which a Japanese student has to express gratitude in English (original source Bou 1998).

(4) E: Look what I've got for you! (maybe a gift)
     JE: Oh!, *I'm sorry.* (in Japanese, 'thank you' may not sound sincere enough)
     E: Why sorry?

Another case of pragmalinguistic failure can be when the learner processes the utterance literally, not recognizing its illocutionary force. The interaction below takes place between the clerk and a Korean student in the Office of Human Resources.

(5) Lee: – Could you sign this document for me, please?
     Clerk: – *Come again...*
     Lee: – Why should I come again? I am here now.

The skill side of conceptual socialization is broader than the pragmalinguistic factors. It is the actual linguistic knowledge of the language learner that enables him/her to perform and process illocutions. The skill side of the conceptual socialization process is measurable.

The content side of conceptual socialization is expected to give information about learners' metalinguistic awareness, interactional style, pragmatic strategies, knowledge of the target culture, and multicultural attitude. In this list I find especially important *multicultural attitude*, which is connected with the willingness and motivation of the bilingual to act according to the socio-cultural rules of the language s/he uses in the given moment. Changes in the content side would be difficult to measure. They are qualitative changes in the content of what the bilingual says, and the way the bilingual behaves in communication. In this sense the content side of conceptual socialization includes sociopragmatic factors.

4.4 Moving through the dynamic continuum of conceptual socialization in L2

From the perspective of conceptual socialization it is important to mention Lave and Wenger's (1991) legitimate peripheral participation. Their approach is based on the assumption that cognition is built from experience through social interaction in communities of practice. It is a process of "incorporation of learners into the activities of communities of practice, beginning as a legitimated (recognized) participant on the edges (periphery) of the activity, and moving through a series of increasingly expert roles as learners' skills develop" (Watson-Gegeo 2004: 341). In activities in the language community, while bilinguals adopt various communicative and social roles in temporarily and spatially situated activities/ practices, at the same time they also develop grammatical, discourse, socio-cultural and general cognitive structures of knowledge. This is how the skill side and content side of conceptual socialization are ideally intertwined. Bilinguals, who begin peripherally in a new language, should be exposed to mutual engagement with the members of the community until they are granted enough legitimacy to be a potential member (Wenger 1998). Moving through this dynamic continuum with its ups and downs, second language users can get from the status of a beginner to advanced roles through gaining and/or being allowed access to social interaction in the dominant language community. However, moving through this dynamic continuum depends both on individual and social factors. *Exposure, quality and quantity of input can be effective only as much as the individual learner allows them to be.* As mentioned above, there can be much control here from the perspective of the bilingual individual.

In her longitudinal study, Ortactepe (2011) examined both the skill side and content side of conceptual socialization. In the qualitative analysis of the content side that she connected to the dynamic changes of social identity, she found evidence against the language myth according to which students learn by osmosis when in the target speech community. Learning through osmosis is the natural way to learn a language. To learn through osmosis means to learn by immersing oneself in a language and culture. Most of the literature on second language acquisition takes for granted that this is the best and most efficient way of acquiring another language. This way of thinking does not seem to take into account the decisive role of the individual learner in the process. An important element of Ortactepe's work is that by analyzing the conceptual socialization process of her subjects one by one, she provided evidence that L2 learners' conceptual socialization relies predominantly – contrary to previous research – on learners' investment in language rather than on extended social networks. This finding demonstrates that not only in language use but also in language development and socialization the role of individual cognition is as important as the role of the socio-cultural environment and social networking.

5 How is pragmatic competence reflected in language use?

Kecskés (2007) argued that using a particular language and belonging to a particular speech community means having preferred ways of saying things and preferred ways of organizing thoughts. Preferred ways of saying things are generally reflected in the use of formulaic language and figurative language. Selecting the right words and expressions in communication is more important than syntax. Language socialization depends on the acquisition of what is expected to be said in particular situations, and what kind of language behavior is considered appropriate in the given speech community. That is why conceptual socialization in L2 requires direct access to the target culture.

Formulaic language is the heart and soul of native-like language use. In fact, formulaic language use makes language use native-like. Dell Hymes (1968) said that "a vast proportion of verbal behaviour consists of recurrent patterns, [...] [including] the full range of utterances that acquire conventional significance for an individual, group or whole culture" (Hymes 1968: 126–127). Coulmas (1981: 1–3) argued that much of what is actually said in everyday conversation is by no means unique. Rather, a great deal of communicative activity consists of enacting routines making use of prefabricated linguistic units in a well-known and generally accepted manner. Successful coordination of social interactions heavily depends on standardized ways of organizing interpersonal encounters because conventional ways of doing things with words and expressions are familiar to everyone in the speech community so speakers can be expected to be understood according to their communicative intentions and goals. Pragmatic competence is directly connected to and develops through the use of formulaic expressions, mainly because the use of formulas is group-identifying. Formulas reflect a community's shared language practices, and so they discriminate those who belong to the group from those who do not (Yorio 1980). This is so because, as Wray and Namba (2003: 36) claimed, "speech communities develop and retain common ways of expressing key messages".

Language socialization studies highlighted the importance of prefabricated chunks in the socialization process both in L1 and L2 development. Ochs and Schieffelin (1984) pointed out that there is much direct teaching of the interactional routines ("elema") among the Kaluli in Western Samoa. Willett (1995) argued that in the first months ESL students relied heavily on prefabricated chunks which they picked up from their fluent English-speaking peers or from adults during routine events. Coulmas (1979: 256–260) gave a summary of the difficulties L2 learners have when using routine formulae. He categorized pragmatic interferences according to the respective process or structural phenomenon giving rise to the mistake in question.

From the perspective of conceptual socialization and change in the pragmatic competence of bilinguals, the development and use of situation-bound utterances (SBUs) are especially important because they are reflections of socio-cultural patterns, cultural models, and behavioral expectations in a speech community. Situation-bound utterances (Kecskés 2000, 2003) are highly conventionalized, prefabricated pragmatic units whose occurrences are tied to standardized communicative situations (e.g. Coulmas 1981; Kecskés 1997, 2000; Kiefer 1995). Many bilingual speakers have an excellent command of the language systems. Besides pronunciation, there are only two things that can reveal that they are not native speakers, i.e. word choice and use of SBUs. SBUs are direct reflections of what is considered appropriate language use in a speech community. Here is an example that was given to me by Roberts Sanders (personal communication).

(6)   He was ordering a pizza on the phone. The woman who answered was fluent in English but had an accent.
Sanders: – I'd like to order a medium pizza.
Woman: – Is that pickup or delivery?
Sanders: – Pickup.
Woman: – *Is that it?*
Sanders: – What?
Woman: – *Is that it?*
Sanders: – Is that what?
Woman: (No response. Silence)
Sanders: – We want three toppings: pepperoni, mushroom, cheese.
Woman: – OK, you want pepperoni, mushroom and cheese.
Sanders: – Right.
Woman: – Okay, about 20 minutes.

Although the woman at Pizza Hut was fluent in English, her inappropriate use of the SBU "is that it?" caused a slight breakdown in the interaction. Normally, "is that it?" is a formula used to close this part of the transaction and move on to something new or closing. But for Sanders, the transaction should not have been moving on, because they were still in the middle of the ordering process. He had not yet told the assistant what toppings he wanted. The woman repeated, "is that it?", and Sanders said "is that what?". This was followed by silence from the woman, who must have been confused. Then Sanders told her what toppings he wanted, she understood perfectly, and they closed the transaction properly. The confusion was caused by the bilingual speaker's inappropriate use of an SBU.

5.1 How are SBUs tied to pragmatic competence?

5.1.1 Situational obligatoriness is culture-specific

Situational obligatoriness of SBUs varies across cultures. This means that certain situations require the use of SBUs in a particular culture, which might not be the case in another culture. There are, for instance, cases when Americans can easily opt for a freely-generated phrase while Japanese or Turks may not do so. This is true the other way around. It is almost impossible to find a Russian, Japanese or Hungarian equivalent to the SBUs: "have a good one", "you are all set", or "I'll talk to you later" in English. Bilinguals not only have to memorize SBUs as linguistic units but also to understand the socio-cultural background (cultural customs, values, attitudes, etc.) these routine expressions are applicable in. This is where most of the influence from L1 occurs. Sometimes the communicative function is culture-specific, which makes it quite difficult to give the functional equivalent of English "you bet", "welcome aboard", or Turkish "gülü gülü oturun" ('stay laughingly'), "gözünüz aydin" ('your eye bright'), "güle güle büyütün" ('raise laughingly') and the like, in other languages because these phrases are the result of the specific socio-cognitive development in the given language and have specific pragmatic features which are usually non-existent or different in the other language(s). For instance, Turkish "gülü gülü oturun" ('stay laughingly') is used to someone who has just bought, rented, or moved into a new house. "Gözünüz aydin" ('your eye bright') is used to someone who has had the good fortune to be visited by a loved one who was far away. It is not that these situations do not exist in other languages. It is that other languages may not find it important to introduce a special SBU in those cases. Hungarians also say something when a friend or relative tells them that s/he has bought or moved into a new house. But they do not insist on the use of a particular SBU in that situation. What they say is usually freely generated. It is hardly possible to find equivalents to these Turkish SBUs in American English, Hungarian, Russian or other languages because they are the representatives of Turkish culture, which finds it important to give voice to one's feelings in the situations described above. "Güle güle büyütün" ('raise laughingly') differs from the other two expressions in that it refers to an event which is considered to be joyful and very special in many cultures, i.e. the birth of a child. This expression is used to the parents of a newborn infant. This situation is lexicalized differently in many cultures. Conceptual socialization means, among other things, that the bilingual becomes aware of these differences and does not look for an equivalent SBU where there is none, and does not try to use the communicative customs of Lx in Ly.

5.1.2 Socio-cultural values expressed by SBUs

SBUs very strongly relate to socio-cultural values. According to Albert (1968: 288), a value system represents "what is expected or hoped for, required or forbidden. It is not a report of actual conduct but in the system of criteria by which conduct is judged and sanctions applied". Even the slightest differences in the socio-cultural value system may result in differences in cognitive mapping and, as a consequence, in lexicalization (Kecskés 2002). For instance, guests are equally valued in American, French, and Hungarian society. But the SBUs that are used to welcome them demonstrate interesting differences:

(7)   English: Make yourself at home.
      French: Faites comme chez vous. ('Do as [you do] at home.')
      Hungarian: Érezze magat otthon. ('Feel yourself at home.')

Although these expressions can be considered as functional equivalents, the use of different verbs (French "faites" is the imperative of the French equivalent of "to do", and the Hungarian "érezd" is the imperative of the Hungarian equivalent of "feel") demonstrates that each language highlights something else as important in one and the same situation.

Coulmas (1981: 11) claimed that "the more tradition-oriented a society is, the more its members seem to make use of situational formulae". However, we must be careful and not accept this claim at face value because it raises the question of how the content of SBUs relates to the situation(s) they are used in. Depending on whether SBUs directly say something about the action and/or participants, or relate them to other situations or agents, Kecskés (2002) highlighted a difference between *situation-bound routines* ("nice to meet you"; "you bet"; "take care"; "you are all set"; "welcome aboard", etc.) and *situation-bound rituals* ("God bless you"; "thank you"). Situation-bound rituals generally relate the actual situation to other situations, events or agents. They are especially frequent in tradition-oriented cultures such as Japanese, Arabic, Chinese, and Turkish. The use of situation-bound rituals is almost obligatory and usually no freely-generated phrases are acceptable instead. They behave like Yiddish psycho-ostensives about which Matisoff claimed that "often it is not so much that the speaker is using an emotive formula that actually belies his true feelings, as that the formula has become a surrogate for the true feeling, an almost automatic linguistic feature that constant usage has rendered as predictable and redundant as the concord in number between subject and verb" (Matisoff 1979: 6). Yiddish psycho-ostensives, just like SBUs, refer to the speaker's attitude to what s/he is talking about. However, Tannen and Oztek (1981) called our attention to the fact that while in Yiddish culture the priority is on verbal inventiveness (consequently, these emotive expressions are productive), in Greek and especially in Turkish culture situation-bound rituals are fixed sets and are usually complete utterances. In tradition-oriented cultures, situation-bound rituals are not considered insincere because these cultures seem to have agreed to accept the surrogate as evidence for the true feeling (Tannen and Oztek 1981). For instance in Turkish:

(8) If someone mentions a bad event or disaster, this should be followed by an expression to erase the effect:
agzindan yel alsin
'May the wind take it from your mouth.'

In contrast to situation-bound rituals, situation-bound routines generally do not sound sincere, and interlocutors are aware of this. They usually say something that is directly related to the actual situation, participants or actions. *They are standardized solutions to coordination problems where no negotiations are necessary.* Situation-bound routines serve an important function in giving people confidence and behavioral certainty in conversation because they can usually be interpreted only in one particular way, which excludes misunderstanding. Future-oriented cultures (like the American culture) as opposed to tradition-oriented cultures generally prefer the use of situation-bound routines to situation-bound rituals. This is one of the reasons why it is so difficult to find the English equivalent to Turkish, Chinese or Japanese situation-bound rituals. The situations that prompt the use of SBUs in tradition-oriented cultures, in many cases, are not even recognized by native speakers of English as events which demand any verbal reaction (cf. Bear 1987). To illustrate this point, Bear (1987) listed several situations where English native speakers usually have nothing to say while Turks find it necessary to use an SBU:

(9) sihhatler olsun
'may (it) be healthy'
(To address someone who has just taken a bath.)

(10) helal
'(it is) lawful, legitimate'
(To someone who choked.)

In contrast, English SBU routines are more "down-to-earth", and there is less attempt in them to establish rapport between participants of conversation. For the future-oriented Americans, expressions such as "See you soon", "I'll talk to you later", "Look forward to seeing you again", "Why don't we have lunch tomorrow?", and others are quite natural.

5.1.3 SBUs and phatic communication (small talk)

Malinowski (1923: 476) defined phatic communication as "[...] language used in free, aimless, social intercourse". It is small talk, a non-referential use of language to share feelings and sympathy, or to establish social rapport rather than to communicate information. Phatic communication is characterized by the use of routinized and ritualized formulas, mainly situation-bound utterances. This term refers to all kinds of acts including greetings, welcomes, questions about work, health, well-being, family and other aspects of life, leave-takes, wish-wells, farewells, compliments about obvious achievements or personal traits of the interlocutors, complaints about things or events with which they are familiar, or those narrations or chit-chat about trivial facts or comments about topics that may seem obvious (Malinowski 1923: 476–479). Why is small talk important for bilingual pragmatic competence? Because it is part of what we referred to as preferred ways of saying things and preferred ways of organizing thoughts in a language. Bilinguals have two sets of small talk, one for each of their languages. However, as we discussed earlier, a bilingual might be more comfortable with the norms and conventions of one of his/her languages than those of the other. Mugford (2011) has shown that his Mexican learners of English transferred local norms and practices and did not adhere to those of the L2 when engaging in phatic exchanges. For instance, unaware of the role of status and distance in the target community, on some occasions Mexican learners made overly personal comments to their instructors, as if assuming they were talking to very close subjects. On other occasions, their small talk displayed local practices, such as lack of expected greetings when entering classrooms, very extended greetings with a profusion of self-disclosure, or the transfer of L1 idiomatic phatic expressions, for example 'fresh as a salad' instead of 'fresh as a daisy' as a reply to a how-are-you question. An effective management of small talk in any language requires an awareness of subtle issues such as when and with whom to engage in it, the underlying reasons and purposes to do so, the topics that can be addressed, or the effects achievable by means of it.

6 Does pragmatic transfer exist?

6.1 The term *pragmatic transfer*

The phenomenon of pragmatic transfer is widely analyzed within the confines of interlanguage pragmatics and cross-cultural pragmatics. The term *pragmatic transfer* usually refers to the carryover of pragmatic knowledge from one language and culture to another language and culture. However, *transfer* may not be the right term to describe what takes place in the bi- and multilingual mind. What really happens is that bilinguals use their L1 cultural models, norms and ways of thinking about the world to formulate or interpret an utterance in their other language, which may result in grammatical, lexical and pronunciation errors at a lower level of proficiency, and grammatically correct but odd utterances or inappropriate use of expressions and formulaic units at a higher level of proficiency. So *transfer* does not seem to be the best way to describe this phenomenon. Here are some examples that are traditionally considered transfers.

(11)   Grammatical transfer
       No plural form after a number (in particular, Chinese and Spanish students make this error because they do not have plural markers in their L1).
       "There are three new student."
       No distinction between subject and object pronouns (Chinese, Spanish).
       "I gave the forms to she."

(12)   Lexical transfer
       A sign in an Austrian hotel catering for skiers (source: Octopus, October 1995, Champaign, IL, p. 144): "Not to perambulate the corridors in the hours of repose in the boots of descension".
       Correctly: "Don't walk in the halls in ski boots at night".

(13)   Conceptual transfer
       Dutch: – What do you know about Kemal's mother?
       Turkish: – His mother was a house woman. Every job used to come from her hand. In making food there was no one on top of her.
       Dutch: – You mean she was a good cook?
       Turkish: – Yes, yes.

Sharwood-Smith and Kellerman (1986: 1) argued that the term *transfer* is inadequate and suggested an umbrella term, *cross-linguistic influence*, that allows "to subsume under one heading such phenomena as 'transfer', 'interference', 'avoidance', 'borrowing' and L2-related aspects of language loss". They recommended that the term *transfer* should be restricted "to those processes that lead to the incorporation of elements from one language into another". In second language acquisition research, Ellis's definition (1994) has been widely used. "*Transfer* is to be seen as a general cover term for a number of different kinds of influence from languages other than the L2. The study of transfer involves the study of errors (negative transfer), facilitation (positive transfer), avoidance of target language forms, and their over-use" (Ellis 1994: 341).

Kasper (1992: 207) defined *pragmatic transfer* as "[...] the influence exerted by learners' pragmatic knowledge of languages and cultures other than L2 on the comprehension, production and learning of L2 pragmatic information". Kasper (1992) revised the two types of pragmatic transfer that Thomas (1983) had spoken about. According to that revision, *pragmalinguistic transfer* refers to those cases in which the functional and social meanings of certain linguistic forms in the L1 affect the comprehension and production of "form-function mappings in L2" (Kasper 1992: 209). *Sociopragmatic transfer* occurs when "the social perceptions underlying language users' interpretation and performance of linguistic action in L2 are influenced by their assessment of subjectively equivalent L1 contexts" (Kasper 1992: 209). In some of her studies Bou-Franch (e.g. 1998, 2012) gave a very useful summary of the understanding of pragmatic transfer in interlanguage pragmatics.

6.2 Bidirectional pragmatic influence

As discussed above, *pragmatic transfer* may not be the best term to describe what happens with pragmatic knowledge and skills in the language use of bilinguals. In interlanguage pragmatics and cross-cultural pragmatics, this phenomenon is usually described as a *unidirectional process*. However, Kecskés and Papp (2000) argued that in the case of bilinguals the two languages mutually affect each other. Pragmatic influence appears to be bidirectional. Consequently, the term *bidirectional pragmatic influence* better describes what happens in the language use of bilinguals (Kecskés and Papp 2000).

An interesting example of bidirectional pragmatic influence is what is called "the intercultural style hypothesis" (Kasper and Blum-Kulka 1993). It refers to a unique development of the common underlying conceptual base in multilingual people. According to this hypothesis (Blum-Kulka 1991; Kasper and Blum-Kulka 1993), speakers fully competent in two languages may create an intercultural style of speaking that is both related to and distinct from the styles prevalent in the two substrata, a style on which they rely regardless of the language being used (Kasper and Blum-Kulka 1993). Kasper and Blum-Kulka claimed that the hypothesis is supported by many studies of cross-cultural communication, especially those focusing on interactional sociolinguistics (e.g. Gumperz 1982; Tannen 1985), and by research into the pragmatic behavior of immigrant populations across generations (e.g. Clyne, Ball and Neil 1991). In a later study Cenoz (2003) investigated the request behavior of fluent Spanish-English bilinguals.

The results showed that these bilinguals make requests in their first language and second language essentially in the same way.

Even if pragmatic influence is bidirectional in the case of bilinguals, the effect of L1 pragmatic competence is usually overwhelming, especially if the L2 was introduced at a later stage. Several researchers (cf. Gonzalez 1987; Schachter 1983; Schmidt 1993) have found that world views, beliefs, pragmatic assumptions, and values are almost always "transferred" from the L1 to the L2 environments. This strong L1 pragmatic influence is demonstrated by He (1988) with the use of the expression "Never mind" by Chinese-English bilinguals when responding to "Thanks a lot. That's a great help". According to Liu (2010), in Chinese people use "没关系" (Mei guan xi) or "不用谢" (Bu yong xie) in response to "Thank you". Thus, some Chinese-English bilinguals fail to see the slight differences among the three English expressions, i.e. "Never mind", "Not at all" and "You are welcome", as in Chinese they could be all translated as "没关系" (Mei guan xi).

7 Conclusion

Discussing the pragmatic competence of adult sequential bilinguals, the paper argued that these bilinguals already have an L1-governed pragmatic competence in place, which is adjusted to accommodate the socio-cultural requirements of the new language as much as the bilinguals allow that to happen. A unique feature of this kind of bilingual pragmatic competence is that bilinguals control what they find acceptable from the norms and conventions of the L2 and occasionally L1. Having a system of pragmatic norms already in place, adult sequential bilinguals may have some kind of resistance toward the use of certain pragmatic norms and speech conventions of (mainly) their L2. Consequently, the language socialization process in subsequent languages may not take place only through osmosis. Contrary to previous research, this paper argues that bilingual conceptual socialization relies predominantly on learners' investment in language rather than just on extended social networks.

This individual control of the pragmatic socialization process is most clearly demonstrated in the use of situation-bound utterances because these formulaic expressions represent the cultural models and ways of thinking of members of a particular speech community. Pragmatic competence is directly tied to and develops through the use of formulaic expressions, mainly because the use of formulas is group-identifying. These expressions reflect a speech community's shared language practices, thus discriminating those who belong to the group from those who do not. This is so because speech communities develop and retain common ways of expressing key messages.

It was argued that bilingual pragmatic competence shows a unique symbiosis of pragmatic rules and expectations of both languages. Bilingual language use is the reflection of this symbiosis. Bilinguals have preferences in the pragmatic rule systems of both languages and act accordingly in communicative encounters.

References

Adamson, H. Douglas. 1988. *Variation theory and second language acquisition*. Washington, DC: Georgetown University Press.

Albert, Ethel. 1968. Value systems. In David L. Sills and Robert K. Merton (eds.), *The international encyclopedia of the social sciences*. Vol. 16, 287–291. New York: Macmillan.

Al-Issa, Ahmad. 2003. Sociocultural transfer in L2 speech behaviors: Evidence and motivating factors. *International Journal of Intercultural Relations* 27. 581–601.

Bardovi-Harlig, Kathleen. 1999. Exploring the interlanguage of interlanguage pragmatics: A research agenda for acquisitional pragmatics. *Language Learning* 49. 677–713.

Barro, Ana, Mike Byram, Hanns Grimm, Carol Morgan & Celia Roberts. 1993. Cultural studies for advanced language learners. In David Graddol, Linda Thompson & Mike Byram (eds.), *Language and culture*, 55–70. Clevedon: Multilingual Matters.

Barron, Anne. 2001. Acquisition in interlanguage pragmatics. Philadelphia: John Benjamins.

Bear, Joshua. 1987. Formulaic utterances and communicative competence. *Journal of Human Sciences* (Insan Bilimleri Degisi.) Middle East Technical University. VI(2): 25–34.

Bialystok, Ellen. 1993. Symbolic representation and attentional control in pragmatic competence. In Gabriele Kasper & Shoshana Blum-Kulka (eds.), *Interlanguage pragmatics*, 43–59. New York: Oxford University Press.

Blum-Kulka, Shoshana. 1997. *Dinner talk*. Mahwah, NJ: Lawrence Erlbaum.

Bou-Franch, Patricia. 1998. On pragmatic transfer. *Studies in English Language and Linguistics*. http://www.uv.es/boup/PDF/Sell-98.pdf (Acessed on 15 April 2013).

Cenoz, Jasone. 2003. The Intercultural Style Hypothesis: L1 and L2 interaction in requesting behavior. In Vivian Cook (ed.), *Effects of the second language on the first*, 62–80. Clevedon: Multilingual Matters Ltd.

Chomsky, Noam. 1978. Language and unconscious knowledge. In J. H. Smith (ed.), *Psychoanalysis and language, psychiatry and the humanities*. Vol. 3. New Haven: Yale University Press.

Clyne, Michael, Martin M. Ball & Deborah Neil. 1991. Intercultural communication at work in Australia: Complaints and apologies in turns. *Multilingua* 10. 251–273.

Coulmas, Florian (ed.). 1981. *Conversational routine: Explorations in standardized communication situations and prepatterned speech*. The Hague: Mouton.

Crystal, David. 1997. *A dictionary of linguistics and phonetics*. 4th edition. Cambridge, MA: Blackwell.

Duff, Patricia A. 2003. New directions in second language socialization research. Korean. *Journal of English Language and Linguistics* 3. 309–339.

Ellis, Rod. 1994. *The study of second language acquisition*. Oxford: Oxford University Press.

Gee, James. P. 1999. *An introduction to discourse analysis: Theory and method*. New York: Routledge.

Grosjean, Francois. 1989. Neurolinguists, beware! The bilingual is not two monolinguals in one person. *Brain and Language* 36(1). 3–15.

Gumperz, John. 1982. *Discourse strategies*. Cambridge: Cambridge University Press.

He, Ziran R. 1988. 语用学概论 [*Pragmatics: An introduction*]. Changsha: Hunan Education Press.

Hymes, Dell. 1972. Models of interaction of language and social life. In John Gumperz & Dell Hymes (eds.), *Directions in sociolinguistics*, 35–71. New York: Holt, Rinehart and Winston.

Kasher, Asa. 1991. Pragmatics and Chomsky's research program. In Asa Kasher (ed.), *The Chomskyan turn*, 122–149. Oxford: Basil Blackwell.

Kasper, Gabriele. 1992. Pragmatic transfer. *Second Language Research* 8(3). 203–231.

Kasper, Gabriele. 2001. Four perspectives on L2 pragmatic development. *Applied Linguistics* 22. 502–530.

Kasper, Gabriele & Shoshana Blum-Kulka. 1993. *Interlanguage pragmatics*. Oxford: Oxford University Press.

Kasper, Gabriele & Steven Ross (eds.). 1996. *Misunderstanding in social life: Discourse approaches to problematic talk*. London: Longman.

Kecskés, István. 2000. A cognitive-pragmatic approach to situation-bound utterances. *Journal of Pragmatics* 32(6). 605–625.

Kecskés, István. 2002. *Situation-bound utterances in L1 and L2*. Berlin & New York: Mouton de Gruyter.

Kecskés, István. 2007. Formulaic language in English lingua franca. In István Kecskés & Laurence R. Horn (eds.), *Explorations in pragmatics: Linguistic, cognitive and intercultural aspects*, 191–219. Berlin & New York: Mouton de Gruyter.

Kecskés, István. 2008. L2 effect on L1. *Babylonia. The Swiss Journal of Language Learning* 2(8). 30–34.

Kecskés, István. 2010. Dual and multilanguage systems. *International Journal of Multilingualism* 7(2). 1–19.

Kecskés, István & Tünde Papp. 2000. *Foreign language and mother tongue*. Mahwah, NJ: Lawrence Erlbaum.

Kiefer, Ferenc. 1995. *Situational utterances*. Keynote presented at the 5th International Pragmatics Conference, Brighton, UK. (Manuscript).

Lave, Jean & Etienne Wenger. 1991. *Situated learning: Legitimate peripheral participation*. Cambridge: Cambridge University Press.

Leech, Geoffrey. 1983. *Principles of pragmatics*. London: Longman.

Leung, Santoi. 2001. Language socialization: Themes and advances in research. *Working Papers in TESOL & Applied Linguistics* 1(1). 1–18.

Liu, Aijuan. 2010. On pragmatic "borrowing transfer": Evidence from Chinese EFL learner's compliment response behavior. *Chinese Journal of Applied Linguistics* 33(4). 26–44.

Lu, Luo. 2001. Understanding happiness: A look into the Chinese folk psychology. *Journal of Happiness Studies* 2. 407–432.

Maeshiba, Naoko, Naoko Yoshinaga, Gabriele Kasper & Steven Ross. 1996. Transfer and proficiency in interlanguage apologizing. In Susan Gass & Joyce Neu (eds.), *Speech acts across cultures: Challenges to communication in a second language* (Studies on Language Acquisition 11), 155–187. Berlin: Mouton de Gruyter.

Malinowski, Bronislaw. 1923. The problem of meaning in primitive languages. In Charles K. Ogden & Ian A. Richards (eds.), *The meaning of meaning*, 146–152. London: Routledge.

Matisoff, James A. 1979. *Psycho-ostensive expressions in Yiddish*. Philadelphia: ISHI Publications.

Mitchell, Rosamond & Florence Myles. 1998. *Second language learning theories*. London: Arnold.

Mugford, Gerrard. 2011. That's not very polite! Discursive struggle and situated politeness in the Mexican English-language classroom. In Bethan Davies, Michael Haugh & Andrew John Merrison (eds.), *Situated politeness*, 53–72. London: Continuum.

Ochs, Elinor. 1986. Introduction. In Bambi B. Schieffelin & Elinor Ochs (eds.), *Language socialization across cultures*, 1–13. New York: Cambridge University Press.

Ochs, Elinor. 1988. *Cultural and language development: Language acquisition and language socialization in a Samoan village*. Cambridge: Cambridge University Press.

Ortactepe, Deniz. 2012. *The development of conceptual socialization in international students: A language socialization perspective on conceptual fluency and social identity* (Advances in Pragmatics and Discourse Analysis). Cambridge: Cambridge Scholars Publishing.

Platt, John. 1989. Some types of communicative strategies across cultures: Sense and sensitivity. In Ofelia Garcia & Ricardo Otheguy (eds.), *English across cultures, cultures across English: A reader in cross-cultural communication*, 13–29. Berlin: Mouton de Gruyter.

Poole, Deborah. 1994. Language socialization in the second language classroom. *Language Learning* 42(4). 593–616.

Rose, Kenneth R. & Gabriele Kasper (eds.). 2001. *Pragmatics and language teaching*. Cambridge: Cambridge University Press.

Schieffelin, Bambi B. & Elonor Ochs. 1986. *Language socialization across cultures*. New York: Cambridge University Press.

Sharwood-Smith, Michael & Eric Kellerman. 1986. Cross-linguistic influence in second language acquisition: An introduction. In Eric Kellerman & Michael Sharwood-Smith (eds.), *Cross-linguistic influence in second language acquisition*, 1–9. New York: Pergamon.

Siegal, Meryl. 1996. The role of learner subjectivity in second language sociolinguistic competency: Western women. *Applied Linguistics* 17. 356–382.

Taguchi, Naoko. 2011. Teaching pragmatics: Trends and issues. *Annual Review of Applied Linguistics* 31. 289–310.

Tannen, Deborah. 1985. Cross-cultural communication. In Teun A. Van Dijk (ed.), *Handbook of discourse analysis*. Vol. 4, 203–215. London: Academic Press.

Tannen, Deborah & Piyale C. Oztek. 1981. Health to our mouths: Formulaic expressions in Turkish and Greek. In Florian Coulmas (ed.), *Conversational routine*, 516–534. The Hague: Mouton.

Thomas, Jenny. 1983. Cross-cultural pragmatic failure. *Applied Linguistics* 4. 91–112.

Watson-Gegeo, Karen A. 2004. Mind, language, and epistemology: Toward a language socialization paradigm for SLA. *The Modern Language Journal* 88(3). 331–350.

Wenger, Etienne. 1998. *Communities of practice: Learning, meaning, and identity*. Cambridge: Cambridge University Press.

Willett, Jerri. 1995. Becoming first graders in an L2: An ethnographic study of L2 socialization. *TESOL Quarterly* 32. 757–761.

Wray, Alison & Kazuhiko Namba. 2003. Formulaic language in a Japanese-English bilingual child: A practical approach to data analysis. *Japanese Journal for Multilingualism and Multiculturalism* 9(1). 24–51.

Yorio, Carlos A. 1980. Conventionalized language forms and the development of communicative competence. *TESOL Quarterly* 14(4). 433–442.

Philipp Wasserscheidt
Construction grammar and code-mixing

Abstract: In this paper I would like to outline a constructionist approach to what is known as code-switching. Taking constructions as the basic elements of language and language production, I show how construction grammar can serve as the starting point for a unified approach to bilingual language use. Constructions as independent linguistic units allow for a decentralized approach which does not take individual languages as a starting point of the contact. I argue that constructions are just as good a frame as the concept matrix-language, while also allowing for the insertion of heads and bilingual constructions. I suggest a constructist explanation of calques and show how the co-occurence of code-switching and calques can be captured.

Keywords: code-mixing/switching, construction grammar, bilingual language use, linguistic transfer, language contact

1 Why a construction grammar approach to code-mixing?

In this paper I would like to undertake the first step in developing a constructionist[1] approach to one of the most interesting phenomena in the study of language, namely code-mixing[2]. The long lasting search for an explanation to the phenomenon of code-mixing has produced a plethora of models, constraints and hypotheses. Hundreds of articles and books have been written on the subject. There might therefore be doubt as to why we would need yet another approach to this field full of puzzling evidence. However, there are at least two reasons why it is nonetheless worth addressing the subject once more. One is mainly grounded in the still nascent theory of construction grammar; the other can be found in the discourse on bilingual speech and code-mixing itself.

---

1 An anonymous reviewer suggested calling the approach 'usage-based'. I completely agree that the version of construction grammar I am promoting here is basically the grammatical component of Usage-Based Linguistics. In this article, however, the focus is on constructions, so that I decided to stick to this term.

2 I use the term *code-mixing* for all instances where overt (phonological) items from two languages appear in one utterance.

Construction grammar has developed over the last 30 years in the works of Fillmore and Kay, Langacker, Goldberg, Croft and many others and has been successfully adopted in various linguistic fields, such as language acquisition, interactional linguistics and historical linguistics. Still, it is a relatively new understanding of language which looks forward to further testing its basic assumptions. It is difficult to come up with any better object for testing a new grammatical theory than the description of bilingual speech. Moreover, construction grammar differs in a number of important assumptions from other theories and their underlying assumptions, which have served as theoretical ground for most of the code-mixing models so far (cf. Gardner-Chloros and Edwards 2004). These differences do not only concern strictly grammatical questions. Indeed, construction grammar does not describe language mainly as a linguistic system in a classical structuralist understanding, but tries to evolve into a theory of linguistic knowledge in general, including its acquisition, representation and processing (Stefanowitsch 2011: 15). It is this aspiration that makes construction grammar a good candidate for a more comprehensive approach to the multifaceted phenomena we encounter in bilingual speech.

The second reason has to do with the ongoing research on code-mixing itself. The literature on this issue concentrates mainly on two questions: *how* do speakers combine items from different languages and *where* do they do it. The latter focuses on grammatical conditions of code-mixing, various sets of which have been proposed by Poplack (1980), DiSciullo, Muysken and Singh (1986), Myers-Scotton (1997) and MacSwan (2001), to name only a few. Naturally, grammar is the focus of all these works, most of which are "concentrated on finding universally applicable, predictive grammatical constraints" (Gardner-Chloros and Edwards 2004: 104). Surprisingly, in contact linguistics there has been little discussion on the appropriateness of the grammatical framework applied or the underlying assumptions about the functioning of language apart from approaches within the generative framework. Reflections on theoretical issues sometimes end in the somewhat disenchanted statement that code-mixing seems to follow no rules whatsoever or should be analysed only within its own rules. Both silence about assumptions and resignation are unsatisfactory insofar as a grammatical theory should be applicable to all varieties of natural language without any changes to its architecture. A search for grammatical constraints on code-mixing therefore has to start with selecting and describing the adopted grammatical model. This includes answering the question as to what exactly the elements of grammar are. Here, construction grammar offers answers that differ significantly from other theories.

The second question is *how* bilinguals combine elements from different languages (cf. e.g. Muysken 2005: 1). Although it is not so obvious from predominantly linguistic works, where both the *how* and the *where* question essentially coincide, this is a question which focuses on language processing. This is why most psycholinguistic models of bilingual language processing, such as Green's Inhibitory Control model (Green 1998) or the Bilingual Production Model (de Bot 1992), Kecskes' Dual Language Model (Kecskes 2006) and Myers-Scotton's Matrix Language Frame Model (e.g. Myers-Scotton and Jake 2010) deal to a great extent with the selection of linguistic elements. They try to explain how a speaker can juxtapose two items from different languages during language processing. Again there is little discussion about the underlying assumption, namely *what* these items actually are. Often, the term *switching* still refers to the transition from one language or code to another and so do the models. But speakers do not produce languages or codes, they produce linguistic units. Although there might be instances of conscious language switches, for example in order to make use of the language's sociolinguistic markedness, in most cases they are not made deliberately. Even if speakers are conscious about their language choice "it is crucial to emphasise that in the production process they select not languages, [...] but words [...]. So it is not languages that compete for selection, but words" (Kecskes 2009: 7). Again the crucial question is *what* exactly speakers select for production, if it is not a language.

As this short discussion about the *where* and *how* questions in code-mixing research shows, it is crucial to determine exactly what we understand by linguistic elements. This question is a theoretical one and can hardly be answered by looking at data alone. As expected in a constructionist framework, I claim that constructions are the basic linguistics elements (cf. Croft 2001: 5). Basically, constructions are the only linguistic elements that have to be taken into account when talking about storage and processing of language.

In the following sections I will outline the theory behind construction grammar and constructions and show how these assumptions can be useful in studying code-mixing. I will firstly discuss the general accordance of constructionist assumptions and the requirement for a bilingual language model followed by specific accounts of bilingual issues, such as the notion of language and language indexation. Then I will outline a constructionist model of code-mixing which I will discuss in more detail focusing on bilingual constructions and the implications of the conceptualization of constructions as complex signs.

2 Construction grammar

Construction grammar is a cluster of closely related approaches to linguistic structure (for an overview cf. e.g. Croft 2007; Goldberg 2006: 213 ff.). Although there are some important differences between the individual accounts, some central assumptions are shared by most researchers (summarized here following Stefanowitsch 2011). First of all, there is the assumption that all grammatical knowledge is acquired, represented and processed in the form of constructions. Secondly, these constructions are conventionalized pairings of form and meaning, whereby the form can be completely captured by referring to what may be called *surface structure*. Thirdly, the semantics of constructions includes all encyclopaedic knowledge and knowledge about the constructions' usage that is necessary to appropriately apply them in communication. This approach to code-mixing also includes the assumption that language has to be acquired through usage (Tomasello 2003; Langacker 2009). This means that language and grammar are nothing other than generalizations over usage and that the only way to assign meaning to a linguistic form or vice versa is to conventionalize this usage in the speech community and to entrench it in the cognitive system of a single speaker. This is said to hold for all linguistic levels, including abstract linguistic entities like paradigms and categories.

Constructions themselves are very close to what is traditionally called a sign. They differ from signs in that they are composite structures (Langacker 2005: 108) which can include smaller constructions or signs in their structure. While some constructionists additionally assume that constructions need to be non-compositional (Goldberg 1995: 4), I adhere to the usage-based position that every form-meaning pairing can "become" a construction if it is used frequently enough. Constructions exist on almost every linguistic level, which means that eventually all linguistic levels can be regarded as being part of a construction. Their form can be both complex and schematic. The complexity ranges from simple lexical morphemes to whole idioms or argument structures and even further. Complex constructions can be more or less schematic, which means that there are slots in the constructions that may be filled by other constructions that are less complex. That is to say, constructions can be nested one into another. The degree of schematicity is low for words or idioms, where the whole of the surface is phonologically predefined by the construction, and high for argument structures or passive constructions. Slots are semantically or pragmatically defined, but mostly lack a formal specification. Regarding their meaning, constructions can be specific or abstract. So, while idioms can be relatively complex, they are not schematic and have a specific meaning. Argument structure constructions as described by Goldberg (1995) are also complex, but highly schematic and abstract in meaning. Construction grammar in principle holds that differences in form tend to reflect differences in meaning and vice versa (cf. Goldberg 1995: 67). However, cross-constructional generalizations can lead to identity of either form or meaning (Stefanowitsch 2011: 18).

Constructions are not universal but have to be conventionalized in the speech community; the inventory of constructions is unique for each language. While it is obvious that the surface form of a construction is different in individual languages and therefore not directly comparable, there are usually also differences in meaning or usage. That is, even if we might identify ditransitive constructions in, say, English and Russian, they are by no means the same construction. Croft even assumes that not only constructions, but all linguistic categories are basically language dependent and can be described only within a language or even only within a single construction (Croft 2001: 170). This would imply that languages are in fact incomparable. While this may seem to be frustrating at first glance, it reflects the puzzling and sometimes contradictory evidence we find in bilingual language use very well. From this point of view, it becomes clear that code-mixing cannot have universal constraints, but depends at the very least on the language pair in question.

3 Construction grammar and code-mixing

Construction grammar offers some promising features for the explanation of bilingual language use without the need of being adapted and even without the need to address code-mixing in any particular way[3]. In the following, some solutions will be discussed that construction grammar can provide to desiderata for a linguistic theory of code-mixing that have been suggested in the code-mixing literature (cf. e.g. Sebba 2010).

Construction grammar is a multi-level approach. Treffers-Daller complained that "there is no term to cover the wide variety of phonological, morphological, syntactic, semantic, and conceptual features, lexical items, phrases, clauses, multiword chunks [...] that can be transferred from one language to another" (Treffers-Daller 2010: 59). The aim of construction grammar is exactly this: to cover all levels of language with one consistent theory and using only one term, i.e. *construction*. Construction grammar has not provided approaches to everything that can be covered by a linguistic theory, yet. But the analysis of bilingual speech will considerably aid to reach this goal.

---

3 One of the anonymous reviewers commented that the article does not make clear the advantages of adopting construction grammar to code-mixing. While I must admit that the reasoning and the empirical part are still cursory, I hope to have made clear at least the potential that construction grammar has in order to cope with a lot of questions within bilingualism research.

Construction grammar avoids the standard language bias (Auer 2006). This holds for a usage-based approach, which is maintained in this outline. Strictly speaking, a "code" or "language" can be defined only by virtue of a frequency-based description of the linguistic means a speech community uses. This makes it possible to account for a code that consists of dialectal, bilingual or emerging elements and to avoid the widely criticised approach to code-switching as the clash of two completely separate grammatical standard systems (Auer 2006: 2). In the end, a usage-based approach, which does not require universal rules, may be able to overcome the matrix language discussion which is partly connected to the question of the separability of "languages" (see below). If a code is described solely on the grounds of the language use of a bilingual community, it may even happen that code-mixing is described by itself, namely when code-mixing is used regularly and certain mixed utterances or expressions become conventionalized. In fact, speakers themselves also rely solely on the community's conventions without reference to standard languages. In this way, analytical flexibility, as demanded by Sebba (2010: 56), is guaranteed: there is no universal *a priori* prediction about the structure of code-mixing.

Construction grammar may help to explain code-mixing by adding another potential motivation for a speaker to switch languages. Since constructions on every level bear some semantic load that is likely to differ between languages, these deviations can help to explain why a speaker chooses, say, an argument structure construction or passive construction from one language and not the other. For example, the alternational type of code-switching is defined without referring to the motivation for the alternate use of linguistic units (Muysken 2005: 96 ff.). A constructionist approach suggests that there may be a straightforward reason for a particular language choice. That is, the properties of constructions may help "determine what switching actually *does* occur" (Sebba 2010: 55, italics original).

In the remainder of the paper, I want to outline more assets of a usage-based constructionist approach to bilingual language processing. These concern the problematic label "language" (Section 4), the process of code-mixing (Section 5), the recognition of bilingual constructions (Section 6), and the integration of the adjacent field of interlinguistic transfer (Section 7).

4 The notion of "language"

In order to be able to apply construction grammar to code-switching, some additional clarifications are necessary. They have not yet been discussed within the theoretical framework of construction grammar but are kept in full accordance with its usage-based principles. The most important one is the question of language marking. There is an abundance of literature on the subject of how a speaker is able to either select a word form from the correct language during production or to assign a heard acoustic form to a language during reception. Many approaches presume that there is a kind of marking on every word that makes this process work. This mark is called *label*, *index* or *tag* (Myers-Scotton 2007: 299; Green 1998: 71; Muysken 2005: 71). In the BIA model family a common language node is assumed (e.g. Dijkstra and van Heuven 1998) that connects all words from one language. But some doubt has been expressed about the existence of such tags. Li (1998) argues that such a label should not allow for any errors in differentiating words from two languages, which, according to empirical evidence, is not true. Paradis questions whether a label like "language" can really be part of the linguistic knowledge of uninformed speakers (Paradis 2004: 204). There have also been some attempts to show that the lexicon can easily do without explicit tagging (Li and Farkas 2002; Meijer and Fox Tree 2003). Paradis argues that there is, in fact, no difference between the brain of a unilingual and that of a bilingual, since unilinguals also have to be able to distinguish between several linguistic entities like dialects, sociolects and pragmatic rules (Paradis 1997: 332). Rather, language affiliation is metalinguistic knowledge, which by its very nature cannot play any role during language processing. Even though it does not seem to be reasonable to assume that every dialect or register a speaker commands should be marked with its own label, it is clear that speakers can easily control these varieties, without having problems selecting the right lemmas. Paradis concludes that words from different languages "are distinguished by phonemic and subphonemic cues in the same way as minimal pairs within the same language" (Paradis 2004: 205) and that no specific marking is necessary.

The approach by Paradis holding that there is no need for language tags (Paradis 2004: 203) is adopted here. It seems logical from the point of view of a usage-based approach that language, just like constructions, is forged together exclusively through the sheer frequency with which all linguistic elements from one language are used together. One could go even further and say that individual languages are the largest constructions we have. If it is feasible to construe everything from morphemes to types of text as conventionalized pairings of form and meaning (or function), then the form-pole of a language is simply the inventory of all its constructions. Since constructions specify linguistic elements only up to the phonological level there is presumably also a set of phonetic forms that are typically used to realize these phonemes. Hence, even if a speaker commands the whole constructicon of a language, he will be labelled as speaking with a foreign accent when he (deliberately or not) fails to choose the right subphonemic features. At the same time it has been shown that speakers are quite good at judging a speaker's L1 based on subphonemic features (Vieru et al. 2011), so phonetics is arguably a cue to "language".

The downside of specifying language solely based on its form is that words or other elements that have the same or a highly similar form in two languages are not assignable. Triggered code-switching, namely the facilitation of a code-switch by, for example, interlingual homophones (de Bot et al. 2009), may be an effect of this ambiguity.

But metalinguistic knowledge should not be underestimated either. Children learn from the very beginning which words are appropriate to say to someone. This is basically the same as with other pragmatic norms. The choice of appropriate language or code is nothing other than knowing how to speak to someone in a certain situation, even if a language has no name or remains as of yet unnamed. But in most modern bilingual societies, language is an openly discussed issue. Bilingual speakers often reflect on their own output and negotiate the language affiliation of words (see Wasserscheidt 2010: 222). This reflection is, of course, not scientific, but certainly helps to shape a more or less clear picture of the borders of each language, even if this border does not coincide with established boundaries of individual languages. This daily negotiation of identities of languages cannot remain without marks in the meaning of the constructions. So, in addition to belonging to a network forming a language, lemmas may also contain direct information about the language they belong to – not as tags, but as one of their (addressee-based) discourse-pragmatic features.

5 Code-mixing with constructions

As should have become clear from the previous remarks, a constructionist approach to code-mixing offers a straightforward answer to the crucial question of *what* code-mixers really mix, namely constructions. The question that arises now is how constructions from different languages can be brought together. At first sight, there are two possible scenarios for combining constructions from different languages. Either they are simply juxtaposed. Or a construction from language B is in some way inserted (nested) into the slots of a construction from language A.

One form of a juxtaposition of two independent constructions is certainly intersentential code-switching. However arbitrary the separation of a speech event and the definition of a sentence may be, the separation supposedly always contains the border of two constructions.

The insertion of constructions into other constructions that are either (more) complex or (more) schematic is obviously very close to what Muysken (2005) calls "insertion". He defines an *inserted constituent* as "a sister to X [that] cannot be licensed by X" (Muysken 2005: 95) and this very much resembles the conception of the form of an open slot in a construction.

What makes a constructionist approach work is the presumed nature of constructions. Constructions are by definition conventionalized and entrenched form-meaning-pairings. The processes of conventionalization and entrenchment in turn are the product of constructions being frequently perceived and produced as complete units. As a matter of fact, there is no meaning without form and no form without meaning. Hence I hypothesize that constructions have to be processed as unseparated entities during language usage. The status of complex constructions in the mental lexicon may be spurious, but during communication speakers cannot split them halfway and have to instead produce the whole construction. Otherwise, they would lose their intended meaning. The particularities of language processing should be basically the same as for words, including, of course, slips of the tongue or other processing errors.

The consequence of this assumption and the language specific nature of constructions in general is that a construction, once it is selected, must be produced entirely in one language. This does not, of course, include slots but only those elements that are in some way (phonologically) specified as the form of the construction. What exactly the form of a construction is still remains to be precisely defined. I will come back to this question below. For the moment it is important to note that these phonologically specified elements of a construction may indeed form some kind of matrix that can be filled with elements from any language. In fact, the very definition of schematic constructions is that of a matrix (or schema), as used by Myers-Scotton (e.g. 2007). Thus, example (1) illustrates a construction, where both dative *–ga* and ablative *–din* are specified and the slots before these components are filled with phonologically integrated elements. This way, the notion of a "matrix language" receives a natural explanation without the need to refer to language at all. The information that the construction is Kazakh and the embedded elements are Russian is facultative. Not languages, but constructions serve as a matrix. In the light of the aforementioned problems with indexing lemmas for language, it is not necessary (though possible) that "the ML [Matrix Language] is selected at the conceptual level" (Myers-Scotton and Jake 2010: 340) since constructions are already language specific and can be selected and processed almost in the same way as speech production models describe the production of single words.

(1) Mašin özimiz *arendi* -ga   alimiz *sel'choztechniki* -din däyu
    Car   self   rent   -DAT take builder's.yard   -ABL say
    'They say they'll rent a car from the builder's yard on their own.'
    (Kazakh-Russian, Muhamedowa 2006: 68)

In line with the Matrix Language Frame Model, I assume that "a given constituent type in any language has a uniform abstract structure and the requirements of well-formedness for this constituent type must be observed whenever the constituent appears" (Myers-Scotton and Jake 2010: 337). This can be easily reformulated in a constructionist fashion: a given construction in any language has a unique form whose requirements must be observed whenever the construction appears. Thus, I hypothesize that constructions are not mixable, at least not more than online processing can mix up linguistic elements anyway.

A "frame construction" can be filled with other elements, most of them being complex signs themselves. The class of elements that can be inserted into a slot is restricted semantically or pragmatically and, to some extent, phonologically. Here, the notion of congruence is crucial. As already mentioned, there cannot be full congruence between linguistic units from two languages in a constructionist approach, even regarding their categorical status. Congruence has to be constructed either by individual speakers or is itself a matter of conventionalization (Sebba 2010). It still has to be evaluated whether current approaches to constructional meaning like frame semantics (see Boas 2010 for a contrastive approach) or collostructional analysis (e.g. Gries and Stefanowitsch 2010) can help to advance the notion of congruence in a constructionist fashion (see also Sickinger 2012).

The two possibilities of combining constructions from different languages via juxtaposition or insertion imply that the form poles of constructions are really incomparable across languages. But there may well be constructions that are identical in two languages. Good candidates are constructions whose elements are marked exactly the same way, for example via word order or a very similar phonological structure (homophones). Other possible examples are constructions that are so highly schematic that they do not contain any concrete form at all. Muysken actually lists some of them in a "preliminary typology of alternation constructions" (Muysken 2005: 102). The list includes clefting, fronting, as well as right- and left-dislocation, all of which employ constructions that do not have a form pole of their own and therefore may have a cognate in another language involved that is just as schematic. Also, diachronically speakers may have lost the capability to distinguish between the formal and/or semantic features two constructions have in their languages, which may lead to "congruent lexicalization" (Muysken 2005). If these constructions also bear a more or less similar meaning, then the language of origin is not inferable from the percept and hence we cannot distinguish between alternation and insertion. That is, the construction can come from any language or from both at a time and does not serve as a linguistically specified frame. Rather, they possibly serve as a kind of trigger for code-mixing itself.

In a constructionist framework, it is not government that regulates the language of the construction. Although heads such as verbs do play a prominent role even in construction grammar, they do not bear any kind of language index that could determine the language affiliation of other elements of the construction. They can be inserted into a constructional frame just like other elements are inserted. Compare, for instance, the infinitive clauses in German and Russian. While Russian only contains the construction V + INF (*pobrobuju uechat'* 'I.try drive.away'), in German the verb can be either followed by an infinitive (*ich will wegfahren* 'I want drive.away': V + INF) or an infinitive clause (*ich versuche wegzufahren* 'I try to drive.away': V + zu + INF). A German-Russian bilingual now has two constructions, one that is somehow equivalent in Russian and German (V + INF) and the German *zu* infinitive. In a code-mixed utterance, it would be totally normal to encounter at least two different patterns: *pobrobuju weggehen* 'I.want go' and *pobrobuju wegzugehen* 'I.want to go'. So while the inflected verb is Russian in both utterances, the construction is Russian in the first and German in the second example. A similar example is discussed by Muysken (2005) regarding the marking of human objects in Spanish-English code-mixing. Spanish requires the marker *a* between the verb and the human object in sentences like (2), whereas English does not. While Muysken predicts the pattern to depend on the language of the verb, his own count reveals that indeed *a* is often (in 3 out of 6 occurrences) used after English verbs (Muysken 2005: 38). This shows that it is not the verb that selects the syntactic frame.

(2) *Veo   a   la   mujer.*
     *Veo   la   mujer
     'I see the woman.'   (Spanish, Muysken 2005: 38)

This shows that code-mixing, just as any other linguistic phenomenon, is basically a statistical one. This means that no linguistic theory about code-mixing should be based solely on the evaluation of single code-mixes but has to include corpus analyses as well. The theory itself can be developed with the help of single examples, but the formulated assumptions should always take into account that the observed rules may at best be mere tendencies. While for unilingual speech it is clear that speakers, however seldom, do produce errors, code-mixing research has no means to determine what an error would look like.

It is to be expected, though, that bilinguals also make errors, especially as they have to cope with at least two codes at the same time, the structures of which being rarely easily compatible. In fact, it is not feasible to argue for or against a proposed model by discussing single utterances, as long as it is not shown that they represent the language use in the community in question.

This short outline of a constructionist approach to code-mixing is, of course, still too simple. In order to provide a useful explanation of the diversity of bilingual phenomena some more elaboration is needed. However, this elaboration must not claim processes or structures that are not already part of the theoretical framework construction grammar offers. The study of bilingual language use may well help to gather new insight into the functioning of constructions and to clarify spurious questions. In the following section I will discuss some concrete examples.

6 Bilingual constructions

It is clear from the material that has been gathered to study code-mixing that bilinguals sometimes use constructions that are not part of the inventory of any language spoken in the community. Many of them are used by bilinguals in order to overcome difficulties in integrating foreign elements into a language. For example, the Turkish community in the Netherlands uses constructions with the Turkish verb *yapmak* 'to do' in order to integrate e.g. Dutch verbs (see example 3; for similar examples cf. Pfaff 1991; Kallmeyer and Keim 2003).

(3) *op   kamers   wonen*   yap-acağ-ım
    on   rooms   live   do-FUT-1SG
    'I'm going to live on my own.'   (Turkish-Dutch, Backus 2010: 229)

The combination of a verb meaning something like 'to do' with foreign elements is a strategy used also in other languages, according to Chan (2010: 190 f.). In the Turkish communities in the Netherlands and Germany this use also extends to the constructions [N yapmak] or [N machen], respectively. Bilingual speakers produce utterances like *ilkokul yapmak* 'elementary school do' in Turkish with the meaning 'to finish elementary school' (Backus, Doğruöz and Heine 2011: 743) or the already famous *Ich mach dich Messer* 'I do you knife' with the intended meaning 'I'll stab you with the knife' (Wiese 2006) in German. Since these combinations are used quite often, they can be regarded as conventionalized or in the stage of conventionalization. Moreover, their meaning is not inferable from the form; hence they are constructions on their own right. Their status as conventionalized constructions will become visible only through a corpus-based analysis.

Other constructions are maybe not the direct outcome of language contact but still differ from the standard language. In my corpus[4], I found sentences from Serbian bilinguals in Hungary where they omit the otherwise obligatory auxiliary in the perfect tense, as in example 4.

(4) Onda od   tog   doba **došl-a**   iz   *ovod*   -e
    Then from that time **came-3SG.FEM** from *kindergarten1-GEN*

   napolje, i   onda ovo.
   outside, and then that.

   'At this time she came out of *kindergarten*, and then this.'
   (Serbian-Hungarian, own corpus)

If one compares the two translations of this sentence into standard Serbian and standard Hungarian (5), one can see that the speaker not only tries to reduplicate the structure of the Hungarian verb (*ki-kerül* 'out-come') but also omits the auxiliary. The correct perfect form of the verb *doći* 'to come' would be *je došla* with the auxiliary *je*. The whole utterance shows varied intertwining of Hungarian and Serbian constructions, including the insertion of the Hungarian noun *ovoda* 'kindergarten'. So it seems natural to account for the omission of the auxiliary *je* in terms of Hungarian influence on Serbian. One interpretation is that the speaker took over the Hungarian perfect-tense construction that does not have auxiliaries.

(5) *Serbian*
   je   *napusti-l-a*   *vrtić*
   AUX   left-PF-SG.FEM   kindergarten.ACC

   Code-Mix
   doš-l-a   *iz*   ovod-e   *napolje*
   come-PF-SG.FEM   from   kindergarten-GEN   outside

   Hungarian
   ki-kerül-t   az   ovodá-ból
   out-come-PF.3SG   ART   kindergarten-ABL

---

4 The corpus is emerging and covers material from the Serbian minority in Hungary. Several subparts are still being processed on different levels, so I cannot offer a full-fledged analysis of the data so far.

However, in the corpus as a whole the omission of the auxiliary is very frequent. In a subpart of the corpus that contains two long discussions with altogether nine speakers, in 186 out of 339 occurrences of the perfect tense construction (i.e. 54.9%) the auxiliary has been omitted. This is already notable and seems to confirm the assumption that there is a Hungarian source – not only ad hoc, but in general. A closer look, however, shows that it is mainly the 3rd person auxiliary that is left out: here the omission ratio amounts to 70% (177 out of 254). For all other forms of the paradigm, speakers formed the perfect tense without the auxiliary in only 11% of all cases (9 out of 76).

As a consequence, the perfect tense paradigm has to be changed for the Serbian of the Serbian minority in Hungary as follows (here for the feminine perfect paradigm of the verb *doći* 'to come'):

1Sg.	sam došla	1Pl.	smo došle
2Sg.	si došla	2Pl.	ste došle
3Sg.	je **došla**	3Pl.	su došle

Another possible explanation could be that the paradigm changes due to the influence of the Hungarian perfect paradigm (exemplified here with the verb *lenni* 'to be'), where the 3rd person singular is the least marked:

1Sg.	volt-am	1Pl.	volt-unk
2Sg.	volt-ál	2Pl.	volt-atok
3Sg.	**volt**	3Pl.	volt-ak

It is feasible that the Serbs rearrange the Serbian paradigm to fit the model of the Hungarian one and make the 3rd person singular form the least marked. But Savić reports the same tendency of auxiliary omission in the Serbian diaspora in the U.S. (Savić 1995: 487). Her explanation is that an "already operating gapping rule has triggered a levelling process in the Serbian grammar of these bilinguals" (ibid.). Indeed, Serbian allows for the omission of 3rd person auxiliaries in some cases, namely when the verb is a reflexive or when it follows the conjunctions *i* 'and' or *a* 'but, and'. However, the linguistic environment for the development of both Serbian codes is quite different, so an explanation would be too speculative at this moment. A usage-based approach that relies on corpus analysis does not have to push made-up hypotheses about the mechanisms of interference or convergence. It only takes account of the fact that the evaluation of bilingual language use must rely on those norms that are conventionalized in the speech community, and the auxiliary omission in the case of the 3rd person singular perfect tense is clearly a convention in the Serbian community in Hungary.

7 Constructions as complex signs

In many cases of code-mixing, a straightforward application of the stated hypothesis that every construction has to be produced in the language it belongs to is not feasible. For instance, speakers often use structures in language A that seem to be a more or less literal translation from structures that belong to language B. This kind of contact phenomenon is called *transference, loan translation* or *calque*. I argue that loan translations play a much more important role in code-mixing than has been assumed to date. First, let us look at loan translations from a constructionist point of view. Backus and Dorleijn (2010) and Backus (2010) provide an interesting approach that relates code-mixing with loan translation and other contact phenomena. I very much agree with their general statement that all contact phenomena are related and may belong to one continuum. I also think that construction grammar can provide even more insight into the underlying mechanisms. Consider one example Backus and Dorleijn provide, i.e. the loan translation *piano oynamak* 'to play the piano'. The correct Turkish version of this expression would be *piyano çalmak* (literally 'piano to.sound'), while the Dutch one is *piano spelen* (Backus and Dorleijn 2010: 77).

(6) Turkish: *piyano çalmak*
     Dutch Turkish: *piano oynamak*
     Dutch: *piano spelen*

The explanation the authors offer is that "only the meaning, and not the overt morphemes, is from Language B, as for example the use of the word for 'to play' (*oynamak*)" (ibid.). This means that the Dutch verb *spelen* 'to play' has been translated to Turkish *oynamak* 'to.play'. However, *oynamak* is indeed a translation equivalent to *spelen*, so there would be nothing wrong with it. Only in combination with *pi(y)ano* it is the case that *oynamak* sounds odd. Indeed, *piano spelen* is obviously an instantiation of a particular construction. The first element of the construction can obviously be replaced by anything that refers to an instrument. So the construction may have the form [X SPELEN]. The meaning of the construction, however, is not the combination of ['instrument' + SPELEN 'to play']. Instead, the concept behind this construction is 'to produce music with an instrument or to be able to master an instrument'. This concept can be expressed in various ways. In Turkish it is a similar (transitive) construction but with a verb signifying 'to sound'. In Hungarian a verbalizing suffix is used, i.e. *zongorá-zni* (literally 'to piano'). So in fact, the combination ['instrument' + SPELEN 'to play'] is the *structure* of the construction as a result of a language-specific construal, not its meaning.

This structure is what Langacker (2005) calls a "composite structure", an idea which has been restated by Verhagen when describing constructions as complex signs: "Thus, a construction can itself also be considered a complex sign, the form-part consisting of elements that are generalizations over actual sound-meaning pairings, i.e. morphemes and paradigms" (Verhagen 2009: 146). The important point in this approach is that constructions are not seen as direct pairings of form and meaning only, but that constructions themselves are combinations of signs (composites) and that this combination in turn serves as signifier for the construction itself. Complex constructions are built partially from single signs which through their co-occurrence prompt a conventionalised interpretation that is referred to as the constructional meaning. A similar approach is Croft's conceptualisation of a construction as "a pairing of complex syntactic structure and a complex semantic structure" (Croft 2001: 204).

For our example, this means that the construction [X SPELEN] consists of two elements: a paradigm, whose elements all belong to the semantic class 'instrument', and the lemma 'SPELEN', which itself is a construction, combining a lexical morpheme and a morphological paradigm. These two elements are the signifiers of the constructional meaning 'to produce music with or to master an instrument'. They form what Verhagen (2009) calls an "intermediate structure" that triggers a corresponding interpretation. Langacker refers to the same relation as phonological and semantic integration of the component morphemes into the composite structure (Langacker 2005: 108). A simplified notation of this construction where both elements are treated as single signs and not as constructions themselves is given in Figure 1:

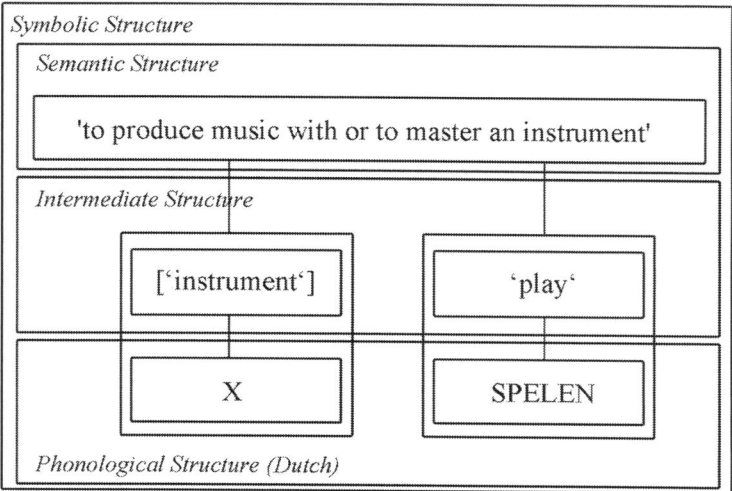

Figure 1: The complex constructional sign of [X SPELEN]

Let us now return to the explanation Backus and Dorleijn (2010) offered for how this loan translation works. The authors claim that "only the meaning, and not the overt morphemes, is from Language B" (Backus and Dorleijn 2010: 77). It is not wrong to assume that the overt morphemes are from Language A (in this case, Dutch). But it is not clear what Backus and Dorleijn are referring to as "meaning". Since constructions are complex signs, we have at least two levels of meaning: the meaning of the construction and the meaning of the component signs of the construction. If the speaker wanted to translate the whole construction with the meaning 'to produce music with or to master an instrument' into Turkish, he would correctly produce *piyano çalmak*, since this is the translational equivalent of the construction. Instead, the speaker translated *spelen* into Turkish without paying attention to the constructional environment. That is, he replaced the independent sign [spelen – 'to play'] with its most appropriate Turkish counterpart – *oynamak*.

However, the simple combination of an instrument with the Turkish verb *oynamak* spoken to a unilingual Turkish speaker would not lead to successful communication, since the unilingual participant would not be able to decode the combination by virtue of his linguistic knowledge. Although the construction is relatively transparent to us, a unilingual could interpret it in a completely different way, just as a combination like *to sound the piano* would hardly be understood in the way a Turkish speaker may have intended. That is, the loan translation in question is only decodable if a speaker knows the Dutch construction. In fact, it *is* the Dutch construction. Thus, in order to produce a loan translation, a speaker uses a construction from Language B including its meaning and its signifiers but translates (some of) the signifiers into Language A (Figure 2). That is, the speaker imitates the Dutch construction.

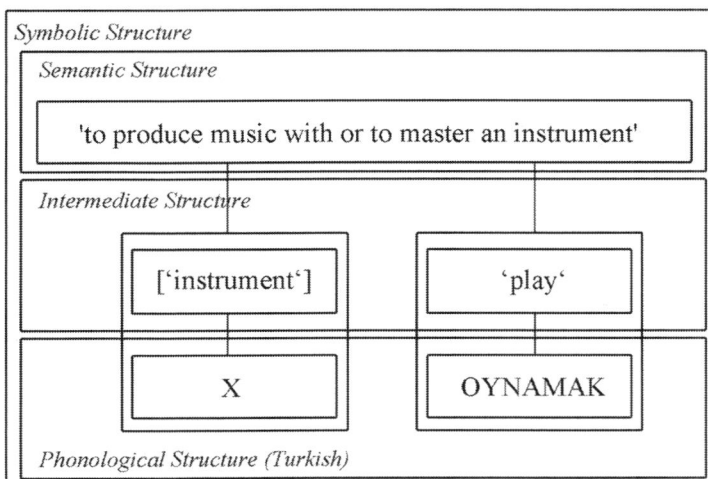

Figure 2: The complex structure of the Turkish loan construction

As a consequence, it is inappropriate to say that only the meaning has been taken over, since meaning cannot come without form. This also holds true the other way round. Backus and Dorleijn state that in interference/transference "only the formal structure comes from Language B" (Backus and Dorleijn 2010: 78). Paradoxically, they add "as in loan translation", although they defined loan-translation to be the transfer of the meaning alone. This paradox (or rather confusion) is, in my opinion, the logical consequence of splitting form and meaning even though one cannot exist without the other. Obviously, it does not make sense to use structures in Language A that do not have a meaning in the language. Rather, form-meaning-pairings are inseparable; otherwise they lose their communicative function. Since meaning is not directly translatable, the only way to transfer the communicative function of constructions is to rebuild their structure by searching for equivalents to their components in language A. This is why I would suggest calling this process 'imitation', in analogy to human imitation which denotes the copying of behaviour with corresponding actions in order to achieve a specific goal. Likewise, bilinguals use the linguistic means of language A to copy a composite structure from language B in order to achieve its constructional meaning. Loan translation as a cultural technique can thus be related to imitative learning.

Loan translation and code-mixing are typically dealt with as separate phenomena. But they belong together in a systematic way and are often used hand in hand. Namely, the strategy of imitating constructions can also occur in instances of code-mixing. The following example of Russian-English code-switching from Broersma et al. (2009) exemplifies this.

(7) No, he is an American citizen, which is going there weird,
potomu chto I have to bring my Ukrainian passport
because

so	*mnoj,*	*kogda*	*my*	*edem*	*tuda*	*v*	Dominican Republic
with	me,	when	we	drive	there	in	

(English-Russian, Broersma et al. 2009: 115)

This example is discussed in Broersma et al. (2009) in the light of trigger words, that is to say interlingual homophones, which might tempt the speaker to switch the language. In this case, the word *passport* functions as a trigger, since it is pronounced similarly in Russian and in English. But my interest is what is going on structurally in this part of the utterance. If we compare the bilingual sequence with its unilingual equivalents, we see that the structure is basically English. Only the last sequence *so mnoj* 'with me' is in Russian.

(8) Russian

mne	*nado*	*vzjat'*	*s*	*soboj*	*svoj*	*ukrajinskij*	*pasport*
Me	must	take	with	myself	my.REFL	Ukrainian	passport

Code-Mix

I have to bring my Ukrainian passport *so mnoj*

English

I have to bring my Ukrainian passport with me

While it easy to recognize a code-switch in this example, a closer look reveals that the Russian elements are actually a loan translation. The structure of the Russian construction equivalent of the verbal complex *bring with me* (*vzjat' s soboj* 'take with oneself') obligatorily includes the reflexive form of the instrumental pronoun *soboj* and hence cannot be the origin of the Russian sequence *so mnoj*, which is non-reflexive. The English construction, however, makes use of the non-reflexive pronoun. The hypothesis that constructions are (by tendency) always produced as a whole is therefore not falsified by this example. Rather, the English construction is produced with all its components (*bring* + *with* + PRON), with the exception that one part (*with* + PRON) has been translated into Russian.

A construction grammar approach seems to be able to account for a simultaneous occurrence of loan translation and code-mixing. As there are arguably a lot more cases like the one discussed (Backus and Dorleijn 2010: 91), an integration of the imitating strategy of loan translation into code-mixing research would certainly yield explanations to code-mixing events that have not yet been accounted for.

To sum up, in order to use the communicative means of two languages at the same time, speakers can either combine both languages or imitate one of the languages or both at a time. What is important in all cases discussed is that constructions are never corrupted, nor are only individual parts of a construction produced. Rather, constructions are used as a whole with their semantic structure, their intermediate structure and a corresponding phonological form.

8 Conclusion

In this paper I outlined a constructional approach to code-mixing with an outlook to bilingual speech in general. The major advantage of an approach utilizing the means of construction grammar is that it comes with some important built-in solutions that foster a compelling explanation of bilingual phenomena. First of all, construction grammar covers all linguistic levels which have been subject to a great diversity of accounts so far. It offers language specific but psychologically plausible and hence generalizable solutions to linguistic structure. The consistent linkage of form and meaning opens the door to explaining not only *where* code-mixing occurs, but also *when* it occurs.

Beyond these advantages, a usage-based approach which takes constructions to be the core elements of language can cope with a lot of phenomena that are still subject to debate in the ongoing research. Most importantly maybe, it does away with the need to assume the existence of a matrix language. Instead, language specific clausal constructions offer a natural frame for the insertion of elements from other languages. Language itself does not need to rely on standard notions of language, but can be determined on the basis of the speech community's language use. This way, bilingual constructions and the functioning of code-mixing as a kind of third grammar can be accounted for.

While the structural implications of a constructionist approach to code-mixing have been, at best, adumbrated, I have demonstrated that an understanding of constructions as complex signs is able to explain not only code-mixing, but also adjacent phenomena like loan translations. Moreover, I have shown that loan-translation can co-occur with code-mixing, a fact which has not been paid enough attention to.

Another promising feature of construction grammar that still has to be developed is that, beyond the structural constraints, constructions potentially offer a direct link to pragmatically and socially driven accounts of code-mixing, which are to date only loosely connected to models focusing on structure.

References

Auer, Peter. 2006. Bilinguales Sprechen: (immer noch) eine Herausforderung für die Linguistik. In: *Sociolinguistica* 20. 1–21.

Backus, Ad. 2010. The role of codeswitching, loan translation and interference in the emergence of an immigrant variety of Turkish. *Working Papers in Corpus-based Linguistics and Language Education* 5. 225–241.

Backus, Ad, Seza A. Doğruöz & Bernd Heine. 2011. Salient stages in contact-induced grammatical change: Evidence from synchronic vs. diachronic contact situations. *Language Sciences* 33(5). 738–752.

Backus, Ad & Margreet Dorleijn. 2010. Loan translations versus code-switching. In: Barbara E. Bullock & Almeida Jacqueline Toribio (eds.), *The Cambridge handbook of linguistic code-switching*, 75–93. Cambridge: Cambridge University Press.

Boas, Hans Christian. 2010. Comparing constructions across languages. In: Hans Christian Boas (ed.), *Contrastive studies in construction grammar*, 1–20. Amsterdam, Philadelphia: John Benjamins.

Broersma, Mirjam, Ludmila Isurin, Sybrine Bultena & Kees de Bot. 2009. Triggered code switching. Evidence from Dutch-English and Russian-English bilinguals. In: Ludmila Isurin (ed.), *Multidisciplinary approaches to code switching*, 104–128. Amsterdam: John Benjamins.

Chan, Brian Hok-Shing. 2010. Code-switching between typologically distinct languages. In: Barbara E. Bullock & Almeida Jacqueline Toribio (eds.), *The Cambridge handbook of linguistic code-switching*, 182–198. Cambridge: Cambridge University Press.

Croft, William. 2001. *Radical construction grammar. Syntactic theory in typological perspective.* Oxford: Oxford University Press.

Croft, William. 2007. 'Construction Grammar'. In: Dirk Geeraerts (ed.), *The Oxford handbook of Cognitive Linguistics*, 463–508. Oxford, New York: Oxford University Press.

de Bot, Kees. 1992. A bilingual production model: Levelt's 'speaking' model adapted. *Applied Linguistics* 13. 1–24.

de Bot, Kees, Mirjam Broersma & Ludmila Isurin. 2009. Sources of triggering in code switching. In: Ludmila Isurin (ed.), *Multidisciplinary approaches to code switching*, 85–102. Amsterdam: John Benjamins.

Di Sciullo, Anne-Marie, Pieter Muysken & Rajendra Singh. 1986. Government and code-mixing. *Journal of Linguistics* 22(1). 1–24.

Dijkstra, Ton & van Heuven, Walter J. B. 1998. The BIA-model and bilingual word recognition. In: Jonathan Grainger & Arthur M. Jacobs (eds.), *Localist connectionist approaches to human cognition*, 55–89. Hove: Erlbaum.

Fillmore, Charles J., Paul Kay & Catherine O'Connor. 1988. Regularity and idiomaticity in grammatical constructions: The case of *let alone. Language* 64. 501–538.

Gardner-Chloros, Penelope & Malcolm Edwards. 2004. Assumptions behind grammatical approaches to code-switching: When the blueprint is a red herring. *Transactions of the Philological Society* 102(1). 103–129.

Goldberg, Adele E. 1995. *Constructions. A construction grammar approach to argument structure.* Chicago: University of Chicago Press.

Goldberg, Adele E. 2006. *Constructions at work. The nature of generalization in language.* Oxford, New York: Oxford University Press.

Green, David W. 1998. Mental control of the bilingual lexico-semantic system. *Bilingualism: Language and Cognition* 1. 67–81.

Gries, Stefan Th. & Anatol Stefanowitsch. 2004. Extending collostructional analysis. A corpus-based perspective on 'alternations'. *International Journal of Corpus Linguistics* 9(1). 97–129.

Kallmeyer, Werner & Inken Keim. 2003. Linguistic variation and the construction of social identity in a German-Turkish setting. A case study of an immigrant youth group in Mannheim, Germany. In: Jannis K. Androutsopoulos & Alexandra Georgakopoulou (eds.), *Discourse constructions of youth identities*, 29–46. Amsterdam, Philadelphia: John Benjamins.

Kecskes, Istvan. 2006. The dual language model to explain code-switching: A cognitive-pragmatic approach. *Intercultural Pragmatics* 3(3). 257–283.

Kecskes, Istvan. 2009. Dual and multilanguage systems. *International Journal of Multilingualism*. 1–19.

Langacker, Ronald W. 2005. Construction Grammars: cognitive, radical, and less so. In: Francisco José de Ruiz Mendoza Ibáñez & M. Sandra Peña Cervel (eds.), *Cognitive Linguistics. Internal dynamics and interdisciplinary interaction*, 101–159. Berlin, New York: Mouton de Gruyter.

Langacker, Ronald W. 2009. A dynamic view of usage and language acquisition. *Cognitive Linguistics* 20(3). 627–640.

Li, Ping. 1998. Mental control, language tags, and language nodes in bilingual lexical processing. *Bilingualism: Language and Cognition* 1. 92–93.

Li, Ping & Igor Farkas. 2002. A self-organizing connectionist model of bilingual processing. In: Roberto R. Heredia & Jeanette Altarriba (eds.), *Bilingual sentence processing*, 59–85. Amsterdam: Elsevier.

MacSwan, Jeff. 2001. The architecture of the bilingual language faculty: Evidence from intrasentential code switching. *Bilingualism: Language and Cognition* 3(1). 37–54.

Meijer, Paul J. A. & Jean E. Fox Tree. 2003. Building syntactic structures in speaking: A bilingual exploration. *Experimental Psychology* 50(3). 184–195.

Muhamedowa, Raihan. 2006. *Untersuchung zum kasachisch-russischen code-mixing. (mit Ausblicken auf den uigurisch-russischen Sprachkontakt)*. München: LINCOM EUROPA.

Muysken, Pieter. 2005. *Bilingual speech. A typology of code-mixing*. Cambridge: Cambridge University Press.

Myers-Scotton, Carol. 1997. *Duelling languages. Grammatical structure in codeswitching*. Oxford: Clarendon.

Myers-Scotton, Carol. 2007. *Multiple voices. An introduction to bilingualism*. Malden, Mass.: Blackwell.

Myers-Scotton, Carol & Janice L. Jake. 2010. A universal model of code-switching and bilingual language processing and production. In: Barbara E. Bullock & Almeida Jacqueline Toribio (eds.), *The Cambridge handbook of linguistic code-switching*, 336–357. Cambridge: Cambridge University Press.

Paradis, Michel. 1997. The cognitive neuropsychology of bilingualism. In: Annette M. B. de Groot & Judith F. Kroll (eds.), *Tutorials in bilingualism*, 331–354. Mahwah, NJ: Erlbaum.

Paradis, Michel. 2004. *A neurolinguistic theory of bilingualism*. Amsterdam: John Benjamins.

Pfaff, Carol W. 1991. Mixing and linguistic convergence in migrant speech communities: Linguistic constraints, social conditions and models of acquisition. *Papers for the Symposium on Code-Switching and Bilingual Studies: Theory, significance and perspective*, 120–153. Strasbourg: European Science Foundation.

Poplack, Shana. 1980. Sometimes I'll start a sentence in Spanish Y TERMINO EN ENSPANOL: Toward a typology of code-switching. *Linguistics* 18 (7/8). 581–618.

Savić, Jelena. 1995. Structural convergence and language change: Evidence from Serbian/ English code-switching. *Language in Society* 24. 475–492.

Sebba, Mark. 2010. On the notions of congruence and convergence in code-switching. In: Barbara E. Bullock & Almeida Jacqueline Toribio (eds.), *The Cambridge handbook of linguistic code-switching*, 40–57. Cambridge: Cambridge University Press.

Sickinger, Pawel. 2012. Mental models and linguistic cues: Investigating the interface between language and mental representation across cultures. In: LAUD Essen (ed.), *Cognitive Psycholinguistics: Bilingualism, cognition and communication*, 125–146. Essen: LAUD Linguistic Agency.

Stefanowitsch, Anatol. 2011. Konstruktionsgrammatik und Grammatiktheorie. In: Alexander Lasch & Alexander Ziem (eds.), *Konstruktionsgrammatik und Grammatiktheorie III. Aktuelle Fragen und Lösungsansätze*, 11–25. Tübingen: Stauffenburg.

Tomasello, Michael. 2003. *Constructing a language. A usage-based theory of language acquisition*. Cambridge, Mass: Harvard University Press.

Treffers-Daller, Jeanine. 2010. Code-switching and transfer: An exploration of similarities and differences. In: Barbara E. Bullock & Almeida Jacqueline Toribio (eds.), *The Cambridge handbook of linguistic code-switching*, 58–74. Cambridge: Cambridge University Press.

Verhagen, Arie. 2009. The conception of constructions as complex sings. Emergence of structure and reduction to usage. *Constructions and Frames* 1(1). 119–152.

Vieru, Bianca, Philippe Boula de Mareüil & Martine Adda-Decker. 2011. Characterisation and identification of non-native French accents. *Speech Communication* 53. 292–310.

Wasserscheidt, Philipp. 2010. Mehrsprachigkeit und Sprachwandel bei Ungarischsprechern im serbischen Banat. In: Christian Voß (ed.), *Ottoman and Habsburg legacies in the Balkans. Language and religion to the north and to the south of the Danube River*, 197–246. München, Berlin: Sagner.

Wiese, Heike. 2006. Ich mach dich Messer – Grammatische Produktivität in Kiez-Sprache („Kanak Sprak"). *Linguistische Berichte* 207. 245–273.

III Input-related cognitive effects in code-mixing

Nikolay Hakimov

Effects of frequency and word repetition on switch-placement

Abstract: This contribution investigates the effects of co-occurrence frequency and repetition priming, or recency, on the structure of naturally occurring bilingual speech. It explores, by way of a case study, patterns of insertional code-mixing in a spoken Russian-German bilingual corpus. In insertional code-mixing, stems from one contact language (embedded language) regularly appear in sentences framed by the other contact language (matrix language) and receive morphosyntactic marking from that language. The resultant mixed constituents alternate with longer embedded-language constituents, usually referred to as 'embedded-language islands' (Myers-Scotton 1993; Auer 2014). In the context of the prepositional phrase, the Russian-German bilingual speaker thus has a choice between inserting a German noun into a Russian prepositional phrase or producing a fully-fledged German prepositional phrase embedded in a Russian clause. The study provides tangible evidence that this choice depends on (i) the frequency with which the examined nouns are used together with specific prepositions in monolingual German, (ii) the degree of competition among these prepositions in monolingual German, and (iii) the occurrence / non-occurrence of the relevant prepositions in prior discourse, i.e. repetition priming.

Keywords: frequency of use, recency, priming, competition, prepositional phrase, code-mixing/switching, embedded-language island, Russian Germans, bilingual speech

1 Introduction

Much research in recent years has focused on the frequency of linguistic structures as a major factor affecting human linguistic behaviour and language organisation. Studies in language acquisition, language processing and language change have accumulated a wealth of evidence that probabilistic information about distributions of linguistic structures is an intrinsic part of language organisation (Barlow and Kemmer 2000; Behrens & Pfänder 2016; Bybee and Hopper 2001; Divjak and Gries 2012; Gries and Divjak 2012; see Diessel 2007; Ellis 2002 for reviews). Both psycholinguistic experiments and analyses of natural spoken language corpora report that (monolingual) language production is influenced by word frequency (Jescheniak and Levelt 1994) and probabilistic relations between neighbouring words (Janssen and Barber 2012; Jurafsky et al. 2001; Kapatsinski 2010; Schneider 2016), as well as the likelihood of syntactic (Tily et al. 2009) and morphosyntactic (Gorokhova 2009) structures with which the word is used. However, attempts to account for bilingual and multilingual production – particularly patterns in code-mixing – by integrating probabilistic information inherent in the codes are still absent from the literature, despite the constantly growing body of work dedicated to bilingualism and multilingualism.

Furthermore, few current models of bilingual and multilingual production take into account cognitive processes operating in online language production in discourse. Priming, an implicit memory effect defined as the influence of the prior presentation of a stimulus on the processing of a subsequent stimulus, has been shown to affect monolingual production on various levels of language (see Pickering and Ferreira 2008, for a review). In bilinguals, experimental studies have focused on cross-language priming effects in lexical access (Dijkstra, Van Heuven and Grainger 1998; Kroll and Stewart 1994; Van Hell and De Groot 1998) and the production of syntactic constructions (Loebell and Bock 2003; Salamoura and Williams 2006; Schoonbaert, Hartsuiker and Pickering 2007). Only recently has experimental research approached priming effects in code-mixing. For example, Koostra, Van Hell and Dijkstra (2010) find that participants in their experiments tended to switch languages at the same position as in the prime sentence, a finding that was shown, in their later study, to be driven by both the presence of cognates in the prime sentence and word repetition (Koostra, Van Hell and Dijkstra 2012). Analyses of naturally occurring code-mixing have traditionally neglected priming effects[1], although the study by Torres Cacoullos and Travis (2016) represents an exception to this trend. The authors assert that in the New Mexico Spanish-English Bilingual corpus, the distribution of syntactic structures in a particular syntactic context – expression of the Spanish first-person singular subject pronoun – largely depends on both language-internal and cross-language priming effects. We can conclude from these few studies that repetition of words and structures in discourse requires due consideration in the analysis of code-mixing. However, the role of repetition in the structure of naturally occurring code-mixing remains unexplored to date.

The purpose of this chapter is to account for patterns of insertional Russian-German code-mixing by taking frequency and word repetition into consideration. In approaching the data, I adopt Auer's (1999, 2011) distinction between the

---

1 To my knowledge, Boumans (1998) was the first to discuss the role of word repetition in code-mixing.

cases of code-switching and code-mixing. In the case of code-switching, conversation participants perceive and interpret the juxtaposition of two codes as meaningful in each individual instance, whereas in the case of code-mixing, language juxtaposition is meaningful for participants in a global sense, i.e. "as a recurrent pattern" (Auer 2011: 467). The present study examines the placement of a switch in the context of the prepositional phrase, which is one of the most frequently reported loci for code-mixing: a speaker can switch the language either at the boundary of the prepositional phrase (Bentahila and Davies 1983: 314; Boumans 1998: 271, 315; Clyne 1987: 757; Haust 1995: 169; Pfaff 1979: 310; Treffers-Daller 1994: 208, 221–224) or within the prepositional phrase, i.e. between the preposition and the noun phrase (Bentahila and Davies 1983: 315; Poplack 1980: 602; Pfaff 1979: 310; Stenson 1990: 173, 178). This variation, which is also characteristic of Russian-German code-mixing, is approached here as an outcome of several factors. First, switch placement is assumed to be influenced by the frequency of the phrase, as measured in a monolingual corpus. That is, a switch at the boundary of the prepositional phrase is likely when high-frequency preposition-noun combinations are produced. With low-frequency combinations, a switch is more probable between the preposition and the noun. The second considered factor is the frequency of the noun being used in the prepositional phrase, which is also measured in a monolingual corpus. Finally, the lexical material constituting the prepositional phrases is considered subject to repetition priming.

2 Previous accounts

Although code-mixing in the context of the prepositional phrase is widely reported in studies of code-mixing involving various language pairs, few scholars have attempted to account for the observed variation between placing a switch within the prepositional phrase and switching at the phrase boundary. Such variation has been of particular interest to the Matrix Language Framework (MLF) model (Myers-Scotton 1993, 2002). The principal tenet of this model is that the structure of a code-mixed clause can be analysed by determining the division of labour between the involved languages.[2] The language responsible for the core clause structure is called the matrix language (ML); the other, dominated language, whose role is usually restricted to the supply of lexical items, is the embedded language (EL) (Myers-Scotton 1993: 75–119). As a result of this asymmetry,

---

2 Muysken (1995, 2000) and Auer (1999, 2014) refer to this type of code-mixing as *insertional* code-mixing.

embedded language content morphemes such as nouns are inserted into constituents framed by the matrix language to form mixed constituents. For instance, in (1), the English noun *city* is preceded by the Croatian preposition *u* 'to' and takes the inflection *-ju* of the accusative case, assigned by the preposition, so that a mixed constituent *city-ju* 'city-ACC.SG.F' emerges.

(1) Croatian-English (Hlavac 2003: 203)[3]

i	iš-l-i	smo	u	*city*-ju...
and	go-PTCP-PL	be.PRS.1PL	to	-ACC.SG.F

'...and we went to the city...'

Embedded language noun stems sometimes lack matrix language case markers, as in (2), where the noun *city*, again preceded by the Croatian preposition *u* 'in', does not take the required locative marker and remains bare.

(2) Croatian-English (Hlavac 2003: 202)

...ja	bolje	vol-im	bi-ti	u	*city*...
I	more	like-PRS.1SG	be-INF	in	

'...I like more to be in the city...'

In code-mixing, prepositional phrases consisting of a matrix language preposition and a mixed constituent, as in (1), and those constituted by a matrix language preposition and an embedded language noun (phrase), as in (2), alternate with prepositional phrases containing only embedded language morphemes. Sequences of embedded language morphemes in the matrix language context, such as prepositional phrases, are called embedded language islands. We can thus analyse the English prepositional phrase *down the stairs* in (3) as an embedded language island.

(3) Croatian-English (Hlavac 2003: 227)

...i	jedan	dan	ja	sam	pa-o	*down the stairs*	i
and	one	day	I	be.PRS.1SG	fall-PTCP.SG.M		and

jedan	je	bi-o...
one	be.PRS.3SG	be-PTCP.SG.M

'...and one day I fell down the stairs and one was...'

---

3 To present examples, italics are employed to highlight the other language material. The Leipzig Glossing Rules are adopted for all the examples. Russian transliteration is done according to the linguistic conventions outlined in Timberlake (2004: 24–25). Hence, the letters «e», «ë», «ю», «я» are transliterated as <e>, <ë>, <ju>, <ja>. However, when «e» and «ë» appear at a morpheme boundary and [j] belongs to the stem, they are transliterated as <je> and <jo>. Example utterances from my bilingual corpus include codes that indicate their position in the corpus.

Myers-Scotton and Jake (1995) explain the appearance of embedded language islands in code-mixed utterances in terms of the premise that grammatical information contained in lemmas (i.e. entries in the mental lexicon underlying lexical items) is distributed at three levels: (i) lexical-conceptual structure (semantic/ pragmatic features), (ii) predicate-argument structure, and (iii) morphological realisation patterns. The lack of congruence at one of these levels between the relevant embedded language lemma and its matrix language equivalent can result in the emergence of an embedded language island (Myers-Scotton and Jake 1995: 1008–1014). According to Hlavac (2003), the embedded language island in (3) is produced because the content morpheme *down* "for most of its uses in English [...] is non-congruent to any Croatian content morpheme equivalent" (p. 227). In other words, the lemmas involved do not match at the level of lexical-conceptual structure. At the same time, Deuchar (2005: 258) contends that semantic/pragmatic differences between lemmas, as in (3), can motivate the appearance of switches, but only grammatical congruence enables code-mixing. In the case of prepositional phrases it is thus congruence at the level of morphological realisation patterns that is relevant in the first place. Different realisation patterns of adposition indeed seem to determine the emergence of embedded language islands in certain language-pairs. For instance:

(4) German-Hungarian (Szabó 2010: 435)
 ich ich war dort (.) ich war dort äh *internátus-ba*
 I   I   was there   I   was there HES boarding.school.SG-ILL
 'I was there, I was there in the boarding school.'

(5) Finnish-English (Lehtinen 1966: 226)
 ja   sitte eh *in the afternoon* isä   vai minä meni...
 and then HES   father or   I   went
 'And then in the afternoon father or I went...'

The Hungarian illative suffix *-ba* in (4) expresses the kind of spatial relations that are coded by the preposition *in* in German. Hence, the Hungarian phrase *internátusba* 'in the boarding school' corresponds to the German prepositional phrase *im Internat* (where *im* is a contracted form, merging the preposition *in* and the determiner *dem*). The phrase *in the afternoon* in (5) is equivalent to the Finnish *iltapäivällä*, which consists of the noun *iltapäivä* 'afternoon' and the adessive suffix *-llä*. We can thus conclude that, if one of the languages involved in code-mixing employs prepositions, and the other relies on postpositions, a possible outcome of code-mixing is the appearance of embedded-language islands. However, explaining this phenomenon by the incongruence in adposition realisation pattern may fail when the involved languages share the same pattern. Such languages include, for example, Russian and German, which both use prepositions to express spatio-temporal relations.

An alternative explanation for the occurrence of the strings *internátusba* 'in the boarding school' and *in the afternoon* in code-mixed sentences (4) and (5) is to assume that these multi-morphemic forms are holistic units, or chunks, in the speakers' mental lexicons. According to the unit hypothesis formulated by Backus (2003), "[e]very multimorphemic EL insertion is a unit, inserted into a ML clausal frame" (p. 91). In this approach, any string of morphemes or words gains the status of unit once it is entrenched in the speaker's lexicon. To qualify as units, multi-morphemic strings have to either (1) demonstrate irregular morphosyntax, (2) express non-compositional semantics, or (3) be of recurrent use (Backus 2003: 90). For the multi-morphemic strings in (4) and (5), which exhibit neither morphosyntactic irregularities nor semantic non-compositionality, it is only the frequency of use that can account for their status as lexical units. Apparently, the morphemes *in, the* and *afternoon*, on the one hand, and *internátus* and *-ba*, on the other, co-occur so frequently in English and Hungarian, respectively, that speakers of these languages store and retrieve them as units. (This idea is in line with Bybee's [2002] Linear Fusion Hypothesis.) Unit status, when it is determined by usage frequency, is a gradient category, because frequency is itself gradient. Although evidence for the unit hypothesis pervades most, if not all, bilingual corpora, to consider any embedded language island a unit is unreasonable (Hakimov, 2015). Consequently, a systematic investigation of embedded language islands requires both statistical analysis and additional evidence, which would establish the unit status of the investigated embedded language islands independently from code-mixing data. I hope to show in the remainder of the chapter that analyses of large monolingual corpora can be remarkably fruitful for obtaining such additional evidence, which would allow us to put the unit hypothesis to a test.

3 Data

3.1 Corpus of Russian-German bilingual speech

This study is based on a corpus of Russian-German bilingual speech recorded in Russian-speaking communities across Germany, i.e. in Freiburg, Hanover, Lahr/ Black Forest and Regensburg[4] (cf. Hakimov 2015). The corpus contains the speech

---

4 Only one speaker from the Regensburg ReBiSlav corpus (Meyer 2011) satisfied the criteria of the study.

of 21 speakers, who migrated from the former Soviet Union to Germany with their parents, ethnic Germans, and are a group officially called *russlanddeutsche Spätaussiedler* 'Russian-German late repatriates' (Brehmer 2007; Meng 2001). The participants of the study are young adults between the ages of 18 and 35. One of the subjects, born in Germany to a Russian-speaking family of German descent, can be classified as a second-generation speaker, whereas the others qualify as the so-called intermediate generation, owing to their young age at which they migrated to Germany (cf. Backus 1996: 58). Although five were exposed to German before emigration, Russian was the first language they acquired. The age of acquisition of German, as measured by the age of migration to Germany, varies: four speakers began learning German before the age of seven, fifteen started between eight and twelve, and one speaker began at the age of fifteen. All but one participant have lived in Germany for at least ten years. One participant has stayed in Germany for only three years, although she started learning German before she emigrated and was living in a half-German family, therefore richly exposed to German. The other control factor for bilingual capacity is school education in Germany: the subjects have either finished school in Germany or were still attending school there. These criteria ensured that all informants were fluent bilinguals.

The total size of the corpus is approximately 28 hours of recorded speech. One half of the corpus contains casual conversations that occurred between one of the subjects and their peers or family members. The other half of the corpus includes informal group interviews, which I conducted with those subjects who were unwilling to record their private conversations. All interviews were carried out in groups consisting of at least two subjects who were very familiar with each other, being either classmates or friends. The subjects' familiarity with one another was intended to enhance the naturalness of the interaction. The subjects were not informed that the phenomenon of interest for data collection was code-mixing. The relevant information concerning the language biographies of the speakers represented in the corpus was made available after the recording.

3.2 Prepositional phrases: Sample characteristics

Prepositional phrases are widely involved in code-mixing in my bilingual Russian-German corpus; a total of 456 pertinent instances were identified. The investigated syntactic context demonstrates a high degree of variability. We first consider the most frequent case. The following structures alternate when Russian provides the clausal matrix:

(6) [R [G P (ART) N G] R]

[R P [G N G](-INFL) R]

where R and G stand for Russian and German, respectively. In the former case, a German prepositional phrase is inserted in a Russian clause, and in the latter case, a German noun is embedded in a Russian prepositional phrase.

The considerable variability that these two structures exhibit in the corpus is due to (i) code-mixing types, i.e. alternation or insertion (Auer 2014; Muysken 2000), (ii) the asymmetry between the participating languages in the case of insertional code-mixing, and (iii) phrase complexity. Twenty-five prepositional phrases partake in alternational code-mixing, for example:

(7) mm   a   jesli *zum*   *warenkorb*   *geh-sch*   (LG0503)
     INTRJ   and   if   to.ART.DAT.SG.M   shopping.basket   go.PRS-2SG
     'Mm, and if you go to the shopping basket?'

In (7), the sequence comprising the Russian conjunction *a* 'and' and the complementiser *jesli* 'if' is juxtaposed with a German string consisting of a prepositional phrase and a finite verb.

The predominant type of code-mixing in the data is insertion: with 431 tokens, it constitutes 94.4 per cent of the sample. For instance:

(8) A: nam   že   zapreti-l-i   kuri-t'   v   škol-e
         DAT1PL   PTCL   prohibit-PST-PL   smoke-INF   in   school-PREP.SG.F

     B: *achso*   daže   *auf dem*   *schulhof*
         PTCL   even   on   ART.DAT.SG.M   playground

     A: v   *schulhof*-e   voobšče   nel'zja
         in   playground-PREP.SG   generally   forbidden

         tol'ko   jesli   vyxod-iš'   *am*   *schulhof*   (LL0517)
         only   if   go.out.PRS-2SG   at.ART.DAT.SG.M   playground
     'A: They prohibited us from smoking in school.'
     'B: Ah, even in the playground?'
     'A: In the playground it is generally forbidden; only if you go outside the playground.'

Lines three and four of example (8) illustrate two major patterns of insertional code-mixing in the examined context in the data: either a German prepositional phrase (*am schulhof* 'at the playground') is embedded in the Russian matrix clause, or a German noun (*schulhof* 'playground') is used in a Russian prepositional phrase (cf. 6). These examples are in line with the observed tendency to use German nouns and prepositional phrases in Russian discourse. By and large, insertions of German items in Russian clauses prevail over Russian insertions in German discourse. Insertion of Russian nouns and prepositional phrases into the German clausal matrix is possible but rare. In (9), for example, German, being the language of the matrix frame, accommodates the Russian prepositional phrase *s kitajtsami* 'with the Chinese'.

(9) *s   kitajts-ami   würd-e   ich   leb-en*   (LJ0526)
    with   Chinese-INS.PL   AUX.COND-1SG   NOM1SG   leb-INF
    'I would live with the Chinese.'

Prepositional phrases that are adjacent to other insertions constitute a special case, for instance:

(10) *ili   ty   v baden-württemberg studier*-uj-eš   *i   potom*
    either   DAT2SG   in Baden-Württemberg study-ST.PRS-2SG and then

    tebe   nado   v irgendein   ander-es   bundesland...
    DAT2SG necessary   to some[ACC.SG] other-ACC.SG federal.state[ACC.SG]

                                  (LR0712)
    'Either you study in Baden-Württemberg and then you have to move to some other federal state...'

In (10), the mixed prepositional phrase *v baden-württemberg* 'in Baden-Württemberg' is followed by the morphosyntactically integrated verbal insertion *studieruješ* '(you) study'. Eighteen tokens of this type (approx. 4.0%) were identified in the corpus. In order to keep the data set homogeneous, these instances were discarded, such that only lone insertions, i.e. those surrounded by the matrix language morphemes, as in (8), were included in the analysed data set.

    Phrase complexity is a further source of variability when Russian is the matrix language. Again, an asymmetry is observed between simple prepositional phrases and those containing expanded noun phrases. The former is more frequent than the latter, comprising 73.1 per cent of the data set. The mixed prepositional phrase *v irgendein anderes bundesland* 'to some other federal state' in (10) exemplifies the case of prepositional phrases with expanded noun phrases. The various patterns reflecting the syntactic variability in the examined context and their counts in the bilingual corpus are summarised in Figure 1. The distribution of the prepositional phrases involved in insertional code-mixing reveals that, with Russian being the matrix language, simple prepositional phrases, whether switched at their boundary or inside, overwhelmingly dominate the other structures described above (χ^2 = 170, p-value < 0.000). Therefore, the present chapter focuses on switch-placement within this type of structure. The data set contains 86 tokens of German prepositional phrases embedded in Russian sentences – [$_R$ [$_G$ P (ART) N $_G$] $_R$] – and 247 German nouns preceded by Russian prepositions – [$_R$ P [$_G$ N $_G$](-INFL) $_R$].

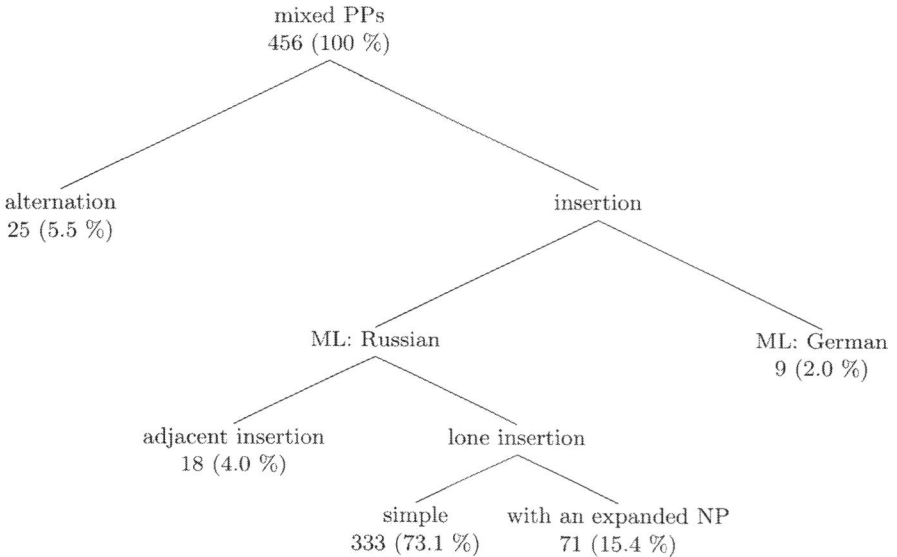

Figure 1: Prepositional phrases involved in code-mixing: variability of structures and proportions

A few of the involved nouns were subject to further analysis since they either participate in word-internal mixing, occur in mixing at a site of non-equivalence, or are considered established loans. Seven German noun stems occurring in Russian prepositional phrases take not only the corresponding Russian inflections but also the Russian diminutive suffix -*ik*, as in *(ot) dart-ik-a* '(from) dart-DIM-GEN.SG'. Such forms were regarded as instances of word-internal mixing and were excluded from the data set under analysis (for more details see Hakimov, 2015). Prepositional phrases resulting from mixing at a site of non-equivalence constitute another equivocal case. Both instances of this case – *na hälfte* '(up to a) half' and *na endeffekt* 'finally'– were produced by the same speaker. The Russian counterpart of the former string is the adverb *napolovinu*, whereas its German equivalent is the prepositional phrase *zur Hälfte*.

The Russian correspondents of the latter string (cf. German *im Endeffekt*) include such expressions as *v (konečnom) itoge* or *v konce koncov*; the unconventional use of the preposition *na* in this context can be attributed to an interference with the adverb *nakonets* 'at last', although its meaning differs slightly from the contextual meaning of the mixed string. Lack of clarity on whether the two instances ought to be subsumed under the category of word-internal mixing or not led me to discard these items from the data set. The last category of noun insertions not included in the final data set consists of three German nouns which have acquired new meanings in the variety of Russian spoken in Germany. The German noun *Sprache* 'language' is used in the corpus in the form *sprachi*, which contains the Russian plural inflection *-i*, to refer to 'language courses'. While entering the vocabulary of German Russian, the meaning of the noun *Heim* 'home' narrowed to that of 'home for late repatriates' (cf. German *Spätaussiedlerheim*). Finally, the German adjective *sozial* 'social' underwent nominalisation and became conventionalised in the meaning 'social benefit'; the noun occurs particularly frequently in the expression *sidet' na soziale* 'to be on supplementary benefit' (cf. Russian *sidet' na [social'nom] posobii*; the examined expression from Germany is yet unattested in Russian Russian). On the basis of the observed semantic changes, we can reasonably assume that these nouns are nativised items in German Russian, or established loans. In total, 233 tokens of German nouns inserted into Russian prepositional phrases were included in the final data set.

3.3 Frequency distribution of the structures in the data set

Specific realisations of German prepositional phrases occurring in otherwise Russian sentences as well as German nouns used in Russian prepositional phrases exhibit varying frequencies of occurrence in the corpus. Most instantiations of the German prepositional phrase appear in the corpus once. A few exceptions nevertheless occur: the string *zum Beispiel* 'for example' is used four times in the corpus, the phrases *am Montag* 'on Monday' and *zum Ausgleich* 'for compensation' occur three times each, and the strings *im Normalfall* 'normally', *am Dienstag* 'on Tuesday' and *am Sonntag* 'on Sunday' appear twice each. Overall, the data set contains 86 tokens of embedded German prepositional phrases, which correspond to 79 types.

German nouns inserted in the analysed Russian prepositional phrases occur in Russian discourse at more variable rates. Some of them are regularly inserted into Russian sentences, whereas others appear in the Russian discourse only once. In order to establish the nonce character of these German insertions, it was necessary to measure their usage frequency in Russian sentences. Every token of a particular German lexical item (type) was counted when it was embedded in the Russian context. For example, the lexical item *Montag* 'Monday' occurs in the corpus in the following contexts:

(11) a. v *montag*   bud-u   rabota-t' (LJ1105)
    in Monday[ACC.SG] AUX.FUT-1SG work-INF
    'On Monday I will work.'

  b. *montag*   bud-u   rabota-t' (LJ1105)
    Monday[ACC.SG] AUX.FUT-1SG work-INF
    'Monday I will work.'

  c. vot ot   *montag* do *freitag* u nas   mnogo škol-y (LN1107)
    PTCL from Monday till Friday at 1PL.GEN much   school-SG.GEN
    'From Monday till Friday we have a lot of school-classes.'

  d. a   my   *chemie* *že* *am*   *montag* pisa-l-i (LJ1105)
    but 1PL.NOM chemistry PTCL at.ART.DAT.SG.M Monday write-PST-PL
    'But we wrote chemistry on Monday.'

As the noun *Montag* 'Monday' occurs three times in the Russian discourse, i.e. in (11a, 11b[5] and 11c) but not in (11d), where it is part of a German prepositional phrase, its frequency in stretches of the Russian discourse amounts to three tokens.

The frequencies with which the examined nouns appear in the Russian discourse in the corpus are given in Table 1. From the table it follows that nonce items, or *hapax legomena*, account for 44.6 per cent of all the inserted German nouns. The most frequent German nouns, which appear ten or more times in Russian sentences, constitute the smallest group (3.1%). The majority of noun lexemes (52.3%) occur as insertions, with the frequency ranging between one and ten and thus falling between the aforementioned groups. Hence, the investigated lexical items constitute a heterogeneous category.

An analysis that includes both nonce and recurrent insertions can be problematic inasmuch as embedded language items recurrent in the matrix language discourse may well be (becoming) established loans (cf. Backus 2013; Myers-Scotton 1993; Poplack and Dion 2012; Poplack, Sankoff and Miller 1988). The

---

5 The noun *Montag* is analysed here as an instance of bare adjunct noun phrase (see Larson 1985 for English, Tajsner 1997 for Polish).

Table 1: Frequencies of German noun insertions in Russian sentences as distributed in bilingual corpus

Absolute word frequency, F	Relative word frequency	Number of lexemes	Number of lexemes, %
1	0.00004	70	44.6
2	0.00008	28	17.8
3	0.00012	20	12.7
4	0.00016	14	8.9
5	0.00020	9	5.7
6	0.00024	6	3.8
$6 < F < 10$	–	5	3.2
10	0.00040	1	0.6
$F < 10$	–	4	2.5
Total		157	100.0

question of whether a given lexical item is undergoing conventionalisation in German Russian cannot be addressed here on the basis of the following considerations. First, in order to examine the conventionalisation of a lexical item a larger sample is needed. Second, frequency counts used for determining the item's status should be complemented by psycholinguistic evidence (cf. Blumenthal-Dramé 2012). A practical question that arises in this context is where to draw the line between items occurring more than once and frequent items. Poplack, Sankoff and Miller (1988) suggest an absolute frequency of ten tokens as a cut-off threshold for a word to qualify as a recurrent item and therefore a potentially established loan. The proposed solution is based on the large size of their corpus, which encompasses approximately 2.5 million words (Poplack, Sankoff and Miller 1988: 98). Expressed in relative terms, the threshold frequency corresponds to the value of 0.000004. The application of this threshold to a small corpus, such as mine, is not feasible because not even a single word in the corpus would count as an established loan. The frequency threshold for German noun insertions in Russian sentences was set at the relative frequency of 0.0002, which amounts to the absolute frequency of five tokens. That is, German nouns which appear at least five times in the Russian discourse were considered frequent and were removed from the data set. The excluded lexical items form a relatively small set, which covers 15.8 per cent of the examined items.

In sum, some German noun insertions occur more frequently in Russian sentences than others. Control over the frequency of such nouns in the Russian discourse was achieved by removing frequent lexical items from the data set.

4 Factors

The remainder of this chapter investigates co-occurrence frequency, noun frequency and word repetition as predictors of switch placement in the context of the prepositional phrase. Specifically, I measure frequencies with which the German nouns identified in the previous section appear together with prepositions in a German corpus. Furthermore, I show that this co-occurrence frequency, noun frequency and word repetition in discourse effectively predict switch placement. The frequency of the preposition is not considered as a predictor of switch placement because the prepositions used in the identified prepositional phrases are all high-frequency items. The factor 'word repetition' is approached in conjunction with the effect of repetition priming.

4.1 Modelling frequency of co-occurrence

Switch placement in the context of a syntactic phrase is hypothesised to be the function of the frequency with which the words constituting the phrase appear together (cf. Bybee 2010: 33). If a preposition and a noun co-occur with a high frequency, they exhibit a strong bond, which is likely to repel a code-switch. Conversely, if the association between the preposition and the noun is loose, i.e. the frequency of co-occurrence between these items is low, a switch is likely to be placed between them. To test these hypotheses, it is necessary to measure the frequencies with which the nouns extracted from the bilingual corpus co-occur with prepositions in German.

4.1.1 Corpus analysis

Associations between words are commonly modelled by utilising large corpora. My bilingual corpus would not suffice for such a task. An approximation of the distributions of preposition-noun combinations in German was therefore inevitable. Hence, co-occurrence frequencies were obtained from deWaC, a large German corpus containing around 1.6 billion words (Baroni and Kilgarriff 2006). Given that this corpus is chiefly based on written language, the measured frequencies can only be considered as rough approximations of spoken language. Regrettably, no corpus of spoken German that matches deWaC in size is available. However, considering the age and education of the participants in the study, we can assume that they have received large portions of their German input from written sources as well.

Nouns participating in the prepositional phrases from the data set were investigated in deWaC in the context of the prepositional phrase. All the syntactic formats of the German prepositional phrase were considered: [PREP N], [PREP ART N] and [PREP.ART N]. The analysis procedure is illustrated by the German prepositional phrase *an einem Seil* 'on a rope', used in a mixed sentence (12).

(12) i   čto   on-i   vs-e   *an*   *ein-em*   *seil*   (LL0510)
      and   that   3-PL.NOM   all-PL.NOM   on   ART-DAT.SG.M   rope
      'And that they are all on a rope.'

Combinations of the noun *Seil* with preposition instantiations, preposition-article contractions and preposition-article combinations were determined in deWaC, and their corresponding frequencies were measured. The results for the item *Seil* are given in Table 2. Since the utilised corpus is not tagged for morphological case, it was impossible to distinguish strings differing in grammatical case. That is, the tokens of the strings *an ein Seil* 'onto a rope [ACC]' and *an ein-em Seil* 'on a rope [DAT]' were automatically collapsed to the pattern *an ein Seil*, where *ein* stands for all the case forms of the indefinite article. The individual patterns were further merged to a less specific pattern with the unspecified article – [an ART Seil] – because the choice of articles largely depends on the sentential context.

Table 2: The use of the noun *Seil* 'rope' in the context of the prepositional phrase in deWaC. The abbreviation *d* refers to all the case forms of the definite article, the abbreviation *ein* refers to all the case forms of the indefinite article

Pattern	Frequency	Pattern	Frequency
am	428	ins	51
an ein	340	durch ein	44
mit ein	250	auf ein	43
auf d	186	über ein	30
mit d	115	ans	28
an d	107	in d	28
mit	84	aufs	23
über	65	um d	17
vom	62	zum	17
ohne	59	durch d	15
im	54	per	15

Table 3: The prepositions accompanying the noun *Seil* in deWaC

Preposition	Frequency	Preposition	Frequency
an	903	*durch*	59
mit	449	*ohne*	59
auf	252	*um*	17
in	133	*zu*	17
über	95	*per*	15
von	62		

In this way I reordered sets of prepositions co-occurring with the investigated nouns and calculated their co-occurrence frequencies. The outcome for the sample noun is presented in Table 3. As suggested by Bybee (2010), the strength of association between a noun and a given preposition realisation was operationalised as co-occurrence frequency. In a set of co-occurrences of a particular noun with an array of prepositions, such as the one in Table 3, the highest frequency value corresponds to the strongest association, as in the combination [*an* – *Seil*], while low frequency co-occurrences stand for loose associations between the string parts, as in [*per* – *Seil*].

4.1.2 Predicting a chunk

To predict an item in production means to determine the likelihood with which it is produced by the speaker. The information about the distribution of a pattern across its specific instantiations is used to model the relationships between these instantiations in terms of probabilities. If one of the slots of a pattern is kept constant, a particular realisation of the whole pattern can be predicted by utilising the information about the distribution of the specific items in the other slot. The predicted realisation is then an outcome of the competition among the specific realisations of the open element. In the present case, prepositions compete with one another in order to become activated together with a particular noun. A co-occurrence distinguished by the highest frequency in a given set has a greater chance of being used in production than a low-frequency sequence. For instance, in the set of the prepositions used with the noun *Seil* 'rope' (see Table 3), the co-occurrence *an* – *Seil* is more likely to be selected than any other co-occurrence.

A novel step was to model the competition in preposition sets by applying odds, based on Fahrmeier et al. (2003: 119–121). Odds are the ratio of the probability that an event will happen to the probability that an event will not happen. Mathematically, it is formulated as follows:

$$odds_1 = \frac{F_1}{\sum F_i - F_1}$$

where F_1 stands for the frequency of a pattern instantiation and $\sum F_i$ denotes the cumulative frequency of the pattern. The index expresses the relationship between an element of a frequency distribution and the remaining distribution elements. Let me demonstrate this by using the distribution of the pattern [PREP ... *Seil*], whose total frequency amounts to 2061 tokens. The preposition slot can be specified by 11 prepositions (see Table 2), and the most frequent co-occurrence is [*an – Seil*] 'on – rope', with a frequency value of 903 tokens. The probability that this realisation is selected in production, as determined by odds, is 0.779. Odds were computed for all the German strings in the data set, *i.e.* nouns preceded by German prepositions. When the preceding prepositions were Russian, odds were calculated for German equivalents of the corresponding Russian prepositions, in order that semantic equivalence might be maintained. For example, in the case of the mixed string *na miete* 'on rent' in (13), the German preposition *von* was selected because its meaning corresponds to the meaning of the preposition *na* 'on' in the context of the verb *žit'* 'to live' (cf. German *von der Miete leben* 'to live on the rent'); the odds ratio was thus computed for the combination [von – Miete], competing with the actually realised string.

(13) on   tol'ko na   *miete* i   živ-ët   (LG05036)
      3SG.M   only   on   rent   PTCL   live.PRS-3SG
      'It is only the rent that he lives on.'

The calculated odds ratios were normalised by employing a logarithmic scale, in order to avoid skewing of the distribution (cf. Baayen 2008: 31). An analysis of outliers (cf. Gries: 258) resulted in the omission of three data points with extremely low odds values: the German phrase *neben dem Haus* 'next to the house' and the mixed phrases *naprotiv straße* 'opposite the street' and *krome kuchen-ov* 'except cake-GEN.PL.M'. The number of excluded data points amounts to 1.2% of the sample. The relationship between odds values and switch placement is represented in Figure 2.

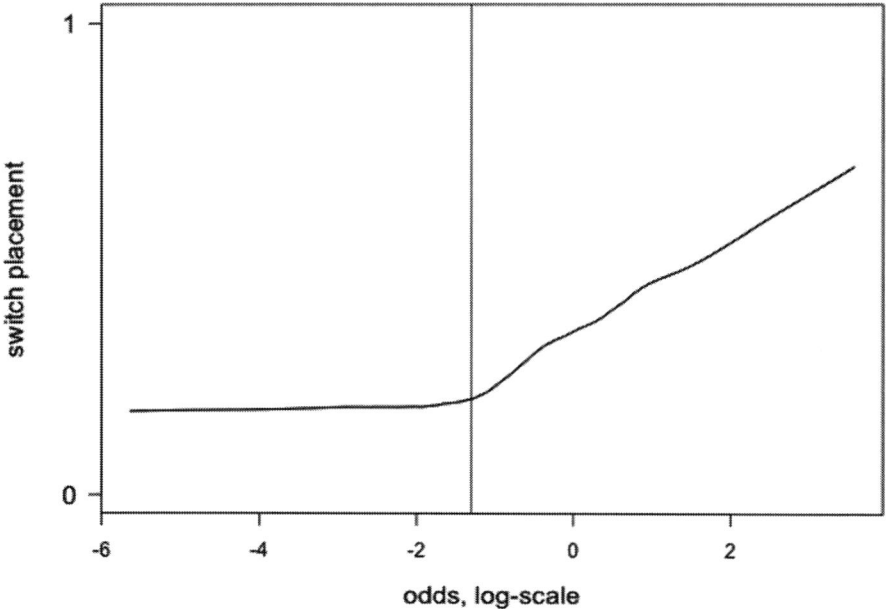

Figure 2: The relationship between switch placement and odds (on the logarithmic scale). The values of 0 and 1 on the y-axis stand for switching within and outside the prepositional phrase, respectively

The binary variable 'switch placement' is on the vertical axis with the values of zero and one, which stand for a switch within a prepositional phrase or at its boundary, respectively; the values of odds are on the horizontal axis. The line depicting the relationship between these variables is a Lowess curve, which represents a function describing the deterministic part of the variation in the data and is generated by locally weighted scatterplot smoothing, a local regression method (Cleveland and Devlin 1988). The Lowess curve shows that the line begins to curve upwards around the logarithmic value of −1.3, which corresponds to the odds value of 0.273. This means that the tendency to switch within a phrase curbs steadily and permanently. With odds reaching the value of 0.273, the phrase boundary gradually becomes a more preferred switch site. That is, the higher the odds, the higher the probability of a switch being placed before the preposition.

4.2 Frequency of the noun

Word frequency has been shown to exert a facilitatory effect in language production (Oldfield and Wingfield 1965) and to operate on the lexeme level (Jeschiniak and Levelt 1994). In other words, frequent words are more accessible in language production. We can assume a relationship between the frequency of a word and the lexicogrammatical patterns associated with it because interactions between lexemes are considered to control syntactic patterns (MacWhinney 1997: 115). Apparently, frequent words can trigger their lexicogrammatical patterns, or chunks, more easily than rare words. Lexicogrammatical patterns of frequent words are thus more accessible than those involving rare lexemes. In the context of the present study, frequent German nouns that occur in the examined prepositional phrases have a stronger tendency to trigger typical prepositions accompanying them than rare German nouns. To test this hypothesis, frequencies of the nouns from the examined prepositional phrases were obtained from the deWaC corpus (see 3.1.1). Table 4 provides some of the prepositional phrases under investigation and the corresponding noun frequencies. The first five prepositional phrases include low-frequency nouns and exhibit phrase-internal switches, whereas the last five prepositional phrases include high-frequency nouns and are switched at the phrase boundary.

Table 4: Prepositional phrases with phrase-internal and phrase-external switches and the frequencies of the involved nouns, measured in deWaC

PPs with switches placed within and outside the PP	F_N
v *erotikshop* 'to the sexshop'	19
na *sporttag* 'on a sports day'	65
s *gummisohlen* 'with rubber soles'	80
za *einzimmerwohnung* 'for a studio appartment'	126
v *prüfungsstress* 'under stress from exams'	249
nach hause '(to) home'	230408
neben dem haus 'near the house'	230408
in der kirche 'in church'	281589
in die stadt 'to the city'	480767
am ende 'in the end'	579078

The obtained frequency values were logarithmically transformed, as suggested in Baayen (2008: 31). The datum *Erotikshop* 'sex shop' was considered an outlier, due to its extremely low frequency in the corpus. The relationship between noun frequency and switch placement is plotted in Figure 3.

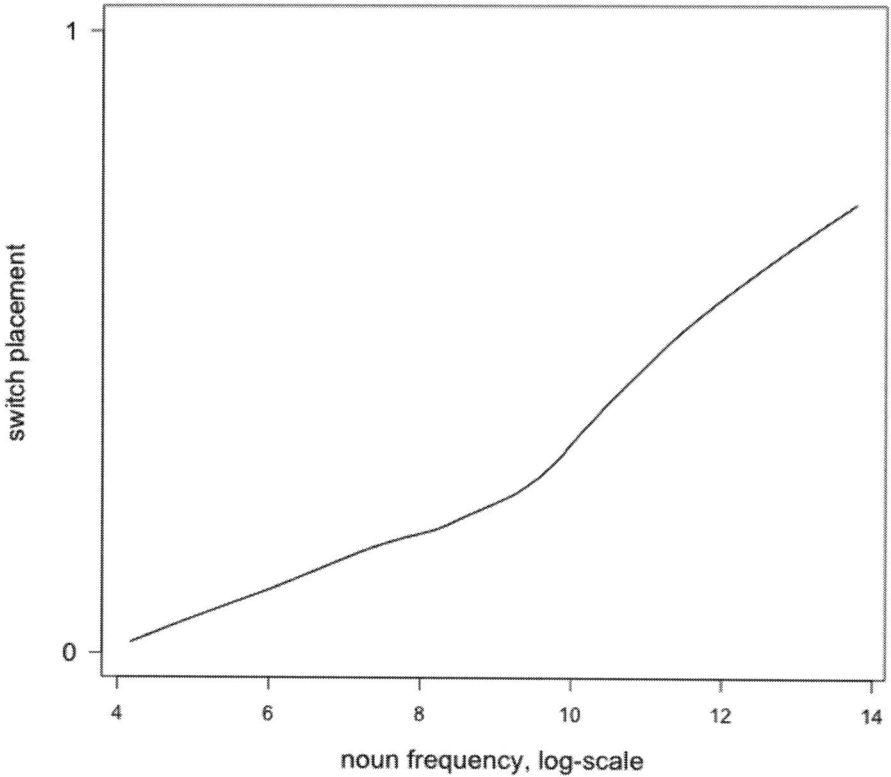

Figure 3: The relationship between switch placement and frequency of the noun (on the logarithmic scale)

The variable 'switch placement' is on the vertical axis, and its values zero and one stand for a phrase-internal switch and a switch at the phrase boundary, respectively; noun frequency is on the horizontal axis. The Lowess curve (see 3.1.2) demonstrates the effect of word frequency on switch placement: an increase in frequency of the noun correlates with a stronger tendency to switch the language at the phrase boundary. This is in line with the aforementioned assumption that the lexicogrammatical patterns involving high-frequency words are more accessible in production. Whether the frequency of the noun contributes significantly to predicting switch placement is tested in a statistical model below.

4.3 Word repetition

The implicit memory effect of priming has been shown to affect monolingual and bilingual language production in various domains of language. The need to give due consideration to word repetition in investigating naturally occurring code-mixing is motivated by both experimental studies and analyses of naturally occurring bilingual speech. Ledoux et al. (2006) provide experimental evidence that effects of lexical repetition persist even when words are embedded in discourse. Support for this finding comes from Koostra, van Hell and Dijkstra (2012), who, in experiments with Dutch-English bilinguals, explored the role of lexical repetition, cognates and second language proficiency in the priming of code-switches. The participants of their study repeated a code-mixed sentence and then described a picture by using a code-mixed sentence. The authors show that lexical repetition between the prime sentence and the target picture and the presence of a cognate in the prime and the target are capable of priming code-switches in sentences. With regard to variation in a particular syntactic context, Torres Cacoullos and Travis (2016) find that specific realisations of syntactic patterns in bilingual speech are subject to priming effects. All this evidence suggests that we need to control for repetition of words in the analysis of code-mixing. The repetition of words that constitute the identified prepositional phrases was therefore examined as one of the factors determining switch placement in the prepositional phrase. Generally, a specific lexical realisation of the phrase is more likely if the prior discourse contains the same lexical material; conversely, a specific lexical realisation of the phrase is less predictable if the prior discourse lacks the lexical items which constitute the target phrase.

In the context of the prepositional phrase, an occurrence of a preposition in discourse can lead to the repeated selection of this preposition in subsequent production, provided that semantic compatibility is maintained. That is, once a preposition is selected, it is highly likely to be selected again in the same language, for instance:

(14) priš-l-o-s   kogda <u>v</u> lahr   zaeha-l-i
be.necessary-PST-SG.N-REFL when in Lahr.ACC.SG.M arrive-PST-PL

perv-ym   del-om   <u>v</u> *krankenhaus*   eha-t'
first-INSTR.SG.N thing-INSTR.SG.N to hospital.ACC.SG.M drive-INF (LG05036)

'First thing when (they) arrived in Lahr they had to drive to hospital.'

The mixed prepositional phrase in (14) consists of the Russian preposition *v* 'to' and the German noun *Krankenhaus* 'hospital'. Alternatively, the speaker may have selected the German preposition *in* 'to' and produced the string *ins Krankenhaus* 'to hospital', with the preposition *in* and the definite article *das* being contracted. However, as the Russian preposition v 'in / to' already occurs in the prepositional phrase *v lahr* 'in Lahr' earlier, the speaker repeats it in the same language in the subsequent prepositional phrase. In other words, the first occurrence of the preposition *v* appears to prime the use of the same lexical item with the German noun *Krankenhaus* 'hospital' in later discourse.

Nouns involved in the examined prepositional phrases are also subject to this pervasive effect, for instance:

(15) tam *welle*   na   nih   polete-l-a   ili poli-l-a-s'
     there wave-NOM.SG onto 3PL.ACC go.over-PST-F.SG or spout-PST-F.SG-REFL

     nu   i   esli posmotr-et' čo   tam *auf der*   *welle* vidno
     PTCL and if   look.at-INF what there on   ART.DAT.SG.F wave visible
                                                                      (LVa0510)
     'A wave went over them or spouted, and if you look at what is visible
     on the wave...'

The noun in the inserted German prepositional phrase *auf der Welle* 'on the wave' in (15) appears in the prior discourse in the same language. Instead of repeating this lexical item in German in the subsequent prepositional phrase, the speaker may have selected the Russian equivalent, i.e. the word *volna*. Nevertheless, we observe the persistent use of the German noun *Welle*. Moreover, the activation of this German noun has presumably coactivated the German preposition associated with it. However, if we assume that the choice of preposition depends on an occurrence of that preposition in the prior discourse, as in (14), we might also expect the Russian counterpart of the German preposition *auf* 'on', i.e. *na*, to appear with the noun *Welle* 'wave', owing to its previous occurrence in the phrase *na nih* 'on(to) them'. The result would have been the mixed phrase *na Welle* 'on wave' (cf. *na volne* 'on the wave'). Inevitably, only the interplay of all the described factors is capable of predicting switch-placement.

The data were coded for the presence or absence of the examined prepositions and nouns in the window of eight seconds in the prior discourse (i.e. 5 ± 3 seconds, cf. Szmrecsanyi 2006: 189). The relationship between switch placement and word repetition in the same language is given in Figure 4, in which the upper panel concerns the repetition of prepositions and the lower panel refers to the repetition of nouns. The proportion of prepositions repeated in mixed

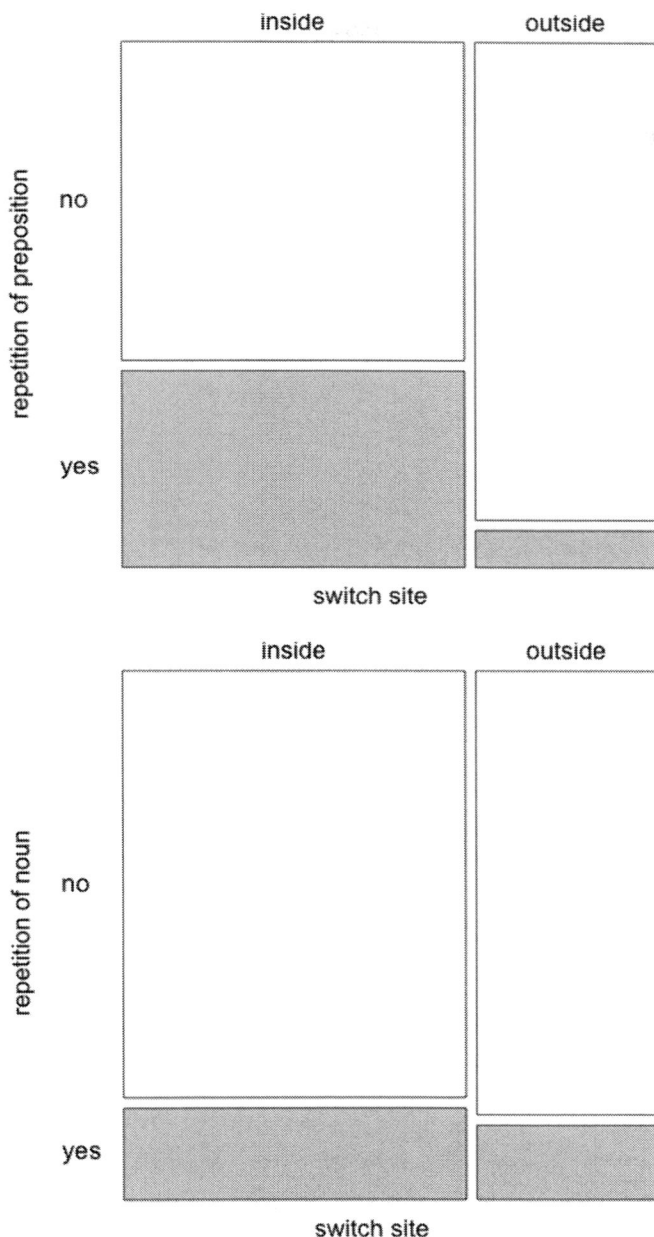

Figure 4: The relationship between switch placement and word repetition in the same language. The upper panel represents prior occurrences of target prepositions, the lower panel demonstrates prior occurrences of target nouns

phrases is skewed; the asymmetry indicates the tendency to switching within the prepositional phrase, given a prior occurrence of a specific preposition in the same language. The relatively similar proportion of nouns that appear prior to the investigated German insertions makes it evident that noun repetition does not affect switch placement. Yet, a possible interaction between the repetition of nouns and the repetition of prepositions cannot be excluded, as in the case of phrase repetition. For example:

(16) ja   im   govorj-u   *wenn ich*   *was*   *von gott*
     1SG.NOM 3PL.DAT tell-prs.1sg if   1SG.NOM something from god

     will   *geh-e*   *ich*   *in die*   *kirche*
     want.PRS1SG GO-PRS1SG 1SG.NOM to ART.ACC.SG church

     a   oni   mne   nača-l-i   *in der*   *kirche*   kak budto s
     but 3PL.NOM 1SG.DAT begin-PST-PL to ART.DAT.SG church as if   with

     gott čo-to   oni   ne tak dela-jut čo   *gott*
     god something.ACC 3PL.NOM NEG so do-PRS3PL what.ACC god[NOM.SG]

     imej-et   v vid-u   (HO1007)
     have.PRS-3SG in view-LOC.SG

     I tell them, if I want something from God, I go to church, but they
     began like, in church people do not treat God as he intends them to.'

Here, the phrase *in die Kirche* 'to church' appears in a German clause for the first time and is then echoed in a mixed clause, albeit with the article in a differing case. Although such a case is relatively rare, an interaction between the variables 'repetition of preposition' and 'repetition of noun' would be able to account for it. Generally, occurrences of prepositions in the prior discourse affect the choice of the preposition in the target phrase. In other words, prepositions prime more strongly than nouns.

    To summarise, I have shown that four factors are predictive of switch placement in the context of the prepositional phrase: odds, based on the co-occurrence frequency of prepositions and nouns; noun frequency; the presence or absence of prepositions in prior discourse; and the presence or absence of nouns in prior, discourse albeit only in conjunction with a repeated preposition. As detailed above, certain instances, such as (15), cannot be explained by taking only one factor into account. This circumstance necessitates a statistical treatment of the subject, such that the aforementioned factors and their interactions are analysed in a multifactorial model.

5 Predicting switch placement

The aim of this section is to examine the factors outlined above as they compete and interact with one another when predicting switch placement in the prepositional phrase. Approaching this issue enables us to answer questions such as these: How predictive is noun frequency of switch placement, all things being equal? Which factor is the most important predictor of the observed variation? Do individual preferences for switch placement override the regularity of the identified linguistic tendencies? These matters are investigated by using the generalised linear mixed model (see Baayen 2008: 278–84; cf. Bresnan et al. 2007). Probabilities of binary outcomes (a switch within a prepositional phrase and a switch at the boundary of a prepositional phrase) will be determined on the basis of the predictor variables, i.e. the considered factors. Significant interactions between these factors and the placement of a switch in the investigated syntactic context will provide objective evidence of the relevance of the factors.

5.1 Model fitting

In a regression model with mixed effects, the joint contribution of all factors is computed by testing each factor individually, while the others remain constant (cf. Szmrecsanyi 2013). In order to obtain a minimal adequate regression model, the common procedure (Baayen 2008; Szmrecsanyi 2013) was employed, which is as follows. The maximal model contained the four considered factors as main effects, i.e. odds, based on the frequency of co-occurrence of the examined nouns and prepositions; the frequency of the noun involved; prior occurrences and non-occurrences of the target noun; and prior occurrences and non-occurrences of the target preposition. The maximal model also included interactions between these factors. The speakers' individual differences in mixing behaviour – a propensity to insert German nouns into Russian prepositional phrases or, rather, a preference for maintaining the integrity of the phrase – may alter the tendencies determined solely by linguistic predictors. These individual differences are considered by introducing the variable 'speaker'. This factor was handled as a by-subject random effect. However, including a random effect for the variable 'item' was impossible owing to the high variation in this variable: 197 various lexemes appear in the 244 prepositional phrases under analysis. The model was thus run without the by-item random variable. The model simplification procedure consisted in the omission of the factors and interaction terms that added no significant explanatory power to the model. Following Baayen (2008: 281), the calculation of the C index of concordance is the basis for estimating the explanatory power of main effects and interaction terms. The process of model reduction resulted in the exclusion of the following two interaction terms from the model: noun frequency × odds and prior noun × noun frequency. Subsequently, the inclusion of the by-subject random effect was justified by the estimation of the C index of a generalised linear model without random effects. The model with the random effect turned out to perform significantly better than the model without a random effect (which is in line with established practice in similar cases; cf. Bresnan et al. 2007; Tagliamonte and Baayen 2012). The final, minimal adequate model is presented in Table 5.

5.2 Model evaluation and model discussion

The minimal adequate model in Table 5 is of high quality. The model correctly predicts 84% of all instances of switch placement in the data set, while the categorical prediction of switch placement by always guessing a switch within the prepositional phrase will be correct in 69% of all cases. The C index of concordance between the predicted probability and the observed binary outcomes is 0.871, which indicates that the model has high predictive power. The performance indicator Somers' D_{xy}, a rank correlation coefficient between predicted probabilities and observed binary response, is 0.725, which again signals the high predictive capacity of the model. Regarding the random effect for the factor 'speaker', we can conclude from its estimated variance and standard deviation that the variation among speakers, although minor, still contributes to the distribution of the examined data.

The main effects in the model provide positive evidence for the assumptions formulated above. The signs of the regression coefficients (b) in Table 4 reveal the direction of the adjustment to the intercept. Hence, a prior occurrence of the target preposition and that of the target noun condition the placing of the switch between preposition and noun, whereas both odds, based on co-occurrence frequency, and noun frequency favour switching at the phrase boundary. Consider the odds ratios reported in Table 5. Among the fixed-effect factors, repetition of the preposition has the largest effect size, which means that if the target preposition appears in the prior discourse, the likelihood of switch placement at the phrase boundary decreases by 97%. That is, there is a high probability that the previously occurring preposition will be selected in the target prepositional phrase. The interaction between a prior occurrence of the target preposition and that of the target noun in the discourse is another strong effect. If both the preposition and the noun appear in the preceding discourse, the odds for switch placement increase by a factor of approximately 25.

Table 5: Predicting switch placement in the context of the prepositional phrase: minimal adequate generalised linear mixed model. Predicted odds ratios are for switches placed at the phrase boundary

	odds ratio	b	p-value
Model intercept	0.012	−4.427	0.000***
Prior preposition	0.030	−3.496	0.000***
Prior noun	0.440	−0.820	0.178
Noun frequency	1.568	0.449	0.000***
Odds	1.359	0.307	0.001**
Prior preposition x prior noun	24.753	3.209	0.007**
Random effect:			
Speaker			
(intercept, N = 19, variance: 0.915, σ = 0.956)			
Summary statistics:			
N			244
% correct predictions (% baseline)			84 (69)
C index of concordance			0.871
Somers' Dxy			0.742

Significance levels: p < 0.001 (***), 0.001 ≤ p ≤ 0.01 (**)

This interaction term accounts for the aforementioned case illustrated in (15). But when the occurrence of the noun and that of the preposition in the prior discourse do not interact, both of them favour switch placement within the prepositional phrase. Although the predictor 'prior occurrence of noun' does not attain statistical significance, it interacts with the factor 'prior occurrence of preposition', enhancing the model's predicative capacity. This is the main reason for retaining this predictor in the minimal adequate model. Another reason is the high level of statistical significance reached by the aforementioined interaction.

After considering the effect sizes of the factors contributing to the minimal adequate model, it is crucial to discuss the overall importance of these factors. This parameter is visualised in Figure 5 by plotting the decrease in the Akaike Information Criterion (AIC) of the model if a factor is removed from the minimal model. According to Szmrecsanyi (2013), more sizable decreases in the AIC criterion of a factor stand for its increased overall importance. In predicting switch placement in the context of 244 prepositional phrases from the data set, the most important factor is 'prior occurrence of the target preposition'. Noun frequency is the second most relevant predictor, followed by 'odds', based on co-occurrence frequency. The model's Akaike Information Criterion sinks drastically when the factor 'noun frequency' is removed from the model. The extent of this decrease appears to substantially exceed the scope of the decrease of factor 'odds'. The interaction between the prior occurrence of the noun and that of the preposition is ranked last. The prior occurrence of the noun is not among the plotted factors owing to its low level of importance for the model, when included without an interaction term.

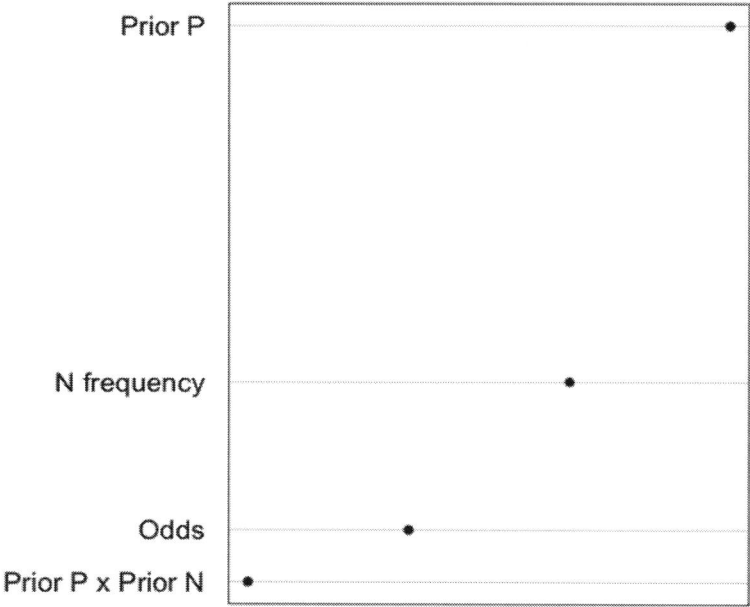

Figure 5: Importance of factors in model: decrease in Akaike Information Criterion (AIC) if factor removed. (The table representation is based on Szmrecsanyi 2013)

A somewhat surprising result of the minimal adequate model is that the predictor 'noun frequency' is more important in accounting for variation in the data than the factor 'odds', which is a measure of competition among co-occurrences of nouns and prepositions. The question then arises as to why 'odds' is a less important predictor than 'noun frequency'. Although 'odds' is the only factor that takes preposition-noun co-occurrences into consideration, it does not perform adequately in the model. A possible reason for such underperformance is the severe competition among chunks involving high-frequency nouns.

Table 6: Prepositions co-occurring with the German noun *Ende* 'end' and their respective co-occurrence frequencies

Co-occurring prepositions	Frequency of co-occurrence
an 'at'	157220
zu 'to'	67684
bis 'by'	22152
nach 'after'	18279
gegen 'towards'	14240
seit 'since'	13063
von 'from'	7214
vor 'before'	6993
ohne 'without'	5242
mit 'with'	5153
für 'for'	3824
ab 'from'	3398
auf 'to'	2408

Table 6 provides a set of prepositions co-occurring with the high-frequency German noun *Ende* 'end'. The noun *Ende* frequently combines with an array of prepositions, so that the competition for activation among them is stiff: summed-up frequencies of the noun's companions, with the exception of the competition winner *an* 'at', outbalance the frequency of the latter. As a result, the top collocate's odds value is lower than 1. A similar situation is observed with other high-frequency nouns. We can thus state that noun frequency does not influence switch placement directly but acts as a leverage for high-frequency nouns, whose numerous chunks, structured as prepositional phrases, are in severe competition with each other.

To summarise, this section shows that such usage-based factors as 'noun frequency' and 'odds', which rely on frequency of co-occurrence, and word repetition (priming), which is related to online processing, act jointly to predict switch placement in the context of the prepositional phrase. The variation among the speakers' preferences for switching the language at the phrase boundary or within the phrase marginally contributes to the variation in the examined data.

6 Discussion and conclusion

This chapter provides evidence that an interplay of usage and processing factors is capable of predicting switch placement in the context of the prepositional phrase in Russian-German code-mixing. The paper demonstrates that a robust account of variation in code-mixing patterns in a specific syntactic context is possible when the following factors are taken into account: exposure to lexical items in the prior discourse, word frequency, and competition among co-occurrences of words. Corpus analyses and statistical modelling were employed to test the assumptions introduced above.

The principal findings of the study include two frequency effects. First, the frequencies with which prepositions and nouns co-occur affect switch placement in the context of the prepositional phrase. If a noun and a specific preposition appear together more frequently than all the other instantiations of the prepositional phrase with this noun, a switch between this noun and the specific preposition is unlikely. Conversely, if the frequency of co-occurrence of a noun and a specific preposition is low, the chance of a switch being placed within the prepositional phrase is high. The fact that high-frequency preposition-noun combinations are not subject to phrase-internal switching is explained by their status in the speakers' mental lexicon as holistic units. Whenever two or more items co-occur on a regular basis in one of the languages involved in code-mixing, speakers store and retrieve these multi-word sequences from memory as units, and their production becomes automatised (cf. Bybee 2010; Janssen and Barber 2012; Schneider 2016). This finding sheds light on the nature of embedded language islands in mixed clauses and provides substantial evidence for the unit hypothesis, formulated by Backus (2003). The use of the odds ratio was a novel method of modelling the competition among multi-word strings structured as prepositional phrases.

The second finding concerns a strong correlation between the frequency of the nouns involved in the examined prepositional phrases and switch placement. I observed that German high-frequency nouns are accompanied by German prepositions in mixed sentences more often than by Russian prepositions. In this case, the switch is usually placed at the boundary of the prepositional phrase. One interpretation of this fact is that high-frequency nouns co-occur within a number of prepositions at a high rate. The stiff competition among these multi-word strings therefore weakens the predictive capacity of odds. As a result, the frequency of the noun appears to be a more important predictor of the variation in the data than odds. Another interpretation is related to the accessibility of high-frequency nouns and their lexicogrammatical patterns, or chunks, in production. Being extremely accessible, these nouns easily co-activate the typical contexts in which they appear. A similar effect has been reported for language comprehension by Arnon and Snider (2010).

The conducted statistical analysis reveals that the most important predictor of switch placement is a prior occurrence of the preposition which is then used in the examined phrase. If this target preposition occurs during the previous eight seconds of the prior discourse, it is likely to appear in the prepositional phrase exhibiting a switch, provided that semantic compatibility is maintained. The effect is so strong that it overrules the effects of frequency discussed above. This fact can be elucidated by the following considerations: First, the investigated prepositions represent the most frequent prepositions, which are distinguished by a wide palette of meanings. Apparently, their frequent use and polysemous nature are interdependent. Second, like pronouns, which are the focus of Torres Cacoullos and Travis (2015), prepositions are function words and can go unnoticed in language production. In other words, function words appear to be stronger primes than content words. Third, code-mixing occasionally co-occurs with self-repair, in which case part of the lexical material remains preserved in the target structure, as in the example below.

(17) *stra- straßebahn*   prijezža-l   v   dvadcat'   četyre   minut-y
      tram[NOM.SG]   arrive-PST.M.SG   at   twenty   four   minute-GEN.SG

      v (.) *also*   *v*   *einundzwanzig*   dvadcat'   četyre   (LR0316)
      at   PTCL   at   twenty-one   twenty   four
      'The tram arrived at twenty-four minutes, well, at nine twenty-four.'

The preposition *v* 'at' appears before the mixed phrase *v einundzwanzig dvadcat' četyre* 'at twenty-one twenty-four' in an instance of self-repair, but also occurs at the beginning of the utterance. Future research should therefore investigate the relationship between switch placement, repetition priming and self-repair.

The present chapter has attempted to provide a usage-based account of switch placement in the context of the prepositional phrase. The results have direct consequences for models of bilingual language production: the choice between inserting a lone German noun into a Russian prepositional phrase and inserting a prepositional phrase appears to depend on the accessibility of linguistic material in discourse and its frequency. This contribution also sheds light on the emergence of embedded language islands in bilingual speech. An embedded language island structured as a prepositional phrase will appear in a mixed sentence if at least one of these factors is present: the noun occurring in the phrase is highly frequent in monolingual usage; it regularly co-occurs with the preposition; and the matrix language preposition equivalent does not appear in the previous discourse.

Acknowledgements

I would like to express my deep gratitude to the research training group GRK DFG 1624/1 "Frequency effects in language" at the University of Freiburg for their support. I am grateful to Peter Auer and Ad Backus for their insightful comments and valuable suggestions, and to Christoph Wolk for advice on statistics. I thank the audiences at the 35th LAUD Symposium and International Symposium on Bilingualism 9 for helpful discussions of earlier versions of this paper.

References

Arnon, Inbal & Neal Snider. 2010. More than words: Frequency effects for multi-word phrases. *Journal of Memory and Language* 62. 67–82.

Auer, Peter. 1999. From codeswitching via language mixing to fused lects: Toward a dynamic typology of bilingual speech. *International Journal of Bilingualism* 3(4). 309–332.

Auer, Peter. 2011. Code-switching/mixing. In *The SAGE Handbook of Sociolinguistics*, 460–478. Thousand Oaks, CA: Sage Publications.

Auer, Peter. 2014. Language mixing and language fusion: When bilingual talk becomes monolingual. In Juliane Besters-Dilger, Cynthia Dermarkar, Stefan Pfänder & Achim Rabus (eds.), *Congruence in contact-induced language change, language families, typological resemblance, and perceived similarity*, 294–334. Berlin; Boston: De Gruyter.

Baayen, R. Harald. 2008. *Analyzing linguistic data: A practical introduction to statistics using R.* Cambridge: University Press.

Backus, Ad. 1996. *Two in one: Bilingual speech of Turkish immigrants in the Netherlands.* Tilburg: University Press.

Backus, Ad. 2003. Units in code switching: Evidence for multimorphemic elements in the lexicon. *Linguistics* 41(1). 83–132.

Backus, Ad. 2013. A usage-based approach to borrowability. In Eline Zenner & Gitte Christiansen (eds.), *New perspectives on lexical borrowing: Onomasiological, methodological and phraseological innovation*, 770–790. Berlin; Boston: De Gruyter.

Barlow, Michael & Suzanne Kemmer. 2000. *Usage-based models of language.* Stanford: CDLI Publications.

Baroni, Marco & Adam Kilgarriff. 2006. Large linguistically-processed web corpora for multiple languages. In *Proceedings of the 11th Conference of the European Chapter of the Association for Computational Linguistics (EACL 2006). Trento, Italy*, 87–90. Morristown, NJ: Association for Computational Linguistics.

Behrens, Heike & Stefan Pfänder (eds.). 2016. *Experience counts: Frequency effects in language.* Berlin; Boston: De Gruyter.

Bentahila, Abdelâli, & Eirlys E. Davies. 1983. The syntax of Arabic-French code-switching. *Lingua* 59(4). 301–330.

Blumenthal-Dramé, Alice. 2012. *Entrenchment in usage-based theories: What corpus data do and do not reveal about the mind.* Berlin; Boston: De Gruyter.

Boumans, Louis. 1998. *The syntax of codeswitching: Analysing Moroccan Arabic/Dutch conversation.* Tilburg: University Press.

Bremer, Bernhard. 2007. Sprechen Sie Qwelja? Formen und Folgen russisch-deutscher Zweis-prachigkeit in Deutschland. In Tanja Anstatt (ed.), *Mehrsprachigkeit bei Kindern und Erwachsenen. Erwerb, Formen, Förderung*, 163–185. Tübingen: Attempto.

Bresnan, Joan, Anna Cueni, Tatiana Nikitina & R. Harald Baayen. 2007. Predicting the dative alternation. In Gerlof Bouma, Irene Krämer & Joost Zwarts (eds.), *Cognitive foundations of interpretation*, 69–94. Amsterdam: Publishing House of the Royal Netherlands Academy of Sciences.

Bybee, Joan. 2002. Sequentiality as the basis of constituent structure. In Talmy Givón & Bertram F. Malle (eds.), *The evolution of language out of pre-language*, 107–132. Amster-dam; Philadelphia: John Benjamins.

Bybee, Joan. 2010. *Language, usage and cognition*. Cambridge, UK: Cambridge University Press.

Bybee, Joan & Paul Hopper. 2001. *Frequency and the emergence of linguistic structure*. Amster-dam; Philadelphia: John Benjamins.

Cleveland, William S. & Susan J. Devlin. 1988. Locally-weighted regression: An approach to regression analysis by local fitting. *Journal of the American Statistical Association* 83(403). 596–610.

Clyne, Michael. 1987. Constraints on code switching: How universal are they? *Linguistics* 25(4). 739–764.

Deuchar, Margaret. 2005. Congruence and Welsh–English code-switching. *Bilingualism: Lan-guage and Cognition* 8(3). 255–269.

Diessel, Holger. 2007. Frequency effects in language acquisition, language use, and diachronic change. *New Ideas in Psychology* 25. 104–123.

Dijkstra, Ton, Walter J.B. & Jonathan Grainger. 1998. Simulating cross-language competition with the bilingual interactive activation model. *Psychologica Belgica* 38. 177–196.

Divjak, Dagmar & Stefan Th. Gries. 2012. *Frequency effects in language representation*. Vol. 2 of *Frequency effects in language*. Berlin; Boston: De Gruyter.

Ellis, Nick C. 2002. Frequency effects in language processing. *Studies in Second Language Acquisition* 24. 143–188.

Fahrmeier, Ludwig, Rita Künstler, Iris Pigeot & Gerhard Trutz. 2007. *Statistik: Der Weg zur Datenanalyse*. 6. Aufl. Berlin; Heidelberg: Springer.

Haust, Delia. 2005. *Codeswitching in Gambia: Eine soziolinguistische Untersuchung von Mandinka, Wolof und Englisch in Kontakt*. Köln: Rüdiger Köppe Verlag.

Hlavac, Jim. 2003. *Second-generation speech: Lexicon, code-switching and morpho-syntax of Croatian-English bilinguals*. Bern; Oxford: Peter Lang.

Gorokhova, Svetlana. 2011. The role of frequency effects in the selection of inflected word forms: A corpus study of Russian speech errors. In Marek Konopka, Jacqueline Kubczak, Christian Mair, František Štícha & Ulrich H. Waßner (eds.), *Grammar and corpora 2009*, 267–286. Tübingen: Narr.

Gries, Stefan Th. 2009. *Statistics for linguistics with R: A practical introduction*. Berlin: De Gruyter Mouton.

Gries, Stefan Th. & Dagmar Divjak. 2012. *Frequency effects in language processing*. Vol. 1 of *Frequency effects in language*. Berlin; Boston: De Gruyter.

Hakimov, Nikolay. 2015. Explaining Russian-German code-mixing: A usage-based approach. Unpublished PhD dissertation. University of Freiburg.

Janssen, Niels & Horacio A. Barber. 2012. Phrase frequency effects in language production. *PloS ONE*, 7(3). e33202.

Jeschiniak, Jörg & Willem J. M. Levelt. 1994. Word frequency effects in speech production: Retrieval of syntactic information and of phonological form. *Journal of Experimental Psychology: Learning, Memory, and Cognition* 20. 824–843.

Jurafsky, Daniel, Alan Bell, Michelle Gregory & William D. Raymond. 2001. Probabilistic relations between words: Evidence from reduction in lexical production. In Joan Bybee & Paul Hopper (eds.), *Frequency and the emergence of linguistic structure*, 229–254. Amsterdam; Philadelphia: John Benjamins.

Kapatsinski, Vsevolod. 2010. Frequency of use leads to automaticity of production: Evidence from repair in conversation. *Language and Speech* 53(1). 71–105.

Koostra, Gerrit Jan, Janet G. Van Hell & Ton Dijkstra. 2010. Syntactic alignment and shared word order in code-switched sentence production: Evidence from bilingual monologue and dialogue. *Journal of Memory and Language* 63(2). 210–231.

Koostra, Gerrit Jan, Janet G. Van Hell & Ton Dijkstra. 2012. Priming of code-switches in sentences: The role of lexical repetition, cognates and language proficiency. *Bilingualism: Language and Cognition* 15(4). 797–819.

Kroll, Judith F. & Erika Stewart. 1994. Category interference in translation and picture naming: Evidence for asymmetric connections between bilingual memory representations. *Journal of Memory and Language* 33. 149–174.

Larson, Richard K. 1985. Bare-NP adverbs. *Linguistic Inquiry* 16(4). 595–621.

Ledoux, Kerry, C. Christine Camblin, Tamara Y. Swaab & Peter C. Gordon. 2006. Reading words in discourse: The modulation of lexical priming effects by message-level context. *Behavioral and Cognitive Neuroscience Reviews* 5(3). 107–127.

Lehtinen, Meri Kaisu Tuulikki. 1966. *An analysis of a Finnish-English bilingual corpus.* Indiana University dissertation.

Loebell, Helga & Kathryn Bock. 2003. Structural priming across languages. *Linguistics* 41(5). 791–824.

MacWhinney, Brian. 1997. Second language acquisition and the Competition Model. In Judith F. Kroll & Annette M.B. De Groot (eds.), *Tutorials in Bilingualism*, 113–142. Mahwah, NJ: Lawrence Erlbaum.

Meng, Katharina. 2001. *Russlanddeutsche Sprachbiografien: Untersuchungen zur sprachlichen Integration von Aussiedlerfamilien.* Tübingen: Narr.

Meyer, Roland. 2011. *ReBiSlav: Das Regensburger Korpus slavisch-deutscher Bilingualer.* http://www.uni-regensburg.de/sprache-literatur-kultur/slavistik/rund-ums-institut/korpora/rebislav/index.html (last accessed on April 15, 2015)

Muysken, Pieter. 1997. Code-switching processes: Alternation, insertion, congruent lexicalization. In Martin Pütz (ed.), *Language choices: Conditions, constraints, and consequences*, 361–380. Amsterdam; Philadelphia: John Benjamins.

Muysken, Pieter. 2000. *Bilingual speech: A typology of code-mixing.* Cambridge, UK: Cambridge University Press.

Myers-Scotton, Carol. 1993. *Duelling languages: Grammatical structure in code-switching.* Oxford: Clarendon.

Myers-Scotton, Carol. 2002. *Contact linguistics: Bilingual encounters and grammatical outcomes.* Oxford: Oxford University Press.

Myers-Scotton, Carol & Janice L. Jake. 1995. Matching lemmas in a bilingual language competence and production model: Evidence from intrasentential code-switching. *Linguistics* 33. 981–1024.

Oldfield, Richard Ch. & Arthur Wingfield. 1965. Response latencies in naming objects. *Quarterly Journal of Experimental Psychology* 17(4). 273–281.

Pfaff, Carol. 1979. Constraints on language mixing: Intrasentential code-mixing and borrowing in Spanish/English. *Language* 55. 291–318.

Pickering, Martin J. & Victor S. Ferreira. 2008. Structural priming: A critical review. *Psychological Bulletin* 134(3). 427–459.

Poplack, Shana. 1980. Sometimes I'll start a sentence in Spanish *y termino en español*: Toward a typology of code-switching. *Linguistics* 18(7/8). 581–618.

Poplack, Shana & Nathalie Dion. 2012. Myths and facts about loanword development. *Language Variation and Change* 24(3). 279–315.

Poplack, Shana, David Sankoff & Christopher Miller. 1988. The social correlates and linguistic processes of lexical borrowing and assimilation. *Linguistics* 26. 47–104.

Schneider, Ulrike. 2016. Hesitation placement as evidence for chunking: A corpus-based study of spoken English. In Heike Behrens & Stefan Pfänder (eds.), *Experience counts: Frequency effects in language*. Berlin; Boston: De Gruyter.

Schoonbaert, Sofie, Robert J. Hartsuiker & Martin J. Pickering. 2007. The representation of lexical and syntactic information in bilinguals: Evidence from syntactic priming. *Journal of Memory and Language* 56. 153–171.

Salamoura, Angeliki & John M. Williams. 2006. Lexical activation of cross-lexical syntactic priming. *Bilingualism: Language and Cognition* 9(3). 299–307.

Stenson, Nancy. 1990. Phrase structure congruence, government, and Irish-English code-switching. In Randall Hendrick (ed.), *The syntax of the modern Celtic languages*, 167–197. San Diego: Academic Press.

Szabó, Csilla Anna. 2010. *Language shift und code-mixing: Deutsch-ungarisch-rumänischer Sprachkontakt in einer dörflichen Gemeinde in Nordwestrumänien*. Frankfurt/Main; Berlin; Bern; Bruxelles; NY; Oxford; Wien: Lang.

Szmrecsanyi, Benedikt. 2006. *Morphosyntactic persistence in spoken English: A corpus study at the intersection of variationist Sociolinguistics, Psycholinguistics, and Discourse Analysis*. Berlin: Mouton de Gruyter.

Szmrecsanyi, Benedikt. 2013. The great regression: genitive variability in Late Modern English news texts. In Kersti Börjars, David Denison & Alan Scott (eds.), *Morphosyntactic categories and the expression of possession*, 59–88. Amsterdam: John Benjamins.

Tagliamonte, Sali A. & R. Harald Baayen. 2012. Models, forests and trees of York English: *Was/were* variation as a case study for statistical practice. *Language Variation and Change* 24(2). 135–178.

Tajsner, Przemysław. 1997. Licensing of bare NP adjuncts. In Raymond Hickey & Stanisław Puppel (eds.), *Language history and linguistic modelling: A Festschrift for Jacek Fisiak on his 60th Birthday*, Vol. 2. *Language modelling*, 1231–1244. Berlin; New York: Mouton de Gruyter.

Tily, Harry, Susanne Gahl, Inbal Arnon, Anubha Kothari, Neal Snider & Joan Bresnan. 2009. Syntactic probabilities affect pronunciation variation in spontaneous speech. *Language and Cognition* 1(2). 147–165.

Timberlake, Alan. 2004. *A reference grammar of Russian*. Cambridge, UK: University Press.

Torres Cacoullos, Rena & Catherine E. Travis. 2015. Two languages, one effect: Structural priming in spontaneous code-switching. *Bilingualism: Language and Cognition*. DOI: http://dx.doi.org/10.1017/S1366728914000406 (published online: 30 April 2015)

Treffers-Daller, Jeanine. 1994. *Mixing two languages: French-Dutch contact in a comparative perspective*. Berlin; New York: Mouton de Gruyter.

Van Hell, Janet G. & Annette M.B. De Groot. 1998. Disentangling context availability and concreteness in lexical decision and word translation. *The Quarterly Journal of Experimental Psychology* 51A. 41–63.

Antje Endesfelder Quick, Elena Lieven, and Michael Tomasello

Mixed NPs in German-English and German-Russian bilingual children

Abstract: Both cross-linguistic priming methodologies and research on code-mixed utterances have been concerned with the nature of the underlying syntactic representations of bilinguals. The present paper investigated code-mixing at the morphosyntactic level (NP) by comparing German-English (G-E) and German-Russian (G-R) bilingual children between the ages of 3;6 and 5;6. Using a language priming paradigm and a monolingual interlocutor in each language, we attempted to elicit mixed NPs from these children. Results showed that G-E bilingual children produced mixed NPs significantly more often than G-R bilinguals, providing support for the importance of structural similarity in this type of mixing. A second finding was that children who were reported as code-mixing at home were significantly more likely to provide answers while children who did not code-mix remained silent. Explanations in terms of individual differences and/or balanced competence are discussed.

Keywords: code-mixing, mixed NPs, child bilingualism, cross-linguistic priming, structural similarities

1 Introduction[*]

Cross-linguistic transfer and the nature of syntactic representations in bilingual children are of great interest to theories of language representation and processing (e.g. Genesee 1989; Volterra and Taeschner 1978). Even though it is agreed that children differentiate their two languages from early on (Lanza 1992; Paradis and Genesee 1996; Paradis and Genesee 1997), many young bilinguals are reported to code-mix both within and across utterances. Research on language transfer and code-mixing within utterances has shown that the two systems interact with each other and are not completely independent (Döpke 1998, 2000; Müller 1998; Müller and Hulk 2001; Yip and Matthews 2000). Code-mixing has often been discussed in terms of grammatical principles that might underlie

* We would like to thank the families and children who participated in this study. We also wish to thank the experimenters and coders Tatjana Welikanowa, Christine Green and Amrisha Vaish.

it and many syntactic and structural constraints have been proposed (e.g. Di Sciullo, Muysken and Singh 1986; Lindholm and Padilla 1978; Meisel 1994; Paradis, Nicoladis and Genesee 2000; Poplack 1980).

There have been two methods used to explore the question of the underlying representations of bilinguals. One is the use of cross-linguistic syntactic priming based on the idea that structures in one language might be able to prime structures in the other. The second is the syntactic analysis of intra-sentential code-mixing in naturalistic speech corpora to attempt to establish the ways in which the syntactic representations in the two languages interact.

1.1 Cross-linguistic syntactic priming

The question to which degree syntactic structures are integrated across languages has been investigated using cross-linguistic syntactic priming paradigms (Bernolet, Hartsuiker and Pickering 2007; Hartsuiker, Pickering and Veltkamp 2004; Schoonbaert, Hartsuiker and Pickering 2007). Syntactic priming describes the finding that speakers tend to reuse previously encountered syntactic structures (Bock 1986). Bock showed that people are more likely to use a passive in describing a picture if they heard a passive before. Priming has also been found in a number of studies with young children (Bencini and Valian 2008; Huttenlocher, Vasilyeva and Shimpi 2004; Savage, Lieven, Theakston and Tomasello 2003). However, using cross-linguistic syntactic priming to investigate syntactic representations in bilinguals has mostly been done with adults. For example, Loebell and Bock (2003) found cross-linguistic priming between German and English. Comparing datives and transitives (active and passive), they found that English datives were primed by German datives and vice versa. However, no priming was observed between passives. The absence of priming for passives was explained by the different word orders in the two languages. Hartsuiker et al. (2004) observed cross-linguistic priming of passives in Spanish/English bilingual adults. After hearing a picture description in Spanish, participants had to describe another picture in English. Hartsuiker et al. (2004) found priming from Spanish to English and argued for an integrated syntactic representation between the languages if the constructions are similar. Bernolet et al. (2007) also used a priming paradigm to investigate whether bilinguals store constructions that are similar in both languages as an integrated representation. If so, they should show cross-linguistic priming effects similar to those Hartsuiker et al. (2004) observed. Bernolet et al. (2007) investigated priming between Dutch, English and German relative clauses and found priming from Dutch to German, which both have verb-final relative clauses. Bernolet concluded that

"[...] because Dutch and German relative clauses have the same word order, they do share a syntactic representation" (Bernolet et al. 2007: 945). However, the authors did not find priming between Dutch and English, which differ in their relative-clause word order, and concluded that each construction is stored separately in the two languages. So the question is whether children show the same cross-linguistic priming effect.

As far as we know there is only one study that addresses this question using a priming paradigm (Vasilyeva, Waterfall, Gámez, Gómez, Bowers and Shimpi 2010). Vasilyeva et al. (2010) tested Spanish-English bilingual children aged 5;2 to 6;5, investigating the use of passive voice. The authors found priming of passive voice from Spanish to English, which parallels the results of Hartsuiker et al. (2004). However, interestingly, they did not find the reverse effect, i.e. priming of the passive from English to Spanish. They explained this by arguing that the Spanish construction, though similar in structure to the English passive, is a rather rarely used alternative to the normal method of passivizing in Spanish. The suggestion was that comprehension in Spanish could drive the priming of the same structure in English but its production in Spanish was inhibited by the low frequency of the construction. Although these results suggest that, even in young bilingual language learners, similar representations in both languages are integrated across languages, they also point to the fact that frequency will be a complicating factor in any experimental paradigm.

1.2 Bilingual code-mixing in children as evidence for interacting systems?

Interaction between the two languages of bilinguals can also be evidenced in intra-sentential code-mixing. Code-mixing is well attested in adult and child bilinguals, although not all children seem to pass through a stage in which they produce code-mixed utterances. There is considerable evidence that children who do produce code-mixed utterances pass through a stage in which they mix more function than content words, as compared to adults who are reported to mix more content words (Deuchar 1999; Deuchar and Vihman 2005; Köppe and Meisel 1995; Liceras, Spradlin and Fernández Fuertes 2005; Liceras, Fernández Fuertes, Perales, Pérez-Tattam and Spradlin 2008; Vihman 1985). A special case of mixing is called *functional-lexical* code-mixing, in which functional and lexical elements within a constituent are from different languages, e.g. mixed NPs such as German – English: *der dog* 'the dog'.

Code-mixed utterances in adults and children have mainly been analyzed in terms of the grammatical principles that might underlie them (e.g. Bernardini and Schlyter 2004; Di Sciullo et al. 1986; Köppe and Meisel 1995; Meisel 1994; Paradis et al. 2000; Poplack 1980). An example is the matrix language approach (Jake, Myers-Scotton and Gross 2002), a theory of production which argues that each sentence or constituent is formulated using the syntax of the 'matrix' language, i.e. that there should be no functional mixing within the constituent. Thus, the underlying syntactic structure of the utterance or of its constituents (the "syntactic glue"; Jake et al. 2002: 79) must come from just one or the other language. A corollary by a number of researchers is that this is the more dominant language (Bernardini and Schlyter 2004; Petersen 1988). A major difficulty with this latter approach is that of establishing dominance (Grosjean 1982; Schlyter 1994). Clearly some children are stronger in one of their languages than in the other, but it is also the case that dominance can change with development, varies as a function of the measure being employed, of whether comprehension or production is being tested and, crucially, of the interactional environment in which the data is collected (Bernardini and Schlyter 2004; Grosjean 1982; Jisa 2000; Lanza 1992, 1997; Petersen 1988; Schlyter 1994).

A special case of functional-lexical mixing is that of mixed NPs. These have been attested both in adults and children and for many different language pairs. They have been mainly studied using recorded spoken language corpora of bilingual children, e.g. Liceras (2005, 2008), Spanish-English, Cantone and Müller (2008), Italian-German, Radford (2007), English-Italian and French-German, and Jorschick, Quick, Gläßer, Lieven and Tomasello (2011), German-English. These NPs are of special interest if one or both of the languages carries grammatical gender, e.g. German-English mixed NPs where the determiner comes from German and carries gender as in the above mentioned example (Cantone and Müller 2008; Jake et al. 2002; Jorschick et al. 2011; Liceras et al. 2005; Liceras et al. 2008; Radford, Kupisch, Köppe and Azzaro 2007). From the perspective of theoretical positions informed by minimalist UG, the issue is how features such as gender can be checked in the 'spell-out' if the settings of these features differ between the two languages. There are various proposed solutions to this problem. The *Accomodation Hypothesis* (Radford et al. 2007) suggests that gender concord with the determiner is achieved either by 'stripping' the imported word of its gender or by according it 'honorary gender' as it is temporarily entered into the syntax of the other language. The *Grammatical feature spell-out hypothesis* (Liceras et al. 2005) is that the language with the most features to be checked will determine the head since this prevents the spell-out from 'crashing'. In the case of a mixed German-English NP, this means that the determiner will be in German, since nouns carry gender in German and not in English. However, Cantone and Müller (2008) in a study of German-Italian mixing report cases where an Italian determiner is used despite the fact that Italian only has two genders while German has three. What is not clear from the research that has been undertaken so far is how these accounts would deal with the situation in which, although one or both languages mark gender, the structure of the NP in the two differs, e.g. one language has a determiner and the other does not. This is the focus of our investigation; we investigate whether the concept of shared representations as proposed from cross-linguistic priming studies can also be extended to bilingual code-mixing.

There are differing positions on the underlying mental representations of the two languages in bilinguals, especially growing bilingual children. The picture remains mixed. According to theories of lexical access, following the language-selective view both languages are accessed and processed independently of each other. However, following the non-selective-language view, lexical representations of both languages are seen as strongly interacting with each other (e.g. Kroll and Stewart 1994; Van Heuven, Dijkstra and Grainger 1998). In discussing syntactic processing we are basically confronted with two opposing views. On the one hand, the separate syntax account, which claims that all constructions are represented separately for each language, also including constructions which are similar across both languages. On the other hand, the shared syntax account, which suggests that rules and constructions that are the same in both languages are represented only once (Hartsuiker et al. 2004; Bernolet et al. 2007). Code-mixing represents probably the most obvious interaction between the languages.

Taking these factors into account the question of total autonomy, shared-ness and integration of the languages remains open. Whereas research on code-mixing and transfer has mainly been concerned with possible points of interaction and underlying rules that guide the phenomenon (e.g. Bernardini and Schlyter 2004; Köppe and Meisel 1995; Meisel 1994; Müller 1998; Paradis et al. 2000), research on cross-linguistic priming has tried to answer the question of whether bilinguals use the same representations and mechanisms to process their different languages or if each of their languages has separate representations and consequently uses separate mechanisms (e.g. Bernolet et al. 2007; Desmet and Declerq 2006; Hartsuiker et al. 2004).

2 NP structure and gender systems in German, English, and Russian

German, English, and Russian noun phrases make an interesting contrast in terms of their overlapping and differing structures. German and English noun phrases are structurally and functionally very similar; they both consist of a determiner which precedes the noun. German determiners are embedded in a three gender paradigm; feminine, masculine and neuter, which is pervasive. English, on the other hand, has no grammatical gender marking on the determiner. Both languages have definite and indefinite determiners. In this respect Russian is different, though, since it has no determiners. However, comparable to German, Russian has a three gender paradigm which is marked on the noun. Thus, taking the two language combinations into account, German and English NPs overlap in form and function, although English marks no gender on the noun. German and Russian NPs differ in their overall form: German NPs consist of determiners and nouns, while Russian NPs consist only of nouns. Both languages mark gender (Table 1).

Table 1: Structure of NP in German, English, and Russian

	German	English	Russian
form	determiner + noun	determiner + noun	noun
grammatical gender	masculine, feminine, neuter marked on the determiner	no	masculine, feminine, neuter marked on the noun
function	referential	referential	referential

First, comparing the overlapping and differing NP structures, we wanted to investigate whether similar syntactic structures might trigger code-mixing. Since German and English NPs overlap in form and function the question arises as to how these constructions are stored in the bilingual mind, i.e. one construction for each language or an integrated construction for both languages.

Second, if language pairs have no overlap in form, does this inhibit mixing? As has been shown in the cross-linguistic priming literature, if there was no overlap in word order, priming did not occur. Although Russian has gender coded on the noun, it does not have determiners. If a child is growing up as a German-Russian bilingual, does this child also produce mixed NPs with a German determiner and a Russian noun?

Thus, our study addresses the following questions: (i) Is it possible to experimentally elicit mixed NPs from bilingual children, using a language priming paradigm? (ii) Does priming the child in one language and thus creating a language imbalance have an influence on children's language choice and mixing? (iii) Are there differences in the production of mixed NPs as a function of the differing NP structures between language pairs? (iv) If children produce mixed NPs with a German determiner, is there correct gender agreement with the translational equivalent?

3 Method

Participants

48 bilingual children (26 boys and 22 girls) who ranged in age from 3;6 to 5;6 years (mean age: 4 years and 5 months) participated in this study. 16 of the bilingual children were growing up with German and English (G-E) (13 in a bilingual household and 3 in an English monolingual household) and 32 bilingual children were growing up with German and Russian (G-R) (13 in a bilingual household and 15 in a Russian monolingual household)[1]. The English bilingual children started attending German kindergarten at a mean age of 1 year and 6 months and the Russian bilingual children at a mean age of 2 years and 5 months. Appendix A gives detailed information about the age and language situation for each priming group. All children lived with their parents in a mid-sized German city, attended German-speaking kindergarten and had at least one parent who spoke either English or Russian from birth. Additionally, 4 children took part in the study but were excluded for the following reasons: 3 were uncooperative, and 1 had a trilingual background. We are aware that our sample combines simultaneous and successive bilinguals; however, due to difficulties in finding enough children, we tested children from both groups and included these different factors in our statistical analysis.

Materials

The experiment included 4 novel objects that were labeled with novel names in each language. All novel nouns were bisyllabic words and were in accordance with their language-specific phonotactics. Since German and Russian encode grammatical gender, two of the nouns were of masculine and two of the nouns were of feminine gender. The gender marking of all novels adhered to the language respective rules. In Russian there exists a strong correspondance between ending and gender of the noun, e.g. Russian feminine nouns end in nominative case with an −a, which is not absolute, e.g. kinship terms ending in −a can also denote a masculine person. However, since our objects were inanimate we adhered to the general rules. Appendix B presents a complete list of the novel nouns and descriptions of the 4 objects. We did not include neuter novels since in German neuter cannot be distinguished from masculine in the accusative case.

---

1 4 G-R families did not fill out the questionnaire concerning language background.

To obtain detailed information about the language background of the families the parents were asked to fill out a questionnaire on the child's language environments. Answers to the questionnaire allowed us to establish the following categories:

1. Whether the household is bilingual or monolingual (i.e. whether it is a 'one parent, one language' household or not)
2. Whether the parents code-mix at home or not
3. Whether the child code-mixes at home or not.

Procedure

Table 2 gives an overview of the outline of each trial. Children received four trials, with each trial a different novel object. In each trial two different games were used. Game 1 was a box with two tubes where the children could make the novel objects slide through. Game 2 was a catapult with which children could make the object fly around. Novel objects were presented in the same order. However, novel names were counterbalanced across trials.

Table 2: Procedure for each trial

Phase/Experimenter	Trial 1 novel object 1
Phase 1 E1	Game 1 L1 10 times named Child 2 times named
Phase 2 E2	Game 1 L2 13 times labeled Child 2 times labeled
	Game 2 L2 12 times labeled Child 2 times labeled
Phase 3	Game 2 E1 asks for object in L1 Child answers

Each trial consisted of three different phases that differed depending on the language used in each phase. Two experimenters took part, one for each of the two languages (E1 for language 1 and E2 for language 2). In phase 1, children first heard the novel object introduced ten times by E1, German always as a full NP with definite determiner and in Russian in the nominative case. They played Game 1 together and the experimenter asked the child twice whether she could repeat the novel name. After E1 had said the novel name ten times she left the novel object and Game 1 on the floor and left the room. Instantly experimenter E2 entered the room, which marks the beginning of phase 2. E2 discovered the novel object on the floor and labeled it in language 2, in the case of German and English always with a full NP and definite determiner, in the case of Russian in the nominative case. They continued playing game 1. E2 labeled the novel object 13 times, also asking the child twice to repeat it in language 2. After that, E2 put game 1 away and took out game 2, the catapult game. She further labeled the novel 12 times and asked the child twice to repeat the name.

Together they played game 2. All in all, children heard the novel noun 25 times in the second phase. After that, E2 silently hid the novel object and E1 came back into the room. In phase 3, E1 discovered the unknown game 2 and asked the child which object was needed in order to play that game. If the child did not answer, E1 asked twice more for the object before continuing with the next trial.

Our aim was to promote the production of mixed NPs by priming language 2 with E2 in phase 2 but then, in phase 3, having E1 ask for which object was needed in language 1.

16 G-R bilingual children were primed in phase 1 in German and in phase 2 in Russian and 16 G-R bilinguals the other way around. 16 G-E bilingual children were primed in phase 1 in German and in phase 2 in English. Unfortunately, due to a shortage of G-E bilingual children, we were not able to test a second group of G-E bilinguals primed in phase 2 on German (see Table 3). All bilingual children were either tested in our child lab or in a separate room in their kindergartens.

Table 3: Participants and experimental phases

Children	Language E1, interlocutor	Language E2 priming	Test situation language E1, E2 silently present
16 G-E bilinguals	German	English	German
16 G-R bilinguals	German	Russian	German
16 G-R bilinguals	Russian	German	Russian

Coding and reliability

The answers children gave were coded into four different categories:
1. No answer
2. Answer in the interlocutor's language (E1)
3. Answer in the language primed in phase 2 by E2
4. Answer with a code-mixed NP, i.e. determiner in one language, noun in the other language.

If children did not remember the label no matter which language, but produced some description in the form of an NP, e.g. *the round thing*, we coded this into the relevant category (2, 3 or 4 above)[2]. However, if children produced a verbal answer, they usually answered with a full NP or just with a noun.

---

2 Only three answers of this kind occured. All were German monolingual, one answer of a G-E bilingual and two answers of G-R bilinguals primed on Russian.

The first coder of the G-E bilingual data was a German monolingual with fluent proficiency in English. 25% of the G-E bilingual children were coded by a second person who was also fluent in English. Coding the data was very straightforward and reliability was high (Kappa 0.91). The few disagreements were resolved easily between the first and the second coder. The G-R data was fully coded twice, once by a German coder with very little knowledge of Russian and a second time by a Russian-German simultaneous bilingual. Again, reliabilities were very good (Kappa 0.98).

3.1 Results

Children's responses were categorized according to the above-mentioned four possible types of answers (see Figure 1). As can be seen from Figure 1, children frequently failed to give an answer but when they did, they most frequently gave a monolingual answer in the language in which they had been primed in phase 2 by E2. Monolingual answers in the language of the interlocutor were relatively infrequent and only the G-E bilinguals primed in phase 2 by E2 with English gave answers with mixed NPs (the 2% of mixed utterances we find in the G-R bilinguals primed on Russian came from one single child who was clearly German dominant). For analyzing the data we used a binary logistic regression.

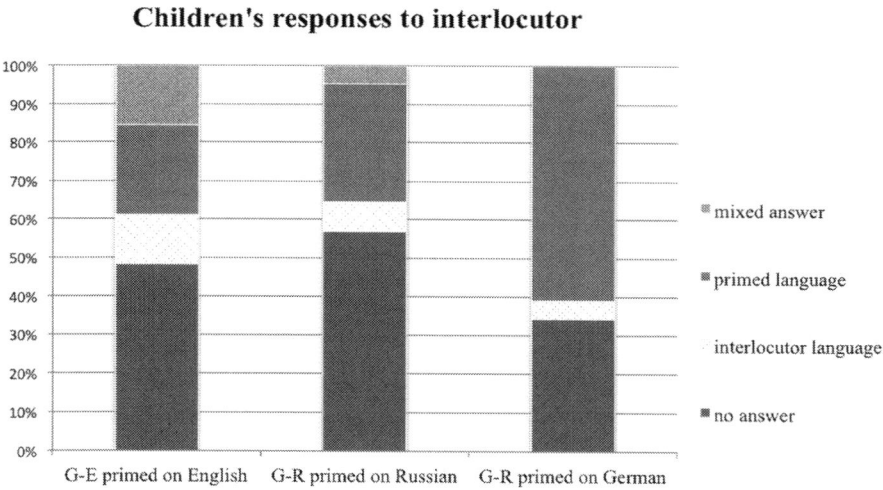

Figure 1: Children's responses to interlocutor

Overall we found that G-E bilingual children primed on English mix significantly more often than G-R bilingual children primed on German (Wald (1) = 7.32, p < .007). If we include only verbal answers into our calculation and leave out the 'no answers' we find that G-E bilingual children mixed significantly more often than both G-R bilingual groups (Wald (1) = 5.20, p < .02). These mixed answers consisted of a German determiner and an English noun even though the children never heard any mixed utterances during the study. They never produced a mixed NP of the reverse kind. In 60% of the mixed utterances the gender of the German determiner correctly matched the gender of the corresponding German novel of the English noun. Although the mixing rate does not seem to be very high, compared to naturalistic corpus data our mixing rate is in a similar range (compare Cantone 2007, and Liceras et al. 2008 concerning general low mixing rates in bilingual children).

Further we found that the G-R bilinguals primed on German answered significantly more often in the primed language, i.e. gave the German label to the Russian interlocutor than the G-R bilinguals primed on Russian and the G-E bilinguals primed on English (Wald (1) = 12.23, p < .001). Interestingly, 82% of the German monolingual answers of the G-R primed on German consisted only of the German novel noun without the German determiner. The remaining 18% included the German determiner followed by the German noun. Gender agreement in these answers was always correct.

3.1.1 Comparing children's answers with parental questionnaire

Using the categories derived from answers to the parental questionnaire, we found that the language constellation of the household (bilingual or monolingual) and code-mixing of the parents revealed only a few significant effects, which however did not hold for all language groups. The language constellation of the household was only significant for G-R bilinguals primed on German in that children coming from a monolingual Russian home answered significantly more often in the primed language (i.e. not in the interlocutor's language) than children coming from a bilingual household (Wald (1) = 10.39, p < .001). We further found a correlation of parent's mixing and children's answer type for G-R children primed on Russian. Children with mixing parents answered significantly more often in the primed language, Russian, than children of non-mixing parents (Wald (1) = 6.39, p < .01), who in turn remained significantly more often silent than children with mixing parents (Wald (1) = 9.02, p < .003). We also found that G-E bilingual children who were classified as children using mixing at home also answered significantly more often with a mixed NP than G-E bilingual children who did not use mixing at home (Wald (1) = 9.13, p < .003). Figure 2 shows the answer categories for the two types of bilinguals comparing children who are code-mixers at home and children who do not code-mix at home.

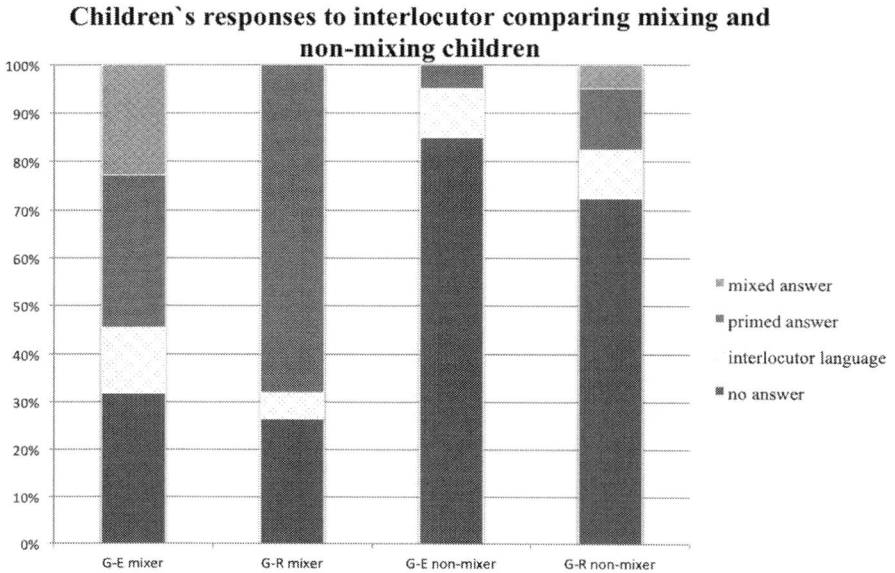

Figure 2: Children's responses to interlocutor comparing mixing and non-mixing children

We found that children who did not code-mix at home remained significantly more often silent (i.e. gave no answer) than children who were mixers (Wald (1) = 29.44, p < .001). Further, children who code-mixed at home answered significantly more often in the primed language, e.g. English answer to the German interlocutor, than children who did not code-mix (Wald (1) = 21.23, p < .001). Finally, we found that G-R children who mixed at home answered significantly more often in the primed language than G-E bilingual children who mixed at home (Wald (1) = 11.80, p < .001). To summarize, children who code-mix at home are more likely to give an answer and more likely to use the primed language than children who do not mix at home, but only the G-E bilinguals who mixed at home produced mixed NPs in the experiment.

3.1.2 Developmental differences

Due to recruiting difficulties we had to choose a very wide age range of two years. So we further divided the children into two different age groups. The younger children, age group 1 (n = 24), ranged from 3;6–4;5, and the older children were categorized as age group 2 (n = 24), ranging from 4;6–5;6. First we compared for age group differences within each language group.

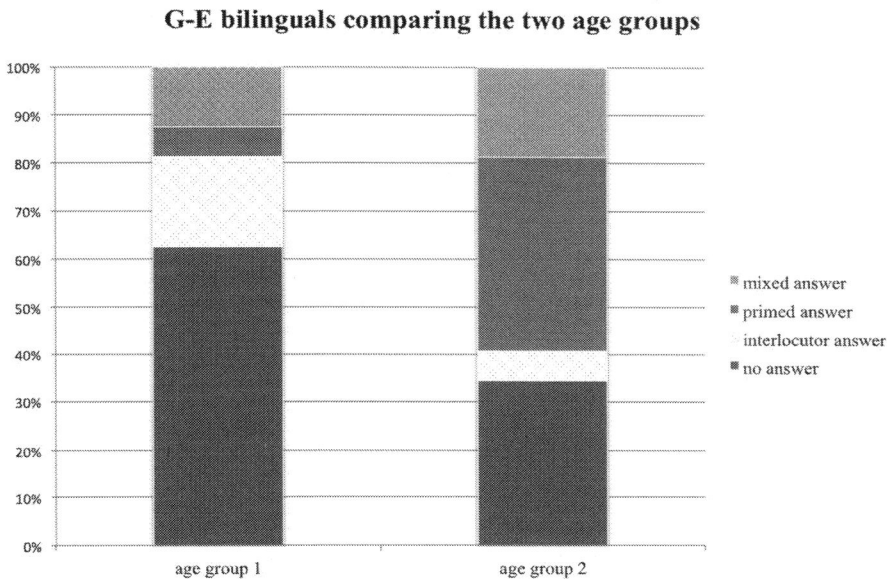

Figure 3: G-E bilinguals comparing the two age groups

Figure 3 shows the differences between the two age groups in the G-E bilingual children. Young G-E bilinguals remained significantly more often silent than older G-E bilingual children (Wald (1) = 5.80, p < .01). They also answered significantly more often in the interlocutor language than the older G-E bilinguals (Wald (1) = 3.98, p < .04). However, older G-E bilingual children answered significantly more often in the primed language than younger G-E bilinguals (Wald (1) = 12.27, p < .001).

We also found an interesting developmental effect of age and code-mixing behavior in the G-E bilingual children. If children did not use code-mixing as a language strategy at home they remained equally silent in both age groups compared to children who use code-mixing. However, children who were classified as mixers did show a difference across both age groups. Young G-E mixers remained significantly more often silent than older G-E mixers (Wald (1) = 7.93, p < .005), and older G-E mixers answered significantly more often in the primed language than younger G-E mixers (Wald (1) = 11.89, p < .001). There were no significant age-related results for the G-R bilinguals.

4 Discussion

Previous studies on cross-linguistic priming have suggested that structures which are similar across the languages may be stored as a single integrated representation. In this study we wanted to investigate whether similar representations might also be a point for code-mixing to occur, especially functional-lexical code-mixing between a determiner and a noun. To investigate this, we tested German-English and German-Russian bilingual children, using a priming paradigm. Results showed that German-English bilingual children produced mixed NPs significantly more often than German-Russian bilingual children. We also found that German-Russian bilingual children primed on German answered significantly more often in the primed language, i.e. German to a Russian interlocutor, than German-Russian bilinguals primed on Russian and German-English bilinguals primed on English. We further found that children who use code-mixing as a language strategy at home showed a different behavior than children who do not mix. The latter remained significantly more often silent in both language groups than children who mix at home. In turn, children who also use mixing at home answered significantly more often in the primed language, i.e. English to a German interlocutor.

Additionally, we also found developmental differences. Young G-E bilingual children remained significantly more often silent than older G-E bilinguals, independent of whether they were classified as mixers or non-mixers. Older G-E bilingual children were more likely to answer in the primed language. Children who were classified as mixers showed the same developmental effect, whereas non-mixers remained silent across both age groups. Finally, we found that children in all conditions were significantly more likely to answer with monolingual utterances in the primed language than in the language of the current interlocutor.

4.1 The representation of mixed NPs

Although there has been considerable research on children's naturalistic production of mixed NPs, this is the first study aimed directly at experimentally eliciting them, allowing greater control over the conditions under which they are produced. Since mixed NPs were produced by the G-E but not the G-R children, this suggests that similarity in the structure of the NP is an important factor in their production. As outlined in the introduction, cross-linguistic priming studies also suggest that similarity in structure is an important factor in whether sentences in one language can prime production of targets in the other language (Bernolet et al. 2007; Hartsuiker et al. 2004, for adults; Vasilyeva et al. 2010, for 5-6-year-olds). These authors suggest that constituents with the same structure have an integrated (shared) representation across languages. Our results could certainly be interpreted in this way. If a single representation indeed triggers code-mixing, we should see less, or no, code-mixing when representations differ across languages. And this is what we found: G-E children produced mixed NPs, G-R children did not produce mixed NPs.

Russian does not have determiners and thus there is no overlap in form between German and Russian NPs. If, as a result, German and Russian NPs are stored separately for each language, there is no stage in production for mixing to occur. However, whether one needs to posit one shared representation or just interaction between the two languages in production depends on the particular model of language production that is proposed and our results cannot address this. There is plenty of evidence for the separate representation of the two languages of bilinguals, but results from priming and code-mixing also provide converging evidence that the systems interact and are not completely autonomous. This interaction can also be seen in the G-R bilingual children primed on German who answered overwhelmingly in German to the Russian interlocutor leaving out the German determiner, which could also be analysed as a language internal mix. But of course it also shows that cultural dominance is a further important factor which could potentially influence results (see Grosjean 2001 on language modes).

Functional-lexical code-mixing within constituents is of special interest because it raises the issue of their grammatical integration. Explanations of this type of code-mixing, which seems to characterize the speech of young bilinguals, vary. One suggestion is that the function words come from the dominant language, another that they reflect the language of the interlocutor, a third that they reflect the language with most features to be checked. We have no information about the dominance of the children but it is certainly the case that the mixed utterances with German function words were produced in answer to a German interlocutor. Note that this goes against our other result that, if children answered at all, they were more likely to do so in the primed language i.e. not that of the interlocutor. Unfortunately, we do not have an English-German condition with which we could check whether children would produce NPs with English determiners and German nouns. However, other evidence suggests that while G-E bilingual children do occasionally do this, they are much more likely to produce NPs in which the determiner is German and the noun English independently either of dominance or the language of the interlocutor (Jorschick et al. 2011). This finding of asymmetry between the language of the function word and that of the content word, especially in code-mixed NPs, has been found in a number of naturalistic studies. The most prevalent type of explanation is in terms of the function word coming from the language which is more 'marked' i.e. has more features to be checked (Liceras et al. 2005, 2008). However, there is considerable dispute in the Generative literature about the implications of functional code-mixing for the grammatical representation of the two languages (i.e. is there a universal grammar for each language or just one through which both languages are produced). Our data cannot speak to this issue, but since German nouns have more features to be checked (gender), this would explain the prevalence of German determiners in the mixed NPs. Syntactic integration of the NP is also supported by the fact that, in the present study, 60% of the children's determiners in mixed NPs agreed with the gender of the corresponding German novel. Jorschick et al. (2011) showed that this was significantly above the level of chance in their study of naturalistically produced mixed NPs.

4.2 Mixing as a communicative strategy

Children who were classified as 'home-mixers' on the parental questionnaire showed a different behavior than children who were classified as non-mixers at home. Figure 2 shows that home-mixers were very much more likely to give an answer, whether mixed or not, and whether in the primed or interlocutor language, than were the 'non home-mixers'. This might suggest that not all bilingual children go through a stage in which they mix, but that children who do use mixing employ it as an additional communicative strategy. It is not likely that this is just a gap-filling strategy because the children who mixed used an English noun (primed in phase 2) with a German determiner in answer to the German interlocutor. Other evidence also suggests that children often have the equivalent word in their other language (Pearson, Fernández and Oller 1995; Quay 1995). It is more likely to result from individual differences in overall 'talkativeness' or from a more balanced competence in the two languages, which allows the children to process both the primed and the interlocutor languages more rapidly and with more confidence than the 'non-mixers'. We cannot really disentangle these two explanations in this study but note that the language constellation of the household (monolingual or bilingual) and parental code-mixing were not related to whether children code-mixed at home or not. However, we also found that the G-E home-mixers were more likely to remain silent the younger they were, possibly supporting the need for greater confidence with both languages. This was not the case for the G-R home-mixers. This might be due to the fact that all but three of the G-E children were growing up in a bilingual home environment while this was only the case for 13 of the 32 G-R bilinguals, the rest of whom heard only Russian at home.

In conclusion, we have shown that NP constructions which overlap in form and function between the two languages of young bilingual children are more vulnerable to code-mixing as compared to when their form differs across two languages. In addition, children who code-mix at home are more likely to produce spoken answers in an experimental situation in which they are addressed in two languages. Finally, the use of a priming methodology to successfully elicit mixed utterances is a methodological innovation that may prove helpful in further research on the underlying representations of bilinguals.

5 References

Bencini, Giulia M. L. & Virginia V. Valian. 2008. Abstract sentence representation in 3-year-olds: Evidence from language production and comprehension. *Journal of Memory and Language* 59. 97–113.

Bernardini, Petra & Suzanne Schlyter. 2004. Growing syntactic structure and code-mixing in the weaker language: The Ivy Hypothesis. *Bilingualism: Language and Cognition* 7. 49–69.

Bernolet, Sarah, Robert J. Hartsuiker & Martin J. Pickering. 2007. Shared syntactic representations in bilinguals: Evidence for the role of word-order repetition. *Journal of Experimental Psychology: Learning, Memory, and Cognition* 33(5). 931–949.

Bock, J. Kathryn. 1986. Syntactic persistence in language production. *Cognitive Psychology*, 18. 355–387.

Cantone, Katja F. 2007. *Code-switching in bilingual children*. Dordrecht: Springer.

Cantone, Katja F. & Natascha Müller. 2008. Un nase or una nase? What gender marking within switched DPs reveals about the architecture of the bilingual language faculty. *Lingua* 118(6). 810–826.

Desmet, Timothy & Mieke Declerq. 2006. Cross-linguistic priming of syntactic hierarchical configuration information. *Journal of Memory and Language* 54. 610–632.

Deuchar, Margaret. 1999. Are function words non-language-specific in early bilingual two-word utterances? *Bilingualism: Language and Cognition* 2. 23–34.

Deuchar, Margaret & Marilyn Vihman. 2005. A radical approach to early mixed utterances. *International Journal of Bilingualism* 9(2). 137–157.

Di Sciullo, Anne-Marie, Pieter Muysken & Rajendra Singh. 1986. Government and code-mixing. *Journal of Linguistics* 22. 1–24.

Döpke, Susanne. 1998. Competing language structures: the acquisition of verb placement by bilingual German-English children. *Journal of Child Language* 25. 555–584.

Döpke, Susanne (ed.). 2000. *Cross-linguistic structures in simultaneous bilingualism*. Amsterdam: John Benjamins.

Genesee, Fred. 1989. Early bilingual development: One language or two? *Journal of Child Language* 16. 161–179.

Grosjean, François. 1982. *Life with two languages. An introduction to bilingualism*. Cambridge, Mass.: Harvard University Press.

Grosjean, François. 2001. The bilingual's language modes. In Janet L. Nicol (ed.), *One mind, two languages: Bilingual language processing*, 1–20. Massachusetts: Blackwell Publishers.

Hartsuiker, Robert J., Martin J. Pickering & Eline Veltkamp. 2004. Is syntax separate or shared between languages? Cross-linguistic syntactic priming in Spanish-English bilinguals. *Psychological Science* 15(6). 409–414.

Huttenlocher, Janellen, Marina Vasilyeva & Priya Shimpi. 2004. Syntactic priming in young children. *Journal of Memory and Language* 50. 182–195.

Jake, Janice L., Carol Myers-Scotton & Steven Gross. 2002. Making a minimalist approach to code-switching work: Adding the matrix language. *Bilingualism: Language and Cognition* 5(1). 69–91.

Jisa, Harriet. 2000. Language mixing in the weak language: Evidence from two children. *Journal of Pragmatics* 32. 1363–1386.

Jorschick, Liane, Antje Endesfelder Quick, Dana Gläßer, Elena Lieven & Michael Tomasello. 2011. German-English speaking children's mixed NPs with 'correct' agreement. *Bilingualism: Language and Cognition* 14(2). 173–183.

Köppe, Regina & Jürgen M. Meisel. 1995. Code-switching in bilingual first language acquisition. In Lesley Milroy & Pieter Muysken (eds.), *One speaker, two languages. Cross-disciplinary perspectives on code-switching*, 276–301. Cambridge: Cambridge University Press.

Kroll, Judith F. & Erika Stewart. 1994. Category interference in translation and picture naming. Evidence for asymmetric connections between bilingual memory representations. *Journal of Memory and Language* 33. 149–174.

Lanza, Elizabeth. 1992. Can bilingual two-year-olds code-switch? *Journal of Child Language* 19. 633–658.

Lanza, Elizabeth. 1997. Language contact in bilingual two-year-olds and code-switching: Language encounters of a different kind? *The International Journal of Bilingualism* 1(2). 135–162.

Liceras, Juana M., Raquel Fernández Fuertes, Susana Perales, Rocío Pérez-Tattam & Kenton Todd Spradlin. 2008. Gender and gender agreement in bilingual native and non-native grammars: A view from child and adult functional-lexical mixings. *Lingua* 118(6). 827.

Liceras, Juana M., Kenton Todd Spradlin & Raquel Fernández Fuertes. 2005. Bilingual early functional-lexical mixing and the activation of formal features. *International Journal of Bilingualism* 9(2). 227–252.

Lindholm-Leary, Kathryn J. & Amado M. Padilla. 1978. Language mixing in bilingual children. *Journal of Child Language* 5. 327–335.

Loebell, Helga & Kathryn Bock. 2003. Structural priming across languages. *Linguistics* 41. 791–824.

Meisel, Jürgen M. 1994. Code-switching in young bilingual children: The acquisition of grammatical constraints. *Studies in Second Language Acquisition* 16. 413–439.

Müller, Natascha. 1998. Transfer in bilingual first language acquisition. *Bilingualism: Language and Cognition* 1. 151–171.

Müller, Natascha & Aafke Hulk. 2001. Crosslinguistic influence in bilingual language acquisition: Italian and French as recipient languages. *Bilingualism: Language and Cognition* 4. 1–21.

Paradis, Johanne & Fred Genesee. 1996. Syntactic acquisition in bilingual children: autonomous or interdependent? *Studies in Second Language Acquisition* 18. 1–15.

Paradis, Johanne & Fred Genesee. 1997. On continuity and the emergence of functional categories in bilingual first language acquisition. *Language Acquisition* 6. 91–124.

Paradis, Johanne, Elena Nicoladis & Fred Genesee. 2000. Early emergence of structural constraints on code-mixing: Evidence from French-English bilingual children. *Bilingualism: Language and Cognition* 3(3). 245–261.

Pearson, Barbara Zurer, Sylvia Fernández & D. K. Oller. 1995. Cross-language synonyms in the lexicons of bilingual infants: One language or two? *Journal of Child Language* 22. 345–368.

Petersen, Jennifer. 1988. Word-internal code-switching constraints in a bilingual child's grammar. *Linguistics* 26. 479–493.

Petrushevskaya, Lyudmila. (online). Linguisticheskie skazochki. Available from: http://lib.ru/PROZA/PETRUSHEWSKAYA/butyawka.txt (Accessed 15 March 2011)

Poplack, Shana. 1980. Sometimes I'll start a sentence in Spanish Y TERMINO EN ESPANOL': Toward a typology of code-switching. *Linguistics* 18. 581–618.

Quay, Suzanne. 1995. The bilingual lexicon: Implications for studies of language choice. *Journal of Child Language* 22. 369–387.

Radford, Andrew, Tanja Kupisch, Regina Köppe & Gabriele Azzaro. 2007. Concord, convergence and accommodation in bilingual children. *Bilingualism: Language and Cognition* 10(3). 239–256.

Savage, Ceri, Elena Lieven, Anna Theakston & Michael Tomasello. 2003. Testing the abstractness of children's linguistic representations: Lexical and structural priming of syntactic constructions in young children. *Developmental Science* 6(5). 557–567.

Schoonbaert, Sofie, Robert J. Hartsuiker & Martin J. Pickering. 2007. The representation of lexical and syntactic information in bilinguals: Evidence from syntactic priming. *Journal of Memory and Language* 56(2). 153–171.

Schlyter, Suzanne. 1994. Early morphology in Swedish as the weaker language in French-Swedish bilingual children. *Scandinavian Working Papers on Bilingualism* 9. 67–86.

Van Heuven, Walter J. B., Ton Dijkstra & Jonathan Grainger. 1998. Orthographic neighborhood effects in bilingual word recognition. *Journal of Memory and Language* 39. 458–483.

Vasilyeva, Marina, Heidi Waterfall, Perla B. Gámez, Ligia E. Gómez, Edmond Bowers & Priya Shimpi. 2010. Cross-linguistic syntactic priming in bilingual children. *Journal of Child Language* 37(5). 1047–1064.

Vihman, Marilyn M. 1985. Language differentiation by the bilingual infant. *Journal of Child Language* 12. 297–324.

Volterra, Virginia & Traute Taeschner. 1978. The acquisition and development of language by bilingual children. *Journal of Child Language* 5. 311–326.

Yip, Virginia & Stephen Matthews. 2000. Syntactic transfer in a Cantonese-English bilingual child. *Bilingualism: Language and Cognition* 3(3). 193–208.

Yip, Virginia & Stephen Matthews. 2007. *The bilingual child. Early development and language contact.* Cambridge: Cambridge University Press.

Appendix A: Age and background information

	German-English	German-Russian primed on Russian	German-Russian primed on German
age range	3;6–5;5	3;6–5;3	3;7–5;6
age span mean age starting German kindergarten	4 years and 5 months 1 year and 6 months	4 years and 3 months 2 years and 3 months	4 years and 6 months 2 years and 7 months
n bilingual house-hold	13	8	5
n monolingual household	3 English	8 Russian	7 Russian*
total n	16	16	16

*4 G-R families did not fill out the questionnaire concerning language background

Appendix B: Novel nouns

Gender German	German	English	Russian	Gender Russian
masculine	der Bokel	the blicket	lorat л о р а т	masculine
masculine	der Alber	the midus	sjapa С Я П а[3]	feminine
feminine	die Nohle	the ression	kluma К Л У М а	feminine
feminine	die Fende	the vasic	pomik П О М И К	masculine

---

3 From Petrushevskaya, L.

IV Input sources in bilingual language development

Catrin Bellay

Musical, audio-visual, poetic, and narrative input: A longitudinal case study of French-English bilingual first language acquisition

Abstract: The chapter explores evidence that children treat the linguistic material in nursery rhymes, songs, stories, and children's television programmes as part of their linguistic repertoire, and readily quote it and deploy it in regular conversation. The data is taken from a longitudinal case study of the French-English bilingual first language acquisition of four siblings living in France. A set of criteria for the profiling of data examples serves to support intuitive judgements identifying items from these sources of input in the children's language production. The criteria enable the classification of four kinds of productive use of phrases from input (verbatim quote, verbatim borrowing, verbatim repetition, and adapted reuse) and three types of response to the ongoing communicative situation (response to the wording of the preceding utterance(s), response to the conversational context, response to the thematic context). The chapter includes a discussion of the way these sources of input may contribute to the process of language acquisition, language representation in the mind, and language use in interaction.

Keywords: input in language learning, child language development, formulaic sequences, language and television

1 Introduction

There is no doubt that infants acquire language in interaction with other people. Furthermore, infants and young children seem well able to acquire more than one language at the same time in this way. But what about other forms of linguistic input to which infants and young children are exposed? In this chapter, I address the question of whether bilingual children can learn about language and language use from a particular source of input which is not a form of interaction in the usual sense of the term. Can bilingual children learn language from nursery rhymes, songs, storybooks, and children's television programmes? What are the characteristics of this kind of input? What do bilingual children learn about language from these forms of input and how do they use that knowledge?

Drawing on data from a longitudinal case study of the French-English bilingual first language acquisition of four siblings, I explore evidence that the children studied treat the linguistic material in nursery rhymes, songs, stories, and children's television programmes as part of their linguistic repertoire, and readily quote it and deploy it in regular conversation. To facilitate the discussion of this subset of input, I use the acronym MAPNI, based on a categorisation of the input sources as Musical, Audio-visual, Poetic, and Narrative Input. The bilingual context of data collection has three important implications for this study. Firstly, the data presented here is bilingual first language acquisition data and since bilingual acquisition and language representation are different from their monolingual counterparts, this specificity must be acknowledged. The context of bilingual first language acquisition can be very variable and must be accounted for in detail as it can impact on the kind of acquisition and use that is observed. Secondly, if we accept that children tap into the linguistic input they are exposed to in order to learn language and its use, and if we accept that MAPNI for children is a part of that linguistic input, then it is reasonable to suggest that children also use the linguistic material in these forms of input to learn language. In the context of bilingual first language acquisition, MAPNI for children is a particular source of Language Alpha[1] linguistic input that children living in a Language A majority environment may draw upon to help them gain knowledge about Language Alpha. If bilingual first language children growing up in the Language A environment rely on one parent speaking to them in Language Alpha as their main source of linguistic input in that language, then the input to which they are exposed, and upon which they can base their knowledge of the language grammar and pragmatic features of its use, will surely be limited. Language Alpha MAPNI can take on a role of additional input providers for such children. Language Alpha input of this nature represents a proportionally larger part of the total input experience in Language Alpha than it does in Language A because Language A is also present in a wide variety of real social interaction contexts.

Thirdly, the context of data collection in the researcher's own bilingual home means that it is easier to spot when the children quote, borrow, repeat or reuse linguistic material from Language Alpha MAPNI because such practice stands out against a backdrop of (mostly) my own interaction-based language input. I am very familiar with a lot of the material the children are exposed to, especially when they are very young, because I read it or sing it to them, or

---

1 *Language A* and *Language Alpha* are the terms proposed by De Houwer (2009: 2) to label the two languages to which bilingual children are exposed simultaneously from birth.

watch it with them. I can spot when this material is used in production and say "I know where that comes from" or "I never say that, so where did he pick it up?"

The aim of this chapter is to present evidence showing that linguistic items from these forms of input are used by bilingual children in language production. In order to do this, I propose a set of criteria for the profiling of data examples. The criteria serve to support intuitive judgements identifying input items in language production.

The paper is structured as follows. In Section 2, I begin by outlining the characteristics of the linguistic material in nursery rhymes, storybooks, and children's television programmes, with particular emphasis on the bilingual context. In Section 3, I discuss the way these sources of input may contribute to the process of language acquisition, language representation in the mind, and language use in interaction. In Section 4, I propose a set of criteria to support intuitive judgements that a particular item of child language production is an instance of use of linguistic material from MAPNI. This set of criteria also enables the classification of different kinds of use of linguistic input material. Section 5 is a description of the case study and the dataset. In Section 6, I present an analysis of examples from the data, using the criteria proposed to validate intuitive judgements about the status of each example as an instance of reuse from MAPNI input sources. For some examples, I also make suggestions about the possible linguistic and pragmatic knowledge learned by the children through exposure to the source item, and discuss the way the children have applied that knowledge to the interaction in which the example occurred. Section 7 presents examples of oral narrative translation by the two older children, and suggests that the translation process can reveal bi-directional cross-linguistic influence.

2 Nursery rhymes, stories, and children's television programmes as sources of linguistic input (MAPNI)

Traditional nursery rhymes, songs, and stories do seem to frequently contain language that could be considered as antiquated grammar (e.g. *be he alive* or *be he dead*) and vocabulary (e.g. *as fast as he could caper*), nonsense (e.g. *lavender blue dilly dilly*), and disturbing or irrational content (e.g. *I'll grind his bones to make my bread*; *the cow jumped over the moon*). But are children sensitive enough to the pragmatics of different genres and presentational contexts to treat nursery rhymes, songs, and the language in children's television programmes as irrelevant to their language acquisition project? Many storybooks for young children (e.g. *Sharing a Shell* by Julia Donaldson) consist of poetic rhyming narrative with regular and symmetrical rhythmic patterns. Others contain texts built around grammatical parallelism (e.g. *Dear Zoo* by Rod Campell). The rhythmic, phonological, and structural elements often present in these forms of input contribute to their interest for children by grabbing and maintaining attention, and facilitating memorisation. For texts which have often been created for entertainment through oral production and transmission, such features are important. Sanches and Kirshenblatt-Gimblett (1976: 102) identify phonological and rhythmic or structural qualities in children's word play, including rhymes and riddles, making them particularly salient for young children who, the authors claim, have a preference for the phonological features of language. Nursery rhymes or chanted narratives often accompany ritualised games involving handclapping, ball bouncing, or group dancing where "the combination of the multiple constraints of rhythm, movement patterns (e.g. handclapping cycles), sound patterns (e.g. rhyme, assonance, alliteration), morphosyntax (e.g. grammatical parallelism) and semantic structuring facilitates the retrieval of information for performers and listeners" (Arleo 2013: 169).

The linguistic material in nursery rhymes, songs, and stories often demonstrate characteristics which distinguish them from the linguistic material in most children's television programmes. However, they do also have some characteristics in common. Input from all these sources is often fine-tuned to match the level of linguistic competence and world knowledge of the intended participants or audience. Some forms of children's television programmes, for example, are scripted to fine-tune the language used to match that of the intended audience (e.g. the BBC series *Teletubbies*, aimed at toddlers, whose characters use babytalk). Children's authors, songwriters, and scriptwriters possibly adapt their language in the same instinctive way as adults using infant or child directed speech in more conversational forms of interaction. Some children's television programmes reproduce language from original nursery rhymes, songs, and stories by including them in the script, sometimes building entire episodes around one such source text. Another way in which the linguistic material of rhymes, songs, and stories is present in televisual media is through filmed or animated adaptations of original texts. Nevertheless, it is undeniable that many examples of children's film and television programmes do not display the phonological, structural, or poetic characteristics of rhymes, songs, and stories. Some narration can occur, but scripted dialogue is also omnipresent. The linguistic material in scripted dialogue may also be fine-tuned to the audience. Bednarek's (2010) textual analysis of adult fictional television programmes includes a list of the linguistic features of scripted fictional television dialogue which distinguish it from naturally occurring dialogue. This form of dialogue seems to share some of the features of child directed speech, such as shorter sentences, a higher frequency of informal language, and the avoidance of unintelligibility. It also contains some of the features associated with children's narrative, such as the aesthetic devices of repetition and rhythm (Bednarek 2010: 64). An analysis of the scripted dialogue in children's film and television programmes, comparing it with naturally occurring adult–child and child–child dialogue, would surely yield equally interesting results.

MAPNI is rich in formulaic language. By *formulaic language* I am referring to such wordstrings as proverbs, idioms, narrative performative sequences (e.g. *Once upon a time*), situation-bound utterances (Kecskés 2003), conversational routines, and sequences which are lexical or grammatical frames, containing variable gaps (e.g. 'the end of the N'; 'as X as Y'). Some sequences may be considered inherently formulaic in a particular language, that is, for the entire speech community who uses that language. Other sequences may be formulaic for particular groups or individuals. In this sense, a partly-fixed grammatical frame that is repeated throughout the text of one song or story, for example, where each instance of the frame contains a variation of one item within that frame, can be seen as formulaic within that song or story, and can become formulaic for the singer, listener, or reader. It is possible that a storybook for very young children such as *Dear Zoo* (Campbell 1982) exposes children to the lexical frame [*he was too* + adjective] in such as way as to ultimately contribute to their knowledge of the underlying grammatical construction [pronoun + *be* + tense + *too* + adjective].

One of the most important characteristics of nursery rhymes, the written text of stories, and children's television programmes, in the context of this study, is their mostly-fixed and immutable nature. Of course, some elements of rhymes, songs, and stories may vary with repeated productions, particularly in memorised oral forms. Children and adults may entertain themselves by adapting the original texts, and discussion based on the texts will most likely vary with each instance of its being shared. Nevertheless, it is generally true that the linguistic material in these forms of input does not change over time. When a parent reads the same storybook to their child regularly over a period of several years, the text of the story will always be the same. At each reading, the child is exposed to an exact repetition of the source text. The same is true for repeated viewing of films or television programmes, provided they are available in a recorded form (video, DVD, or digital recording) and accessible to the child on a regular basis. However, the same cannot be said for everyday conversation, co-constructed by speakers as the speech event unfolds, and therefore open to an extremely wide degree of variation. Repeated exposure to fixed linguistic material undoubtedly contributes to its memorisation, and this in turn may contribute to the building up of a mental repertoire or corpus which enables language acquisition and use. Also, despite their young audience and the informal, unprestigious context of their transmission, nursery rhymes, songs, stories, and television programmes for children can be considered as having certain literary and cultural qualities. Since language and culture are intimately linked, folklore, nursery lore, and popular media that provide children access to both is valuable, particularly for bilingual children living in a monolingual community.

MAPNI can help children learn language by providing a favourable context for them to practise understanding and producing language in a repetitive, context-based way. Because the context is frequently shared with other family members and care-givers, it then enables the infant to take on a communicative role. Songs and rhymes can accompany other activities, often with semantic relevance as well as practical utility, for example, saying the *Five Fat Sausages* rhyme while waiting for the sausages to cook. Sharing and talking about MAPNI is a context within which parents and children can discuss the meaning of words and phrases, as well as the different situations in which they can be used. They might also enable children and adults to address issues of different practices and beliefs. Indeed, as children grow and their linguistic skills and world knowledge progress, rhymes, songs, stories, and television programmes can become relevant to them in ways that extend beyond form or the immediate mapping of here-and-now experience onto linguistic symbols. Stories and television programmes can provide children with experiences that are not possible within the confines of their own limited environment, and can enable them to deal hypothetically with issues that they have not yet encountered in reality.

3 Learning language from musical, audio-visual, poetic, and narrative Input

The notion of *convergence*, the idea that children imitate members of the surrounding speech community, being motivated by a desire to sound like them and be recognised as belonging to that community, is relevant in the context of bilingual children's exposure to MAPNI. The notion of convergence can be applied to the way children assign roles to themselves and others in order to act out scenes from MAPNI. These kinds of input can provide models for role play, in which the model may or may not be adapted to the child's own life. In the case of bilingual children growing up in a monolingual Language A community, if we consider that characters from Language Alpha MAPNI represent the Language Alpha speech community, and that this form of Language Alpha input is a proportionally major source of children's contact with that community (instead of regular, real, physical contact), then it is not unreasonable to suggest that when children imitate those characters and adopt their manners of speech, they are identifying with the represented speech community and wishing to be a part of it.

From a pragmatic perspective, children can learn about phrases as they appear in dialogue and specific situations by encountering them in stories, films, and television programmes. Situation-bound utterances are contextualised and culturally embedded. Conversational routines are played out in a variety of settings. Since it has been demonstrated that children can learn language which is not addressed to them by overhearing it (Lieven 1994), then it is not impossible that they can also learn language from 'overhearing' book characters and film or television actors communicating with each other. Also, some children's television characters deliberately elicit verbal reactions from viewers (e.g., Miss Hooley in the BBC children's programme *Balamory* asks viewers, "How are you today?", waits for a reply, and then responds as if she has heard it). While Roseberry, Hirsh-Pasek, Parish-Morris and Golinkoff (2009) have demonstrated that very young infants cannot learn language from a television screen, it may be the case that older children do gain linguistic benefits from television viewing. As far as adult viewing is concerned, Bednarek (2010) claims that "the dialogue featured in fictional television series can have a significant influence on learners of English in non-English speaking countries" (Bednarek 2010: 10). She quotes Mittman (2006) and Quaglio (2008), who argue for the use of television dialogue in the English language classroom. Bednarek suggests that "the language shown on television may also have an impact on native speakers" (Bednarek 2010: 10). Such an impact can be explained by mental corpus theory (Taylor 2012) and the analysis of repetition in discourse (Tannen 2007).

From a cognitive perspective, learning formulas and constructions is possible through exposure to and productive practice with language in MAPNI. Taylor's mental corpus theory states that "our knowledge of a language [...] is in large part constituted by (mostly implicit) memories of past linguistic experiences [...] [and that] learning a language consists in building up this memory store and that [...] our performance on a linguistic task – be it producing language in speaking or writing, comprehending language when listening or reading [...] – is a function of our accumulated memories" (Taylor 2012: 2). In line with Taylor's theory, the sources of input examined in this chapter may contribute to children's building up a repertoire of phrases and constructions from input and reusing them in conversation. The natural human tendency to repeat the speech of others is convincingly demonstrated by Tannen (2007). According to Tannen, prepatterning, formulaicity, and idiomaticity are all terms for "the many ways that any current utterance can be seen as repeating prior utterances" (Tannen 2007: 3). For Tannen (2007: 2–3), "repetition is at the heart not only of how a particular discourse is created but how discourse itself is created". Tannen (2007: 8) also refers to the notion of intertextuality, claiming that "meaning in language results from a complex of relationships linking items within a discourse and linking current to prior instances of language". Intertextual quotation in Swedish-American bilingual family discourse is examined by Beers-Fägersten (2012: 81), who notes that "intertextual quotation is the proposed term for the practice of appropriating exact bits of media text and integrating them into conversation" and that it occurs across communicative events, unlike intratextual repetition, which occurs within one communicative event. According to Beers-Fägersten (2012), the identification and recognition of intertextual quotation across communicative events is only possible when participants have shared knowledge of prior or source texts. In this sense, the prior text is a form of common ground or common knowledge, and it is transformed into a source text "through a process of appropriation" (Beers-Fägersten 2012: 82). Beers-Fägersten (2012: 91) demonstrates that both conversational and thematic repetition trigger quotation, and intertextual quotation also occurs "as a direct response to the wording of the utterances preceding it [...] building on previously employed lexical items or syntactic structures, which trigger a memory of prior talk from a media source".

Bellay (2013) shows that bilingual children can learn and reuse phrases from Language Alpha storybooks read to them by a parent, particularly when the phrases are defined and discussed during reading, reused by the parent in other contexts, and the children are provided with opportunities to reuse the phrases themselves. It is sometimes difficult to ascertain whether all the reuse examples documented by Bellay (2013) are instances of intertextual quotation, with conscious reference to the source texts and the common ground they represent, or the result of implicit memory of source texts being triggered by conversational and thematic contexts and/or as a response to the wording of preceding utterances. The process of parental teaching and then modelling the use of phrases from storybooks in other contexts described by Bellay (2013) does not necessarily function as intertextual quotation in the same way as described by

Beers-Fägersten (2012) since the parent's ultimate intention is to encourage the children's appropriation of phrases from the source text in order to build up their Language Alpha linguistic repertoire. However, the features of intertextual quotation presented by Beers-Fägersten (2012) are relevant to the data presented in this chapter, since the element of parental teaching is either much less marked or absent from the context of appropriation.

4 Criteria for identifying the productive reuse of items from input source texts

In this section I discuss criteria to support intuitive judgements that a particular item of child language production is a quote, repetition, or reuse of linguistic material from a nursery rhyme, storybook, children's film, or television programme. Wray and Namba (2003: 27) propose a set of criteria for identifying formulaic sequences in datasets. The aim of their "criterion-based exploration is not to influence the judgement so much as to shed light on why that judgement has been made". Similar difficulties exist in the identification of formulaic sequences as are present when attempting to identify instances of productive reuse of items from input source texts. As Wray and Namba (2003: 26) point out, "the main reason for this difficulty is that the majority of formulaic sequences are, to the casual ear or eye, indistinguishable from novel strings because they are grammatically unexceptional and their meaning is entirely predictable". As a response to this difficulty, I propose a methodology which takes intuition, based on the researcher's detailed knowledge of the subjects' linguistic repertoire, as its starting point. Intuitive judgements about the status of examples from the dataset are backed up by a classification procedure which lends weight to the identification of the reuse of phrases from specific input sources. The criteria I propose classify examples of reuse of linguistic items from input as one of four possible types of phrase use, which can each be one of three possible types of response to the ongoing communicative situation.

4.1 Types of phrase use

A. *Verbatim quote* is the exact repetition of a phrase from a source text, with conscious and intentional reference to the original source. If knowledge of the source text is shared by the speaker and hearer, the verbatim quote may be a way to refer to that shared knowledge or a particular shared meaning that the source or the phrase from it may have taken on for those particular speakers/hearers.

B. *Verbatim borrowing* is similar to a verbatim quote but does not carry the additional meaning associated with common knowledge of the source text. The hearer may have no knowledge of the source text and the speaker does not intend to refer to the source text. The speaker may borrow the phrase because she likes the sound of it or finds that it accurately describes the event, opinion, or emotion that she wishes to convey.

C. *Verbatim repetition*. While the phrase is an exact repetition of one from a source text, no reference to a source text is intended, and the speaker does not seem to be aware that she is repeating.

D. *Adapted reuse*. In this case the repetition is partial in the sense that some of the source phrase may be repeated verbatim, while other elements may be altered and thus adapted to suit the ongoing communicative situation.

4.2 Types of response to ongoing communicative situation

1. *Response to the wording of the preceding utterance(s)*. Something about the preceding utterance(s), on a phonological, lexical, and/or syntactic level, triggers a memory of prior talk from, or about, a source text. The use of a quote, borrowing, repetition, or adaptation constitutes interactive alignment with the speaker of the trigger utterance (it is possible to align with oneself).

2. *Response to the conversational context*. The conversational context triggers the use of an appropriate phrase (e.g. situation-bound utterances, conversational sequences).

3. *Response to the thematic context*. The thematic context triggers a memory of a prior text, the use of which may or may not be appropriate to the ongoing communicative situation.

Phrase use types A to D are proposed as a diagnostic and classification tool in conjunction with informed intuitive judgements. They are not to be considered as an immutable identification label for the status of phrases in any dataset, since the speaker's referential or non-referential intentions, or indeed lack of intention, as is suggested in the definition of phrase use C, is extremely difficult for the hearer to ascertain. Any judgement of this nature is necessarily speculative. Nevertheless, it is interesting to speculate on the level of consciousness with which the phrases are reused by the children in this study, since the notion of unconscious reuse can lead to debate about the extent to which linguistic items from input can become part of an individual's implicit memory and the place they may hold in an individual's mental corpus. It is always useful to analyse examples of phrase use in the context of the ongoing communicative situation in which they occurred, and to take into account the context in which the phrase was originally encountered. This is because the proximity to, or distance from, the context of the source text can be indicative of the degree of referential intention with which they are applied to another context.

5 Data

The children studied here are Loïc, born in 2003, Meriel, born in 2005, Owen, born in 2006, and Léonie, born in 2010. All four children were born and live in France with their British mother and French father. They are simultaneous bilinguals who are exposed to direct, interactional input in English from me, their mother, and in French from their father and the community, and input in the form of stories, songs, film, and television programmes in both languages. The family home is not equipped with an aerial, so television viewing is restricted to DVDs, videos, or digitalised media, including online viewing and gaming. Growing up with two languages in this way means that the children are learning to navigate their way along the bilingual language continuum (cf. Grosjean 2008, 2010). While at home alone with their mother, they may move closer to the monolingual English end of the continuum, particularly when reading, singing, watching English-language films or television programmes, or playing together in English. French is never completely deactivated or inhibited in such situations. However, the children know they can call on their linguistic resources in both languages to ensure successful communication. Their only, and infrequent, experience of monolingual English-language situations are if one child finds him/herself alone with a monolingual family member or friend, either during a visit of the latter to the French home, or during family holidays to Wales. Most of the time, the children are either in bilingual language mode or monolingual French mode, as is the case when they are at school or with the childminder. The One-Person-One-Language strategy, which was adopted by the children's parents at the birth of the eldest child, proved successful during the early years of each child, but has gradually been replaced by a less rigid One-Person-Two-Languages strategy, which reflects the bilingual reality of life in this mixed-couple family. Because of the influence of school and the wider community, French has become the dominant language of the home and sometimes the language chosen by some of the children when addressing their native English-speaking mother. However, the children's language choice is a fluctuating variable that is dependent on the personality of each child, their current relationship with their two languages, and the amount of time they spend interacting with their mother or engaging in English-language activities such as reading, singing, and watching television in English.

As the main provider of English interactional input for the children, the way I respond to and negotiate language choice with them is influential. During the early years of bilingual family life, I would respond to French or mixed child utterances with a minimal grasp strategy, including feigning incomprehension, making expressed guesses, and expanding on child utterances (see Lanza 2001, 2007 for an analysis of parental strategies in bilingual parent-child interaction). I also stuck rigidly to English when addressing the children, even when in the presence of other, French-speaking, people, including their father. As time went on and the family grew bigger, monolingual English interactional situations became more complex. The early dyadic mother-child interactions, became triadic mother–child–child interactions, then multiparty interactions. And as the older children started attending school in France, they began to introduce more French items into the interactions, even when their father was not present, and began to address each other in French more than in English. Their French-speaking father began to borrow English terms and insert them into his French sentences.

In addition to the increasing complexity of bilingual family interaction at home, my studies of bilingualism and discussion with other parents of bilingual children, led me to readjust my ideas about parental language strategies and I began to adjust to the reality of bilingual communication in the home. This meant taking away the notion of obligatory language choice based on the addressee and allowing the children the freedom to choose which language to use. Feigning incomprehension of French child utterances no longer felt comfortable, nor did only addressing the children in English, even when monolingual French-speakers were present. Watching the older children become increasingly competent speakers and then readers of English also resulted in the disappearance of the initial fears I had had that they would only succeed in learning to use two languages if I was strict about their use of English. Over a period of ten years, communication in our bilingual family has evolved from dyadic parent-child English-only interactions, to multiparty bilingual interactions, where both the children and the parents are free to choose whichever language they prefer and can switch freely between the two during conversations, including mid-sentence, without meeting refusal to understand or disapproval of a particular language choice. In this sense, then, language choice is truly that: a choice. When the children occasionally tell each other, or their mother, which language to speak, or not to speak, I intervene by reminding them that we do not have to adhere to rules about language choice in our family. I tell them that they do need to learn to negotiate their language choice when outside the home, taking into account the linguistic competence and preference of the other people present. I encourage them to practice their English so that they can communicate with monolingual family and friends.

The corpus, which I have been compiling for the last ten years, comprises a mixture of diary notes and transcribed video recordings. I do not attempt to record everything the children say or to provide a description of the bilingual acquisition process. The focus on the role of MAPNI in bilingual acquisition and language use is a way of providing a framework within which to examine the relationship between input, intake, and output. Most of the more interesting examples are in the form of diary notes. There is often a delay between hearing something interesting and being able to write it down, so some error in transcription may occur. A certain amount of luck is required to capture relevant examples on video. For this reason, some video sequences were set up with specific purposes in mind, for example, recording parent–child conversation while reading or watching a film together.

The difficulties of capturing relevant examples of language use on video are far outweighed by the advantages of being present as the children's mother and not just a researcher on weekly visits. I am able to hear examples in many contexts, at any time of day (or night!), and analyse them with rich interpretation thanks to my detailed knowledge of the children's linguistic experience, particularly concerning their exposure to, and use of, English. Most importantly, I am very familiar with the text of all the nursery rhymes, songs, stories, and television programmes to which the children are exposed in the home from an early age. As the children get older, I do not always sit and watch television with them, so my knowledge of the scripts is less than for early years viewing. However, the fact that the children only watch DVDs, videos, and digitalised recordings means that the same films and programmes are frequently repeated, and I can easily check the contents of a film or programmes if necessary. Similarly, as the children learn to read alone, my knowledge of their exposure to input from books is less detailed. But again, the English-language books in the home are a permanent feature which I can read and refer to if needed, unlike the French-language books which are regularly borrowed from the local library or school.

One of the advantages of being a parent-researcher is that I am able to make judgements based on the conversational or thematic context in which the example takes place. I am present when examples of the use of phrases from input occur and so can hear any phonological clues which might indicate quotation, borrowing, repetition, or reuse. I have detailed knowledge of the children's linguistic capacities and their input experience, something which helps particularly with the identification of the use of phrases from input. By focusing on MAPNI, the identification in the children's productive use of source input material becomes much easier than if one were attempting to trace more general, conversational input. This does not mean that the children only use linguistic material from these sources. It is probable that the types of use observed here also occur with phrases of a more general nature. However, identifying that relationship would be much more difficult. Finally, it is important to point out that ours is not a family in which an inordinate amount of time is devoted to exposure to such input, or in which the children receive priming in the process of using the linguistic material in it.[2] The examples presented here have arisen from the observation of the children's behaviour in natural interaction.

6 Analysis

In this section, I present examples from the case study data and use the criteria proposed in Section 4 to classify the form of phrase use and the type of response to the ongoing communicative situation in which the phrase was uttered. In the examples, I am referred to as Mo and the children are referred to by the first two letters of their names. The age of each child, at the time the example occurred, is included in brackets. The examples, source texts, phrase use types and response types are summarised in Table 1 at the end of the chapter.

(1) (Meriel is stepping on her sister's coat, which is lying on the floor)
Mo: *Don't just step on it!*
Me (7;11,18): *Don't just grab it!*

In the first example, the mother's utterance reminds Meriel of a line from the storybook *Chocolate Mousse for Greedy Goose*. This rhyming narrative is a firm family favourite that has been read over and over, and recited and quoted many times. Meriel quotes the line verbatim (phrase use type A) in response to the preceding utterance which is almost identical to the source text phrase (response type 1). Indeed, my preceding utterance is an adapted reuse of the source text phrase, no doubt caused by frequency effects in the input. Response to the wording of a preceding utterance is a common response type for examples

---

2 An exception to this general rule is presented in Bellay (2013), where parental priming of the use of phrases from a storybook was carried out in order to explore its effect on the children's use of target phrases.

of verbatim quoting, and as is the case here, quotes of this nature do not always correspond to the ongoing communicative situation.

(2)   Lé (2;6,28): *The big bad mouse!*

Example (2) is also a verbatim quote (phrase use type A), but this time Léonie is role-playing, imagining that her brother, who is chasing her at the moment she utters the example, is a character from a storybook, *The Gruffalo's Child*, the animated adaptation of which she had also watched many times on DVD. Léonie reproduces the intonation employed by the animated character on the DVD, thereby making the identification of the utterance as a verbatim quote possible. Role-playing is a common context for the occurrence of verbatim quotes and the utterance can be classified as a response to the thematic context (response type 3).

(3)   Mo: *Put your hood up. It's raining.*
       Ow (2;2): *It's pouring?*

In (3) Owen's utterance is a response to both the thematic context (response type 3) and to the immediately preceding utterance (response type 1). Owen appears to be reminded of the nursery rhyme,

> It's raining, it's pouring,
> The old man is snoring.
> He went to bed and bumped his head
> And couldn't get up in the morning.

Owen's use of the phrase "it's pouring" aligns with my own preceding utterance, "it's raining". The strong intuition that this is an example of verbatim borrowing (phrase use type B) from the nursery rhyme, rather than an instance of productive speech is based on two things. Firstly, at the age of 2 years and 2 months, when he produced this utterance, Owen had only encountered the phrase "it's pouring" in reference to rainfall, through exposure to that specific nursery rhyme. If I, like most native speakers, were referring to heavy rainfall in a conversational situation, I would not say "It's pouring".[3] As an isolated description of heavy rain, I would say "It's tipping down," my own preferred,

---

3 A quick *Google* search of "it's pouring" confirms the non-occurrence of this phrase in isolation, the co-occurrence of the two phrases "it's raining, it's pouring," and their link to the source song.

and a widely used, formula for describing such an event. Secondly, Owen produced this utterance with a rising, interrogative intonation. This suggests he was seeking further information about the extent of the rain, rather than consciously quoting the nursery rhyme. Furthermore, if this utterance was an instance of productive language use, he should have asked "Is it raining?" with the subject-verb inversion typical of English closed questions. It is possible to argue that Owen's use of the affirmative form to ask a question is an instance of cross-linguistic influence from French, a language in which such usage is common. However, the atypical use of the phrase and its co-occurrence with the preceding utterance in the source text point rather to an instance of verbatim borrowing from input.

An analysis of (3) cannot isolate the child's production from the adult's. Not only is it an occurrence of co-construction in a pragmatic sense, it is also a form of co-construction of a fixed formula in two parts, of which the second part is difficult to dissociate from the first. Before this example occurred, Owen had been repeatedly exposed to the co-existence of the two phrases "It's raining, it's pouring" in the song, which he had heard me singing during, and as a descriptive response to, the event of heavy rain. For him, then, the second phrase follows on from the first in the event script which accompanies heavy rain, and this occurs with sufficient frequency for him to come to predict such co-occurrence. We can posit that, as a result of such exposure, contrasted with the occurrences of only the first phrase "It's raining" used to describe lighter rainfall, Owen has realised that the first phrase establishes the existence of the event, while the second phrase provides additional information about the nature of the event. Owen appears to use the phrase, adding an interrogative intonation, "It's pouring?" in order to request confirmation of the existence of a possible additional quantifying feature of the event I have just described. In other words, he has understood that it is raining and wishes to know if it is raining heavily. He may have inferred the possibility of this additional feature by the instruction to "put your hood up", which implies a causal relationship between the event of heavy rain and the result of one's head getting wet if it is not covered. Or, he may simply be reminded of the co-existence of the two phrases in the song. His question may be a result of frequency in the input; the first phrase acting as a memory trigger which invokes the second. Whatever the cause, it could be that in this way, he is able to infer the relationship between an object concept "hood", an event concept expressed by a memorised formula "It's raining, it's pouring" (with the adult meaning 'It's raining heavily'), and one possible, conditional, result of the event "My head might get wet if I don't cover it with my hood".

In (4) we see an example of code-switching, where it appears that the quoting or borrowing phenomenon triggered the code-switch.

(4)   Ow (6;5,21): *Il pleut. Good Heavens!* 'It's raining.'

The first sentence, in French, comments on the event. The second, in English, is either a quote (phrase use type A) or a borrowing (phrase use type B) from the storybook *Why?* My intuition at the time was that Owen was borrowing the phrase, but I cannot confirm that he was not actually quoting. His intention to quote was not obvious from any intonational clues. Owen's older sister had been reading him the story, from which the phrase "Good Heavens!" has been quoted or borrowed, only a short time earlier. The phrase was used to comment surprise at the heavy rain, so in response to the thematic situation (response type 3).

Example (5), taken from Bellay (2013), is an example of verbatim repetition of a phrase from the storybook *Dumpling* (phrase use type C) to match the conversational situation of mother complaining (response type 2).

(5)   Me (5;9,28): *Some people are never satisfied!*

This idiomatic phrase was one of nine target phrases which were isolated for special parental treatment during and between repeated parent–children reading sessions of two storybooks. This particular phrase was only commented on once during reading, when I asked the children if they knew what the phrase meant. Loïc replied by providing a translation in French. Meriel's use of the phrase, a few days later, was identifiable as an example of verbatim repetition since no reference to the source text was made by her, and the thematic context in which she used it did not correspond in any way to the context in which she had encountered it. From her exposure to the phrase in the story, she had, however, gained some knowledge about the pragmatic, conversational use of the phrase, as a response to a complaint.

Example (6) illustrates how the repetition phenomenon is also observable in the children's Language A, French, and at an early stage of language development. Here, Léonie repeats part of a line from a French nursery rhyme. Her repetition (phrase use type C) accompanied her showing a plastic fish to her mother and brother.

(6)   Léonie (1;9,24):   *Poisson.   Dans l'eau.*
                           'Fish.   In the water.'

       Owen (5;9,19) (sings):   *Les petits poissons dans l'eau...*
                                'Little fish in the water...'

It seems that the first word *poisson* triggered an association with the rest of the line from the nursery rhyme and caused her to add *dans l'eau* as a reponse to her own preceding utterance (response type 1). It is possible to surmise this because there was a marked pause between the two sentences and she did not sing them. Interestingly, her brother recognised the source text and Léonie's utterance triggered his singing of it. This sort of inverted triggering of the memory of a source text is a very common occurrence in our family, with mother and children frequently bursting into song or quotations when reminded of a source text by something someone says or something that is going on.

The phrase in (7) is said in response to the thematic context Loïc is observing on the television (response type 3). On this occasion, the television programme was viewed directly on the BBC children's channel, *CBeebies*, during a visit to the grandparents' home in Wales.

(7)   Lo (4;3): *Raindrops keep falling on his head.*

It is an example of an adapted reuse (phrase use type D) of a line from a song that we sang frequently at the time the utterance was produced. We sang it by way of accompaniment to the weather.

> Raindrops keep falling on my head
> Just like the guy whose feet
> Were too big for his bed
> Nothing seems to fit
> These raindrops keep falling on my head
> They keep falling
> Because I'm free

The song originally featured in the 1969 film *Butch Cassidy and the Sundance Kid*, but it was not through exposure to the film that Loïc had encountered it. The melody is played by a wind-up musical toy radio that I had had as a child; the lyrics of the song are printed on the back of the toy. The toy radio is at the grandparents' home and we play with it, and sing along to it, while staying there, including at the time (7) was produced.

My strong intuition that this phrase is an example of adapted reuse of a phrase from input is based on the conversational intonation with which it was uttered. It was neither sung, nor said with the marked pause or intonation of a quote. It is not a verbatim borrowing since Loïc adapted the phrase, changing *my* to *his*, thereby demonstrating his understanding and command of the underlying grammar of the construction. His retention of the main verb of the phrase, *keep*, is specific to the lyrics of the song's original text. A more conventional way of expressing the event would be "raindrops *are* falling on his head". Therefore, I propose that Loïc's schematisation of the underlying construction is partial. He retains the main verb of the original formula, not realising yet that it is pragmatically inappropriate, while being able to appropriately adapt the possessive pronoun. The reasons for this partial acquisition may be the result of frequency features in the input; he has heard "raindrops keep falling on my head", thanks to his exposure to the song, more often than "raindrops are falling on my head", which is not a commonly occurring sequence in everyday speech. Herein lies a paradox, since "raindrops are falling on his head", while being grammatically correct and appearing to be more conventional, is arguably less common in real usage than "raindrops keep falling on my head". This is because the formula with *keep* is one of many such items which make up the shared cultural store of a large part of English speakers, particularly native speakers. The formula has become part of the shared cultural store precisely because of its title role in the well-known song. It could be argued that exposure to unconventional formulas such as this are unhelpful in the language development process, leading the child into inappropriate usage. I prefer to focus on the communicative advantages gained by the bilingual child by using all the resources in his (limited) Language Alpha linguistic repertoire, regardless of the subtleties of some details. Such an approach is highlighted in Wong-Fillmore's case study of naturalistic child second language acquisition (1976, 1979: 190), where she identifies successful strategies such as "make the most of what you've got" and "work on big things; save the details for later".

Example (8) is also an instance of adapted reuse (phrase use type D). Loïc had been watching an *Oswald* cartoon in which Oswald does some baking with his friend Daisy. Daisy lists the ingredients in the following way, "flour, butter, sugar".

(8)   Lo (2;1;18): *(upon seeing a flower) flour, butter, and sugar.*

In his reuse of the phrase, Loïc adapted the source phrase by adding "and". It is possible to see this utterance as an example of semantic confusion arising from homophones. It is also possible that, when he saw the flower, Loïc said or heard the word "flower" in his mind. This then triggered a response to the phonetic characteristics of this internal utterance. We can classify his reuse of the phrase from input as a response to the preceding utterance (response type 1). In the same period, Loïc had been watching French-language cartoon adaptations of the popular *Babar* stories. When we talked about the cartoons together in English, I couldn't remember the English name of the character "Flora", who is called *Fleur* in the French version. When it is not being used as a name, the French word *fleur* is translated as 'flower'. Example (9) shows how crosslinguistic influence between a bilingual child's two languages can interact with an inter-textual memory trigger (response type 3), linking two separate children's television input sources. My utterance reminds Loïc of the phonetic association in (8) which he had made the day before (response type 1) and he produces another adapted reuse (phrase use type D) from the *Oswald* cartoon.

(9)   C: *Babar's children are called Alexander, Pom and Fleur.*
          Lo (2;1;18): *butter and sugar.*

In the classic English children's story *The Tiger Who Came to Tea*, Sophie and her mother are interrupted during tea by a tiger who asks to be invited in because he is hungry. The tiger eats and drinks everything in the house and then says, "Thank you for my nice tea. I think I'd better go now". The children in this study not only enjoyed having the story read to them many times, they also had fun role-playing the story, taking it in turns to play the different charac-ters. In (10) the children adapt and borrow, quote, or repeat the dialogue from the story (phrase use types D and A, B, or C) as their own means of communica-tion in response to the conversational context (response type 2). I had made some soup for dinner, but the children did not like it. They could see I was dis-appointed so when leaving the table they thanked me and excused themselves politely.

(10)   a.   Lo (5;5): *Thank you for my nice dinner. It was very nice.*

       b.   Me (3;3): *Thank you for my nice dinner. I'd better go now.*

This example illustrates the way conversational context (response type 2) can trigger the memory and adapted reuse of phrases encountered in a story. It is interesting to note the way the original version of the first phrase was slightly altered to suit the interaction for which it was reused, so that "tea" becomes "dinner". Loïc's phrasing in (10a) is probably, although not necessarily, inspired by the story and could simply be a polite formula, a situation-bound utterance, that he has acquired. It is impossible to ascertain whether his adapted reuse was made with conscious reference to the source text. The similitude with the source text, combined with the intensive exposure to the source text at the time the example occurred, makes it highly likely that the phrase had become part of Loïc's mental corpus. He was then able to call upon it in a relevant context, and his knowledge of the internal grammar of the phrase made it possible for him to adapt it (phrase use type D).

Meriel appears to be reminded of the story both by the context and by what Loïc has just said (response types 1 and 2). Her utterance in (10b) is a response to the preceding utterance (response type 1). She repeats Loïc's adaptation of the (tiger's) polite formula and then adds a phrase which could be a verbatim, if incomplete, quote from the tiger. However, my intuition at the time was that she was not pretending to be the tiger at that moment. I believe she was borrowing a phrase she had encountered in the story and which, through intensive exposure in reading and role play, she had appropriated as part of her own mental corpus. She then used it in a way she had construed to be appropriate thanks to its use in the story (phrase use type B). In fact, Meriel's second sentence is not really suitable to the context in which she produced it, another indication that she was borrowing dialogue. This example also demonstrates the way children sometimes use phrases from stories in inappropriate ways, thus pointing to a process of linguistic appropriation by experimentation, tentatively trying out different formulas that have been encountered but possibly not fully understood, in the hope that successful communication will take place. Example (10) clearly demonstrates the way a story can help children acquire the necessary "institutionalised routines, such as thank you and bye bye", routines which "set up significant social signals of the child's compliance with the expectations of the adult world" (Wray 2002: 18).

Example (11) illustrates the inappropriate adapted reuse of a phrase encountered in the storybook *Sharing a Shell*. Owen seems to have understood the message of the story, which is teamwork. However, he has associated this notion with a frequently repeated phrase in the text, "two/three friends sharing a shell," and has gone on to partially adapt the phrase to another context ("friends" becomes "boys").

(11) (Watching Loïc at football training)
      Ow (2;8;18): *Two boys sharing a shell*
      Mo: *What do you mean?*
      Ow: *Two boys sharing a shell.*
      Mo: *Where?*
      Ow: *There. (Points to group of boys on pitch)*
      Mo: *I don't understand, Owen. How are they sharing a shell? Where's the shell? There are more than two boys.*
      Ow: *Two boys sharing a shell, there. (points)*
      Mo: *Do you mean they are in a team?*
      Ow: *Yes, in a team.*

This is an instance of adapted reuse (phrase use type D) in response to the thematic context (response type 3). I was able to work out Owen's intended meaning thanks to our shared knowledge of the source text. Examples (10) and (11) demonstrate the way that the children can identify a variable gap in a frame and then slot in a new lexical or grammatical item to suit the context of reuse. Many other examples from the corpus illustrate this phenomenon. The lines "Sit up nicely now, be good" and "oops a daisy, mop it up", from the baby board book *Time for Dinner* were frequently quoted by Meriel, when aged 2;8. During and after intensive reading of the book, which was a favourite for a few months, these lines quickly became mealtime usage (response type 2), clearly with reference to the story we had shared. Whenever I asked a child to "sit up" or "sit nicely" at the table, Meriel would invariably add "be good", echoing the line from the book. Meriel did not content herself with merely echoing the text of the story. Her repeated quoting (phrase use type A) of the line "oops a daisy, mop it up" when a drink was spilled (12a) enabled her to then move on to her own adaptation (phrase use type D), (12b), which she said when an object was dropped on the floor.

(12) a. Me (2;8;15): *Oops a daisy, mop it up.*

     b. Me (2;8;21): *Oops a daisy, pick it up.*

Meriel's adaptation of the phrase demonstrates the way such formulas can be acquired from stories and applied to equivalent real-life contexts, particularly when the context is relevant to the child and forms a regular part of their personal experience. Meriel's ability to produce a new version of the original source text, combining the idiomatic first phrase with a variation on the verb in the second phrase, is a good illustration of the way children learn that it is possible for a formula to have gaps within the formulaic frame which can be filled according to the context. This example is a case of limited lexical variation on closed sets such as pronouns or a small group of interchangeable words (see Wray and Namba [2003: 33] for a classification of the possible types of variation within a formulaic frame).

The corpus also contains examples of the children playing with variable gaps in formulaic frames from songs with apparently no function other than amusement and creativity. The last two examples in this section demonstrate one of the ways in which songs can provide a means for children to experiment with language, discovering what is semantically (im)possible and what is creatively acceptable.

(13) Lo (2;4): *Oh do you know the muffin elephant?*

Example (13) shows creative lexical variation of the noun phrase from the first line of the nursery rhyme *Do you know the muffin man?* where the noun *man* has been replaced with the noun *elephant.*

(14) Lo (2;6): *Old MacDonald had a chair, e-i-e-i-o. With a sit down here and a sit down there.*

Example (14) shows creative lexical variation of the noun phrase and the verb phrase from the song *Old MacDonald had a farm.* In the original version, Old MacDonald has many different animals and each verse introduces a new animal and the sound it makes, e.g.,

> Old MacDonald had a pig, e-i-e-i-o.
> With an oink-oink here and an oink-oink there,
> Here an oink, there an oink,
> Everywhere an oink-oink.

In Example (14), Loïc's creativity is more effective than in (13), since his variation respects the rhythmical constraints of the original and so is easy to sing in addition to being funny.

7 Bilingual translation of stories

In a bilingual family, children may often translate when passing on messages, or code-switch to repeat information to another person, as do the children in this study, but what interests us here is their translation of stories. In our bilingual family, reading storybooks sometimes provides a terrain for experimenting with translation and talking about the challenges involved as parent and child try to translate a story together. Through activities such as this, the children learn about the often slippery nature of translation equivalents, particularly concerning things like emotion terms or abstractions. They become aware of the fixedness and culture-specific nature of some phrases, and the possibility that in some cases the notion stays the same while only the words change. It may be thanks to such exercises that the child bilingual (who is bilingual since childhood) is equipped to provide culturally appropriate translations for terms and ideas whose subtleties may remain more elusive to the adult bilingual (who became bilingual as an adult). Or it could be the case that understanding and translating such subtleties require the maturity of the adult mind. The notion of dual cultural knowledge for bilinguals (Kaya 2007) is open to discussion when referring to children, and depends on definitions of culture, and the exposure to culture in childhood. The study of the relationship between the acquisition of language and manifestations of culture traditionally aimed at children (i.e. nursery rhymes, songs, stories, and children's television programmes) may provide some insight into this question. Is the bilingual child, who is exposed to bicultural input of this kind, able to produce culturally appropriate translations? What can the translation process tell us about the child's developing lexicons and the organisation of their two languages?

At the time of the examples presented here, the subjects were pre-literate, natural translators/interpreters, who did not produce written translation (for the notions of 'natural' and 'native' translator see Harris and Sherwood 1978 and Toury 1995). In this chapter, the focus is on oral narrative translation. The pre-literate bilingual child can produce an oral translation of a written text when that text has been read aloud to him/her in one language, and the child in turn tells the same story in another language. In this case, the young translator uses skills other than those used for the interpreting of spoken, conversational-type language acts, since he/she is truly translating a text, with all its textual specificities, even if the translation is presented in a spoken form. However, the child is not able to go through the construction and reorganisation process carried out by the literate translator, working with a written text, so the translation will remain spontaneous and instinctive.

For very young children, access to written stories is through being read to by a literate person, usually an adult, sometimes an older sibling. Most of the time, children look at a book while listening to the story and the illustrations are complementary, helping them to understand the text. Some children's books rely so heavily on the illustrations that simply reading the text, without referring to the pictures, would hinder full comprehension of the story. This is particularly the case when the text of a story consists entirely of dialogue. The translation of such a story could resemble the translation of an account of an experience, an ongoing event, or something heard in conversation, for example. More complex, traditional fairy tales, on the other hand, may be accompanied by illustrations, but do not depend on them for their meaning. The whole story is presented in the text, the language is more literary with the use of narrative formulas and, in the case of French, the past historic tense. In order to translate these texts, equivalents must be found which have a corresponding register in the target language. The translation requires knowledge of textual language, knowledge that the child can only acquire if a literate person reads aloud to them. In his preface to Dalgalian, Weinreich calls this knowledge "oral textual competence" (Dalgalian 2000: 12).

Wray's (2002: 133) explanation of the balance of analytic and holistic language processing from birth to adulthood could lead us to hypothesise a parallel development of the manner in which bilingual children approach translation acts. During the first, holistic, processing phase (from birth to age 2), the bilingual child might tend to translate formulas, or entire sequences, which are stored whole in the bilingual memory. During the second phase, of analytic processing (age 2 to 8), the child may break up sequences in order to process and translate them. As a result, the child may have to produce a greater effort to generate new sentences from their components and the language's grammar, with a translation of components, rather than sequences, taking place. In this case the child will be confronted with the difficulties of analytically translating fixed formulas and idioms. In the third phase of language processing (age 8 to 18), the child might then gradually return towards a more holistic translation strategy which, in the fourth phase (adulthood), would involve a balance between the translation of equivalent sequences and equivalent components.

In this section, I present several examples of the children's narrative translations. Example (15) is a translation by Loïc (5;7) and example (16) a translation by Meriel (3;5) of a story they had co-constructed with the other pupils and the teacher at school. The text of the original book, *Toutes les Couleurs*, is composed of simple dialogue in the first and second persons. There is, in fact, no narrative text. However, since the narrative had been created orally by the pupils, using the text and illustrations as a guide, the translation Loïc and then Meriel gave me was in narrative form.

(15)   Lo (5;7): *First the little rabbit rolls in the green grass and when he gets up his bottom is all green. He sees some strawberries and then his mouth is all red. Then he sees some mud. He splashes his feet in the mud. Then his feet are all brown. He picks some flowers and then he has his hands all yellow. He gives them to his mummy.*
Mo: *What does he give?*
Lo: *The flowers. Then his mummy says, "You need some blue. Go in the bath." And then the little rabbit doesn't have any colours any more.*
Mo: *Does he become a particular colour after that?*
Lo: *White. White is his normal colour.*

(16)   Me (3;5): *The little rabbit's all white. And the rabbit's got every colour but not blue. He's go in the grass and get his botton [bottom] wet. He's step in the mud for get his feet all brown. How about the flowers. I not say. He give the flowers to his mummy and he's got all yellow. He's need some blue. He's eat some strawberries and get his mouth all red. Something else. But not the same. I go to bed!*

Meriel had been listening to her older brother and then wanted to tell the story too. It is probable that she was largely influenced by Loïc's version. I found these translations so interesting that I borrowed the book from the teacher who explained to me how the group of children had told the story together, with the help of the illustrations, adding their comments to the dialogue which had been read aloud. When Loïc and Meriel switched to English to tell the story, were they translating the speakers or the text? To what extent did they understand that they were dealing with a text, and what influence did this understanding have on their translation strategy? The following example provides us with some clues. Meriel had another go at translating the same story. This time, I gave her the book and asked her to tell the story first in French and then in English. I recorded her on video; here is a short extract from her English version:

(17)   Me (3;5): *Yeah! Um, youpi! Oh! J'ai, um je, I've got my bottom all green!*
       Oh! Yum yum! Je vais manger quoi?
       Mo: *Strawberries.*
       Me: *I gonna eat the strawberries, and then I'm gonna get my mouth all, all*
       Mo: *Red.*
       Me: *Red.*
       Mo: *That's right.*
       Me: *Oh! J'ai la bouche toute rouge. Oh! J'ai les pieds tout marrons.*

Firstly, we can note that here Meriel provides a translation of the text of the book and not a narrative. This may be because she is 'reading' to me from the book and I can see the action for myself in the pictures. She might assume I don't need narrative explanation of the events, or she may be reproducing what she remembers hearing her teacher say when reading aloud. When translating the book into English she code-switches frequently, and not always in the usual direction. In this extract we can see how she code-switches to French to ask me a question, whereas at that time she usually spoke to me in English. The code-switch may have been triggered by the French word *fraise* being the first to come to mind, since in her earlier telling of the story in French she had no trouble with this word, and a memory lapse concerning the English equivalent *strawberries*. Meriel's use of "I've got my bottom all green" instead of "my bottom is all green" (which is the way I translate it later on), is a more appropriate one, since it can include the meaning of having caused oneself to become green, an element of cause and effect, which is a pertinent interpretation of the story. It is more likely due to luck than design, nevertheless it works. It is possible to argue that Meriel's frequent exposure at home to the variable frame in expressions like "you've got your sleeves all wet" or "you've got your face all mucky", has directly enabled her to produce this very natural translation by taking into account the reaction of the little rabbit's mother, of chiding the little rabbit for having got himself in a mess, a reaction that Meriel could firmly identify with!

The next set of examples come from a bilingual *Sleeping Beauty* book that Loïc and I made together, using his drawings, when he was aged 5;5. At this time, Loïc's exposure to the classic fairy tale was in the form of two DVDs, the French-language Disney animation, *La Belle au Bois Dormant*, and the Abbey Home Media animation, *Sleeping Beauty*. I had never read the story to him from a book. Loïc began by telling the story to me in French, using his drawings as a basis for the narrative. When he had finished, I read aloud my transcription of his oral narrative, which he then translated into English, sentence by sentence. I also transcribed the English translation. The resulting bilingual story contains examples of formulaic story-telling phrases such as "Once upon a time, a long time ago" and its translation equivalent, *Il était une fois, il y a longtemps*. Sometimes no equivalent is provided, as with "and they lived happily ever after", which Loïc did not translate. We can see that Loïc's fairytale vocabulary is extensive in both languages. He correctly uses the terms *roi, reine, princesse, prince* and *king, queen, princess, prince, chaudron* and *cauldron, sorcière* and *witch*, *dragon* and *dragon, château* and *castle*. He has trouble with *rouet* and *spinning wheel*, although I am certain he had heard the English term *spinning wheel* in stories before. To replace his lexical gap, Loïc gives a functional definition, which differs slightly across languages, demonstrating the issue of translation equivalents.

(18) a. *un objet pour faire de la laine*

    b. *another object to do some cotton*

Does Loïc believe that *laine* and *cotton* are the same thing? Or does he choose an English option from the same lexical group, with similar properties, because the real translation equivalent of *laine* 'wool', or the more appropriate *fil* 'thread' are unavailable to him? Sometimes Loïc's vocabulary is more precise and suitable for a fairytale in one language than the other (19) and sometimes cultural influence is detectable in his vocabulary choices (20).

(19) a. *Le roi enferma sa fille dans*   *une petite* **chambre.**
        'The king locked his daughter in a little bedroom.'

    b. *The king locked his daughter in*   *the* **cellar.**

(20) a. *Elle tomba sur   le **carrelage**.*
          'She fell on   the tiles.'

    b. *She fell on   the **floor**.*

The example (20a) conjures up images of French homes, where floors are commonly tiled and the floor is often referred to as *le carrelage*, 'the tiles'. In the next example, Loïc produces a linguistically correct but culturally inappropriate translation. It would have been more appropriate to use a phrase such as "don't worry" or "it's alright", since in the situation he has created in his story the speaker is comforting the princess.

(21) a. *C'est pas grave.*

    b. *It doesn't matter.*

Loïc's translation is influenced by the common French usage of *Ce n'est pas grave* when comforting a child. A literal translation would be 'It's not serious'. A pragmatic translation in this context would be "It's alright" but in a different context could be "It doesn't matter". Despite his understanding of the phrases in both languages, and his otherwise correct choice of whole phrase translation equivalent, he cannot see the cultural inappropriateness, even though he would never have heard me, or any other English speaker he knows, say "It doesn't matter" to a crying child.

Taylor refers to translation in his discussion of speaking idiomatically: "Translators are aware that the transfer of conceptual content is not just a matter of replacing the words in the source language with words in the target language [...] rather a matter of selecting a form of words with respect to the conceptualization which it symbolizes" (Taylor 2012: 103). He illustrates the point with the different ways of describing motion events in English and Romance languages:

> [I]n describing motion events, English speakers like to make use of verbs describing specific manners of motion (rush, dash, hurry, crawl, jump, limp, scuttle, and many more), with the path or direction of motion expressed in a prepositional phrase (into the house, out of the room, up the stairs, across the field). Speakers of Romance languages, on the other hand, express the path and direction by means of a verb (enter, exit, ascend, cross) with the manner of motion expressed in an optional adverbial adjunct (running, in a hurry, on all fours, and the like). Thus in English, one 'runs out of the house', while in French 'on sort de la maison en courant', that is, one 'exits the house running' [...] it is not the idiomatic way to describe the event. (Taylor 2012: 103)

Examples (22) and (23) illustrate how these differences can complicate the bilingual child's translation process.

(22)   a.   *Le prince *vu dans le canal un dragon qui vola jusqu'au prince.*[4]
           'The prince saw in the canal a dragon which flew up to the prince.'

       b.   *The prince saw a dragon which came up to the prince, flying.*

In (22) the crosslinguistic influence works in the expected direction, with a translated English version which reproduces the French motion event preference, instead of the more idiomatic 'a dragon which flew up to the prince'. However, in (23), something unexpected occurs.

(23)   a.   *Il *coura jusqu'à l'autre côté de la forêt.*[5]
           'He ran all the way to the other side of the forest.'

       b.   *He ran all the way to the other side of the forest.*

The English version (23b) is quite idiomatic, whereas the French version (23a) would have been better expressed as *Il traversa la forêt en courant*, that is, 'He crossed the forest running'. The preferred English way of expressing the motion event has influenced the French version, despite the fact that the French version was produced first during the initial telling of the story, and (23b) was produced later as a translation of (23a).

In (24) we find a formula which Loïc had first encountered in the storybook *Thomas and James* as "That'll teach you a lesson". Documented examples in the corpus of the adapted reuse of this phrase demonstrate that Loïc was able to adapt the phrase to the context by modifying the personal pronoun when required, as in the following example from his bilingual *Sleeping Beauty* story:

(24)   a.   *Ça   *l'apprendra   cette petite fille.*
           'That   will teach   this little girl.'

       b.   *That will teach her a lesson.*

Not only does Loïc use this phrase repeatedly, in many different situations, but he also attempts to translate it into French as it is, rather than using a more appropriate, equivalent French expression.[6] Such an example seems to reveal

---

4 The correct past historic form of the verb is *vit*.

5 The correct past historic form of the verb is *courut*.

6 A more idiomatic phrase would be *Ça lui servira de leçon à cette petite fille.*

cross-linguistic influence from English to French. It may also suggest that Loïc was entering the second phase of acquisition, moving towards more analytical processing, breaking down strings and trying to translate them component by component, rather than seeking a holistic translation equivalent. Concerning the last three examples, it is important to emphasise that Loïc produced his French version of the *Sleeping Beauty* story first, and then translated it into English. Thus, the cross-linguistic influence observed here is not a product of the translation process, but rather the translation process reveals the existence of cross-linguistic influence.

8 Conclusion

In this chapter I have discussed a fascinating phenomenon observed in the linguistic productions of my own four bilingual children, that is, the quotation, borrowing, repetition, and adapted reuse of phrases from nursery rhymes, songs, stories, and children's television programmes. In order to illustrate the phenomenon, I have presented examples from my corpus which can be categorised as one of four types of phrase use in one of three types of response to the ongoing communicative situation. By proposing these classification criteria, I hope to support the essentially intuitive judgements I have made about the status of the examples as evidence of the ways the children use the linguistic material in these forms of input. The bilingual context of the case study has also provided insights into the development of natural translation competence in these young simultaneous bilinguals, and its application to the specific skill of oral narrative translation.

MAPNI is a particular source of Language Alpha linguistic input that bilingual children living in a Language A majority environment might draw upon significantly more than monolingual children do in a monolingual context. They might do this because, in this specific context, Language Alpha input of this kind represents a proportionally larger part of the whole input experience than it does for monolingual children in a monolingual environment. In other words, the children reported on here get most of their English input from their mother and from MAPNI. Of course, they also listen to and read stories, sing songs, and watch films in French, but this form of input represents a fraction of their overall French language input experience which is also provided through almost all other direct human contact, including, from the age of four, six hours at school, four days a week, with several teachers and lots of friends. A significant part of their English language input experience, other than conversing with me, or "business talk" (language used to get things done), involves reading stories together (most evenings for about half an hour, sometimes more) and watching English-language films (about three hours a week on average, often more). Even with very young children, Language Alpha MAPNI can provide a basis for further interaction in that language. There is also the added element of the eldest child now reading extensively to himself in English and looking at English-language internet sites, something which will merit further investigation.

The twin arguments of the proportion of input and the capacity for the parent-researcher to know where a phrase in the output has come from, are peculiar to the bilingual context of this case study. Unfortunately I cannot compare my data to similar monolingual data because, to my knowledge, no one has yet looked at the way monolingual children (or other bilingual children) use the linguistic material in MAPNI in their own language production. Therefore, I cannot claim that the bilingual children in this study are using the linguistic material in these specific forms of input more than monolingual children would, although I intuitively suspect this is the case. Nevertheless, I have provided some evidence that the children in this study use the linguistic material in these input sources, and it is thanks to my position, as a minority-language parent-researcher raising bilingual children in a majority-language community, that I have been able to observe them doing so.

References

Arleo, Andy. 2013. Investigating the universal children's rhythm hypothesis: data, issues, perspectives. In Jean-Luc Leroy (ed.), *Topicality of musical universals/Actualité des universaux musicaux*, 157–170. Paris: Éditions des archives contemporaines.

Baker, Colin. 2006. *Foundations of bilingual education and bilingualism*. Clevedon: Multilingual Matters.

Bednarek, Monika. 2010. *The language of fictional television: Drama and identity*. London: Continuum.

Beers-Fägersten, Kirsty. 2012. Intertextual quotation: References to media in family interaction. In Ruth Ayass & Cornelia Gerhardt (eds.), *The appropriation of media in everyday life: What people do with media*, 79–104. Amsterdam: John Benjamins.

Bellay, Catrin. 2013. Bilingual children's reuse of formulaic phrases encountered in storybook reading: The effect of rich definition, parental reuse, and parent-initiated reuse. *E-Crini* 4. http://www.ecrini.univ-nantes.fr (Accessed on 15 April 2013).

Dalgalian, Gilbert. 2000. *Enfances plurilingues*. Paris: L'Harmattan.

De Houwer, Annick. 1990. *The acquisition of two languages from birth: A case study*. Cambridge: Cambridge University Press.

De Houwer, Annick. 2009. *Bilingual first language acquisition.* Bristol: Multilingual Matters.

Grosjean, Francois. 2008. *Studying bilinguals.* Oxford: Oxford University Press.

Grosjean, Francois. 2010. *Bilingual: Life and reality.* Cambridge (Mass.) & London: Harvard University Press.

Harris, Brian. 1980. How a three-year-old translates. In Evangelos A. Afendras (ed.), *Patterns of bilingualism,* 370–393. Singapore: Singapore University Press.

Harris, Brian & Sherwood, Bianca. 1978. Translating as an innate skill. In David Gerver & H. Wallace Sinaiko (eds.), *Language, interpretation and communication,* 155–170. New York: Plenum Press.

Kaya, Bruce. 2007. The role of bilingualism in translation activity. *Translation Journal* 11(1). http://www.bokorlang.com/journal/39bilingual.htm (Accessed 15 April 2013).

Kecskés, István. 2003. *Situation-bound utterances in L1 and L2* (Studies on Language Acquisition). Berlin: De Gruyter.

Lanza, Elizabeth. 2001. Bilingual first language acquisition: A discourse perspective on language contact in parent-child interaction. In Jasone Cenoz and Fred Genesee (eds.), *Trends in bilingual acquisition,* 201–229. Amsterdam: John Benjamins.

Lanza, Elizabeth. 2007. Multilingualism and the family. In Li Wei and Peter Auer (eds.), *Handbook of multilingualism and multilingual communication,* 45–67. Berlin: Mouton de Gruyter.

Lieven, Elena. 1994. Crosslinguistic and crosscultural aspects of language addressed to children. In C. Gallaway and B. Richards (eds.), *Input and interaction in language acquisition,* 56–73. Cambridge: Cambridge University Press.

Robinson, Peter & Nick C. Ellis. 2008. *Handbook of cognitive linguistics and second language acquisition.* New York & Abingdon: Routledge.

Roseberry, Sarah, Kathy Hirsh-Pasek, Julia Parish-Morris & Roberta Michnick Golinkoff. 2009. Live action: Can young children learn verbs from video? *Child Development* 80, 1360–1375.

Sanches, Mary & Barbara Kirshenblatt-Gimblett. 1976. Children's traditional speech play and child language. In Anthony Backhouse & Barbara Kirshenblatt-Gimblett (eds.), *Speech play: Research and resources for studying linguistic creativity.* Philadelphia: University of Pennsylvania Press.

Tannen, Deborah. 2007. *Talking voices: Repetition, dialogue, and imagery in conversational discourse.* Cambridge: Cambridge University Press.

Taylor, John. R. 2012. *The mental corpus: How language is represented in the mind.* Oxford: Oxford University Press.

Tomasello, Michael. 1992. *First verbs. A case-study of early grammatical development.* Cambridge & New York: Cambridge University Press.

Toury, Gideon. 1995. *Descriptive translation studies and beyond.* Amsterdam: John Benjamins.

Wong-Fillmore, Lily. 1976. *The second time around: Cognitive and social strategies in second language acquisition.* Stanford, CA: Stanford University PhD thesis.

Wong-Fillmore, Lily. 1979. Individual differences in second language acquisition. In Charles J. Fillmore, Daniel Kempler & William S.-Y. Wang (eds.), *Individual differences in language ability and language behaviour,* 203–228. New York: Academic Press.

Wray, Alison. 2002. *Formulaic language and the lexicon.* Cambridge: Cambridge University Press.

Wray, Alison. 2008. *Formulaic language: Pushing the boundaries.* Oxford: Oxford University Press.

Wray, Alison & Kazuhiko Namba. 2003. Use of formulaic language by a Japanese-English bilingual child: A practical approach to data analysis. *Japan Journal of Multilingualism and Multiculturalism* 9(1). 24–51.

Children's books and films

Awdry, Wilbert. 2000. *Thomas and James*. (Adapted from *Thomas and the breakdown train* [1946]). London: Egmont Children's Books.

Camp, Lindsay (text) & Ross, Tony (illustrations). 1988. *Why?* London: Andersen Press.

Campbell, Rod. 1982. *Dear Zoo*. London: Campbell Books.

Donaldson, Julia (text) & Monks, Lydia (illustrations). 2003. *Sharing a shell*. London: Macmillan.

Donaldson, Julia (text) & Scheffler, Alex (illustrations). 2007. *The Gruffalo's child*. London: Macmillan.

Donaldson, Julia (text) & Sharrat, Nick (illustrations). 2006. *Chocolate mousse for greedy goose*. London. Macmillan.

Henley, Claire (text) & Sully, Katherine (illustrations). 2001. *It's time for dinner*. London: Marks and Spencer.

Kerr, Judith. 1968. *The tiger who came to tea*. London: Harper Collins.

King-Smith, Dick (text) & Davies, Jo (illustrations). 2002. *Dumpling*. London: Puffin.

Sanders, Alex. 2001. *Toutes les couleurs*. Paris: Ecole des Loisirs. Children's television programmes and films

Balamory: Daisy bus days. 2005. CBBC Scotland. DVD.

La belle au bois dormant. 1959. Walt Disney. DVD.

Oswald: A sticky situation. 2004. Viacom International and HIT Entertainment PLC. DVD

Sleeping beauty. 1994. Abbey Home Media. DVD.

Teletubbies. 1997–2001. *CBBC. Television.*

The Gruffalo's child. 2011. Orange Eyes Limited. DVD.

HuiPing Chan, Wander Lowie & Kees de Bot

Input outside the classroom and vocabulary development: A dynamic perspective

Abstract: Facilitated by the Internet, smart phones, and computers, input outside the classroom is increasingly becoming an essential means of promoting
second language acquisition. These channels increase the exposure opportunities for learners of English and enable language learning independent of time
and place. The current longitudinal study describes the development of lexical
sophistication of four low-proficient English learners, who received differing
degrees of quantitative input over five months. We used a dynamic mathematical
model to explicitly investigate the three dynamically interacting factors that
shaped the process of the lexical development: initial value, learning rate, and
carrying capacity. Our results, focusing on the process rather than the product
of vocabulary learning, demonstrate that each learner's vocabulary learning
process was variably dependent on input outside the classroom.

Keywords: vocabulary learning, language modeling, dynamic systems theory

1 Introduction

Both the frequency (quantity) and quality of the input are crucial for the successful development of a second language. However, in many classrooms
around the world, English language instruction often occurs within a non-
authentic context. In Taiwan, language learning syllabi are constructed around
the grammar-translation method, and the main focus is on word-list translation
or textbook reading. Whilst students attend eight hours of English classes a
week, they rarely hear a complete English sentence or produce any spoken
English themselves. This level of in-class English input is not quantitatively sufficient in terms of the number of repetitions necessary to memorize new vocabulary. In addition, it does not qualitatively support contextual comprehension of
the words.

Receiving input outside the classroom could potentially overcome the short-
comings of such English classes in Taiwan. Exposure to English in an unstruc-
tured setting increases the amount of input learners receive, which in turn
increases the number of words learners are exposed to. Learners can watch

English episodes, listen to English radio, read online news, play online games, and chat on Facebook. These sources, combined with the ubiquity of TV, computers, iPads, or smart phones, have resulted in an environment where learners can receive English input whenever and wherever they choose. These rich and varied opportunities could potentially lead to an improvement of the learners' English proficiency beyond in-class learning.

The importance of input outside the classroom has been emphasized in several studies. Xu (2010) found that input outside the classroom is influential in supporting the retention of English words. Dutch learners, who receive lots of English input in everyday life, have a higher retention rate of English words than Chinese learners, who have limited access to authentic English input in everyday life. Another study in the Netherlands (de Bot et al. 2004) elucidated the factors determining the English proficiency of thirteen to sixteen-year old lower secondary pupils. 1574 pupils were tested on four skills of English proficiency: listening ability, reading ability, speaking ability, and writing ability. This study showed that the prime determiner of English proficiency was not school-based teaching but rather exposure to English through the media (TV, music, computers, and the internet) outside the classroom. Listening to pop songs, especially when the listener understood the lyrics, had a strong effect on their aural comprehension skills. Watching TV programs, with either English subtitles or spoken English, also had an impact on language proficiency, especially on listening ability.

These findings reflect the main argument of Ellis (2002) and Larsen-Freeman (2002) in that the input, operationalized as the frequency of occurrence, is key in successful language acquisition. The ability to use English fluently can be seen as a cumulative effect of interacting within an authentic English environment. The more learners connect themselves with a naturalistic English context (environment), the more likely they are to develop a good command of English. With increased amounts of contact time with English through various channels outside the classroom, learners enhance the possibility of successfully learning English.

However, the large-scale quantitative studies reported on earlier have not been able to provide a satisfactory explanation of what exactly occurred during the language learning process. The explanatory power of the study by de Bot et al. (2004) was limited, as only 14% of the variance was explained. Moreover, these and other studies have concentrated on the outcomes of the process (i.e. the product), rather than on the process itself. Therefore, a more detailed study is needed in which learners are followed extensively and longitudinally to observe the development of language over time. It is not feasible to carry out such research at a large scale due to limited time and resources. A smaller-scale longitudinal study should, however, be able to give us sufficient insight into the real-time process of language learning as it is influenced by input outside the classroom. The developmental process can be investigated by the longitudinal data with the application of a dynamic mathematical model. In this context, our study intends to answer three research questions:

1. Do learners of English improve the quality of their written language samples (operationalized in terms of lexical sophistication) when they receive additional exposure to input outside the classroom?
2. Does the quality of the written language samples (operationalized in terms of lexical sophistication) of learners of English decrease when the learners receive reduced exposure to input outside the classroom?
3. Can the logistic model meaningfully interpret the development of lexical sophistication for each individual learner?

We followed four Taiwanese learners of English longitudinally for five months, who produced a time series of fifty-six pieces of writing. These pieces of writing were analysed as an indication of the development of the learners' lexical sophistication. We then compared the writing development (in terms of lexical sophistication) with the differing degrees of amount of input the learners had received outside the classroom.

This paper begins with a general review of research into vocabulary learning and focuses on the differences between our study and previous studies on this issue, followed by a focus on vocabulary learning from a dynamic systems theory perspective. The description of data collection combines detailed information regarding the participants, the materials, and the procedures with the time series of writing production. Finally, the analyses and results pertaining to the concepts of dynamic systems theory lead to the discussion and conclusions about the application of a dynamic approach to investigating the influence of input outside the classroom on lexical sophistication.

2 Vocabulary learning

2.1 Lexical sophistication

Vocabulary has long played an essential role in studies of second language acquisition. Learners of English need around 8000 to 9000 word families (all morphologically related lexical items are counted as one family) for a coverage of about 98% of authentic texts such as novels or newspapers (Nation 2006). As for listening comprehension, they need about 90% coverage of the vocabulary to sufficiently understand the spoken discourse (Laufer 1989). A large number of lexical items are required to read and comprehend English as a second language. The number of lexical items, referred to as vocabulary size, is regarded as an important indicator of the capacity to operate in English.

The use of Lexical Frequency Profiles (LFP), developed by Laufer and Nation in 1995, is an approach to estimating the productive vocabulary size of English learners from their writings. LFP generates a profile of the writing productions by describing the lexical content of the text in terms of frequency bands. For example, a profile of a writing production could report that 92% of the vocabulary falls in the frequency band of 1 to 1000, 5% of the vocabulary falls in the frequency band of 1001 to 2000, and 3% of the vocabulary falls in the frequency band of 2001 to 3000. Calculating the percentage of the vocabulary that falls into each frequency band makes it possible to characterize each text in a standardized way. However, Meara (2005) argues that whilst LFP may be able to distinguish the differing percentages of lexical items within each frequency band that occur between beginning and intermediate learners of English, it may not be able to detect small differences between the texts generated by the same learner during the same period. That is, we may not find a significantly different percentage of lexical items in LFP within one individual learner because the features of the writing productions by the same learner during the same period are identical. Therefore, a longitudinal study of intensive writing productions, based on an average of two to three observations per week, may not generate a significant improvement in different frequency bands in the LFP.

V-Size (Meara and Miralpeix 2004) is an alternative approach to estimating vocabulary size from writing samples. V-size gives an indication of the productive vocabulary size of the subjects who produced the text by shaping the text profile directly. Take, for example, pieces of writing of a subject who has a productive vocabulary of approximately 3000 words. V-size assumes that a learner with a smaller vocabulary size will use more frequent lexical items while a learner with a larger vocabulary size will use more infrequent lexical items. Applying Zipf's law (1935), V-Size fits the number of words in different frequency bands with the mathematical model generated from Zipf's law and generates one value indicating the level of lexical sophistication, i.e. vocabulary size. The higher the value of vocabulary size, the higher the lexical sophistication is. V-size allows us to explore the characteristics of the texts produced by subjects who use different levels of vocabulary.

2.2 Intentional and incidental vocabulary learning

To enlarge the number of the lexical items, two major approaches to acquiring vocabulary have been investigated, i.e. intentional and incidental vocabulary learning. Intentional vocabulary learning (explicitly drawing the learners' attention to the lexical items themselves) is especially effective for the retention of words. Smith (2004) found that learners retained more novel lexical items that were learnt in an Internet chat program, in which words were largely used through the interaction between the subjects. Walter and Bozkurt (2009) also found that learners have better retention of words when the words on the notebook are first previewed and later incorporated in the classroom. Maximizing the engagement with words is the main principle in designing intentional learning activities (Schmitt 2008).

On the other hand, incidental learning (implicitly exposing learners to meaning-focused input) increases the number of word repetitions and allows learners to consolidate their contextual knowledge of the vocabulary. Hulstijn and Laufer (2001) investigated the incidental learning that results from reading. They compared the short-term and long-term receptive vocabulary retention between three levels of involvement loads, i.e. reading comprehension, comprehension plus filling in target words, and composition-writing with target words. Their results showed that words which were processed with composition-writing were more successfully retained than words which were processed with comprehension or comprehension plus filling in target words. Knight (1994) also found that Spanish intermediate-level language learners increased their English vocabularies by reading and deducing meaning through guessing or using a dictionary. In the light of these studies, it can be argued that acquisition of vocabulary could be enhanced by intentionally or incidentally engaging learners with the words to greater degrees.

These studies, focusing on either intentional or incidental learning, mostly investigate what type of "in-class input" learners are engaged in and draw conclusions based on how many lexical items learners are able to recognize or produce after the treatment. However, the potential impact of natural exposure to English input on promoting the acquisition of vocabulary, especially with in-depth longitudinal observations, remains largely unknown. Input outside the classroom may potentially enhance vocabulary learning by exposing learners to the words more frequently, which would maximize their lexical engagement in a context-based environment and raise the chances for learners to retain and then produce the words themselves. Therefore, it would seem that there is a need for a study that investigates the potential effect of input outside the classroom on vocabulary acquisition.

Bulté and Housen (2012) systematically distinguished four different categories of lexical measures for the purpose of observing writing productions. They found that lexical diversity was the most common measure across or within the writing studies (e.g. type token ratio, D) in which the number of different words used in the writing productions is investigated. Other measures, such as lexical sophistication (measuring the difficulty level of word use), have not been as widely used as a complexity measure of writing productions. In our study, we focused more on lexical sophistication (the number of less frequent words used) than on lexical diversity, as we assume that the exposure to input outside the classroom may bring about more immediate effects on lexical sophistication than on lexical diversity.

3 Vocabulary development

3.1 A dynamic perspective of vocabulary development

The application of dynamic systems theory (DST) to the study of second language development includes several basic characteristics (de Bot and Larsen-Freeman 2011). One of the starting points of the dynamic systems approach is that there is a sensitive dependence on the initial conditions of the individual. It features a non-linear development with interconnected variables, and these variables change through internal reorganization and interaction with the environment. *Dynamic*, in fact, refers to the changes that occur in a system as a result of internal forces and "energy from outside itself" (de Bot and Larsen-Freeman 2011: 8).

DST has been applied to first and second language learning (Larsen-Freeman and Cameron 2008; Larsen-Freeman 2006; van Geert and Steenbeek 2005) and human cognitive systems (Elman 2004; Spivey 2007). These studies intend to depict the tendencies, patterns, and contingencies of language development, which is iterative, non-linear, time-dependent, and interconnected. These are also the key characteristics assumed by DST.

3.2 Modelling vocabulary development

One way of investigating dynamic development is to build a mathematical model that quantifies the dynamic relationships between the variables. To apply a mathematical model, we start by observing the developmental patterns of the data. This helps us determine which mathematical model we could choose to describe the trajectory. The trajectory generated from the model must resemble the trajectory of the data. Second, we look into the theoretical background of the model, which must be compatible with the concepts on which our data is based: iterativity, non-linearity, and time-dependency.

Vocabulary development as a dynamic non-linear process is iterative, and is limited by the availability of resources. The size of the vocabulary in time $t + 1$ depends on time t, which implies that each data point depends on the previous data point in time. The way in which the variables interact unfolds step by step. Learners have a limited learning capacity (working memory), limited input (external resource), and limited motivation. Consequently, the vocabulary does not increase infinitely but stagnates in the end. The logistic model presents a dynamic theoretical equation where it models iterative growth and allows us to model on the basis of initial conditions, carrying capacity, and learning rate.

The logistic model was originally used to describe the population growth over time by Verhulst (1845). The population varying over time can be described as:

$$dP/dt = rP(1 - P/K)$$

Equation 1: Population logistic model equation

The left part of the equation demonstrates that the population (P) changes with time (t). The right part of the equation demonstrates that the growth rate of the population (r) changes with time and that the population (P) is limited by its resources (K).

The pattern of the logistic model is likely to match that of vocabulary development in that the development is slow in the initial state, is faster in the middle state, and is slow again when the maximum capacity is approached in the final state. This is demonstrated in Figure 1. The growth pattern changes with three variables: the initial value (the beginning value of the development), the learning rate (the slope of the development), and the carrying capacity (the maximum final value of the development). We illustrated how the adjusted values of three variables change the trajectory in Figure 1. When changing the value of the carrying capacity (K) from 1 to 1.5 and holding other parameters constant, we find the difference between line 3 and line 1. Changing the value of the learning rate from 0.3 to 0.4 and holding other parameters constant, we find the difference between line 3 and line 4. Changing the initial value (the beginning value of the development) from 1.2 to 2.0 and holding other parameters constant, we find the difference between line 3 and line 2.

Previous applications of logistic equation modelling have shed important light on the dynamic interactions of components within dynamic systems. Caspi

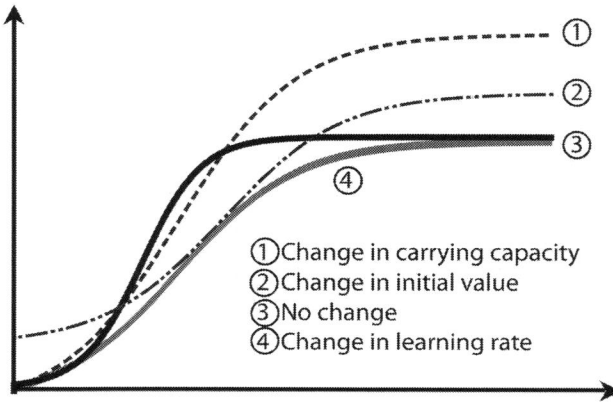

Figure 1: The change in the trajectory of adjusted values of three variables

(2010) utilized the logistic model to describe the academic vocabulary development of four advanced learners of English. She found that the more receptive vocabulary knowledge acted as a conditional precursor for the more productive vocabulary knowledge. Chan (2010) used the logistic model to describe the vocabulary development of three different levels of vocabulary knowledge for learners of English. In both studies, the logistic model successfully interprets the vocabulary development of different levels of vocabulary knowledge using three variables: initial value, learning rate, and carrying capacity. The carrying capacity represents all of the learner's resources in the time frame.

4 The study

4.1 Method

We followed four beginning learners of English for five months through their log of input outside the classroom and their fifty-six pieces of writing. Based on their logs and the input given by the experimenter, we defined low, intermediate, and high degrees of input outside the classroom, operationalized as hours of English input per week. The learners freely produced two to three pieces of writing per week without any time limit on a Facebook writing club that was set up for the experiment. Measuring the lexical sophistication (with the measure of V-size) from their writing productions, we observed the general trajectory of the data, smoothed it, fitted the smoothed data with the logistic model, and then obtained the value of the three variables. We also compared the mean V-size with high, intermediate, and low degrees of input exposure.

4.2 Participants

Four Taiwanese beginning learners of English participated in the study: Skid, Grace, Gloria, and Tina. At the start of the experiment, their receptive vocabulary size was approximately 2260 words, according to the General English Proficiency Test they passed (Wu 2012). This figure (2260) provided us with a rough idea of the English proficiency level of these learners. Through interviewing the subjects' English teacher, several details were already known about the participants. Skid (age 32) could read well, but could not comprehend fast-paced English conversation, speak fluently, or write smoothly. Tina, Grace, and Gloria (age 15) were very close friends. They had an equal capacity in four aspects of English: speaking, listening, writing, and reading. Tina was particularly good at speaking fluently, and Gloria was particularly good at writing error-free sentences.

4.3 Materials

The four learners made use of five material resources. They read online news written for ESL learners on Breaking News English, watched free online movies in English with Chinese subtitles on Tube+, watched the latest English music videos on YouTube, chatted with friends on Facebook in English, and listened to English songs with iTunes. Among the five resources, movies and readings constituted the two main types of English input.

In this study, the larger part of the input was experimentally manipulated; some of the input was selected by the participants themselves. We kept track of the learners' input from their logs, which convey the history of input outside the classroom. The participants wrote down what type of input (e.g. movie), how long they were exposed to the input (e.g. 2 hours), and what they did with the input (e.g. "I looked up two words from the movie"). The fifty-six written language samples were analysed as an indication of the learners' development of lexical sophistication.

4.4 Input stages

From the participants' logs, we categorized three degrees of input outside the classroom: low (less than 2 hours of English input per week), intermediate (2 to 5 hours of English input per week), and high (more than nine hours of English input per week). Within five months, Skid went from a low level of input to an intermediate level of input, mostly receiving the input from movies and reading.

Tina, Grace, and Gloria spent most of their time together and went from a low level of input to an intermediate level (mostly through reading), then a high level, and then back to an intermediate level (mostly through movies).

In the first stage, classified as low input, where Skid completed writing productions 1 to 19, he did not have any English input. In the second (intermediate) stage, from writing productions 20 to 38, he mostly watched movies as English input. In the third (still intermediate) stage, from writing productions 39 to 56, he mostly read online news as English input.

In their first, low-input stage, from writing productions 1 to 10, Tina, Grace, and Gloria only had English songs as their English input. In the second (intermediate) stage, from writing productions 11 to 20, they mostly read online news as their main English input. In the third stage, from writing productions 21 to 37, they read online articles every day, watched two to three English movies a week, and frequently chatted with friends on Facebook or face-to-face in English. This was the stage with a high-level of input. In the fourth stage, from writing productions 38 to 56, they fell back down to an intermediate level of input, watching two English movies per week as their main source of English input.

4.5 Writing tasks

The four participants wrote approximately 200 words for each piece of writing. The topics of the 56 pieces of writing were all TOEFL writing topics[1]. These topics were related to expressing opinions, for instance agreeing or disagreeing with a statement, or comparing the advantages and disadvantages of a particular subject. For example, they produced one writing piece on comparing the advantages of having friends who are different from them with the advantages of having friends who are similar to them. They also produced another writing piece on whether they agree with the statement that parents are the best teachers. For our intensive longitudinal study, it was important to keep the level of difficulty of different writing topics consistent. These topics, which are highly related to the learners' life experience, could potentially elicit an equal amount of words from each learner. Although the topics varied, they were invariably general in nature and required little topic-specific vocabulary. Moreover, as our participants had a comparatively small vocabulary pool, the topics were limited in word choice and thus many of the words used largely overlapped.

---

1 TOEFL writing topics can be found here: http://www.ets.org/Media/Tests/TOEFL/pdf/989563wt.pdf

4.6 Procedure

Over five months, the four participants posted two to three 200-word pieces of writing per week on a Facebook writing club set up for the purpose of the experiment. Participants were able to read each other's posts and to comment on what they had read or written. As could be observed from the content of the pieces of writing, the four participants demonstrated very little imitation of each other's work. Some of the participants may have learnt new vocabulary from the productions of the other participants, but this new vocabulary could also have been learnt from alternative English input. Regardless, there was no significant evidence of imitation apparent in the writing productions. The participants could choose whether or not to respond to each other if they received feedback on their posts. There was no requirement to correct their grammatical or lexical errors.

All writing productions were transformed into text files, so we could utilize V-size v2.0 (Meara and Miralpeix 2004) to estimate the development of lexical sophistication with the value generated from this tool, i.e. vocabulary size. Following the guide of V-size, errors including incorrectly spelt words were excluded from the text; proper names, like Taiwan and Japan, were recoded as the highest frequency band to avoid an overestimation of the productive vocabulary size; hyphenated words, e.g. *well-known*, are counted as two words in V_size, thus we edited these down to one word.

4.7 Design and analyses

We assumed that our four participants would increase their lexical sophistication (V-size) whilst receiving more input outside the classroom and that the development of lexical sophistication would be stagnant during the phase of no exposure to input outside the classroom. We closely observed the learners' amount of input outside the classroom from their logs and analysed their writing productions in terms of lexical sophistication. In order to construct a dynamic concept of the development, each individual, taken as a constantly changing complex system, has a set of variables that interact over time. In our study, two variables were selected for observation: the amount of input outside the classroom, and the vocabulary in the written language samples, operationalised as lexical sophistication. The basic assumption was that with more contact with an English context, learners would increase their lexical sophistication over time, while with less input outside the classroom, learners' lexical sophistication would be stagnant or even decrease. Input outside the classroom is supposed to interact with the writing productions over time, causing change in the individual's complex system. Input outside the classroom is assumed to promote the use of more advanced words in the writings; in turn the writings, consolidating the use of the words, may facilitate the comprehension of the input outside the classroom at the next time point. The previous output (writing productions) becomes the current input. This concept of a constantly changing, interacting, and self-organising complex system is an essential characteristic of dynamic systems theory.

Our study attempts to reveal the relative importance of the interconnected variables, i.e. input outside the classroom and vocabulary development. We will describe the system in which the development is iterative and the pattern is non-linear through modelling. In order to do so we first observed the developmental patterns in the data and decided that the logistic model was suitable for our study. Further research into the theoretical background of the model demonstrated that it was compatible with the concepts on which our data is based, i.e. iterativity, non-linearity, and time-dependency. Applying the logistic model to interpreting the trajectory of the data enables us to obtain the values of the three main variables, which meaningfully quantify the vocabulary development.

4.8 The modelling procedure

The general impression of the first look at the trajectory is usually fluctuant as there is a lot of variability. It is natural to find variability in the trajectory as there are many factors influencing the performance of the learners. However, to obtain a clearer idea of what the general trajectory looks like, it is necessary to remove some of the variability from the data sets, whilst at the same time ensuring there is no loss of crucial information from the data. One technique to remove the variability is data smoothing. We opted for one commonly accepted smoothing method, i.e. smoothing spline (Green and Silverman 1994), which locally fits a cubic smoothing spline to the data sets and is more dynamic than creating linear trendlines.

After obtaining the smoothed data, we proceed with the model fitting. In order to fit the logistic model with the smoothed data in order to obtain the values of the three variables. To find the best fitting, the smallest difference between the logistic model and the smoothed data must be ascertained. This difference usually refers to the smallest sum of squares. The values of the three variables are entered into the equation of the logistic model to generate the model trajectory, and the difference between the model trajectory and the smoothed trajectory is calculated in terms of the sum of squares. This process is repeated until the smallest sum of squares is found. It is not feasible to manually enter the values of three variables thousands of times to find the least sum square. A curve-fitting program, Amoeba (Press et al. 1986) is applied to execute the fitting task to automatically find the smallest sum of squares and then generate the values of the three variables.

5 Results

We intended to investigate how the lexical sophistication (represented by the measure of V-size) of writings was affected by different degrees of input outside the classroom. We first observed the trajectory of the data and the smoothed data of the V-size, then obtained the values of the three variables (initial value, learning rate, and the carrying capacity) in order to determine the logistic model, and then compared the mean V-size for each degree (low, intermediate, high) of English input.

5.1 Developmental trajectory

The development of raw data is depicted in Figure 2. Skid's data has more variability than the other three participants' data. Tina's, Grace's, and Gloria's data

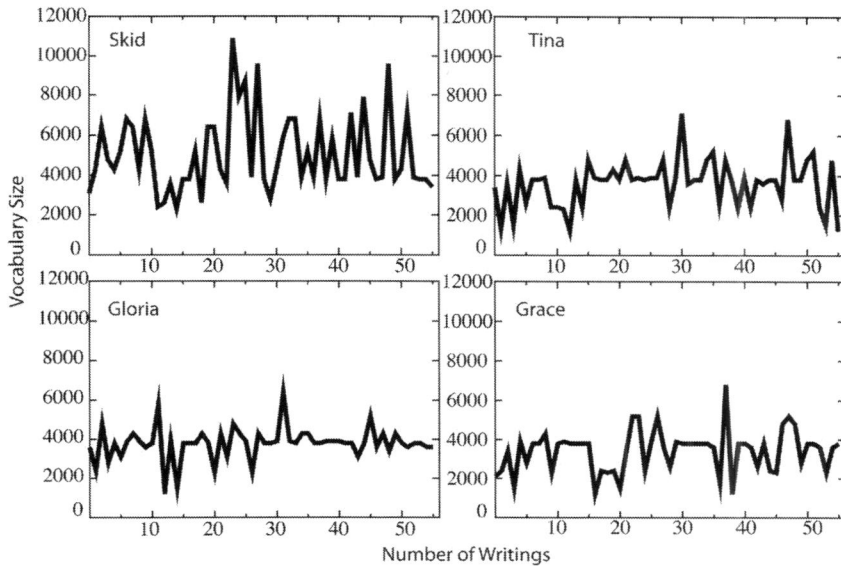

Figure 2: Trajectory of the measure of lexical sophistication (V-size) of the four learners

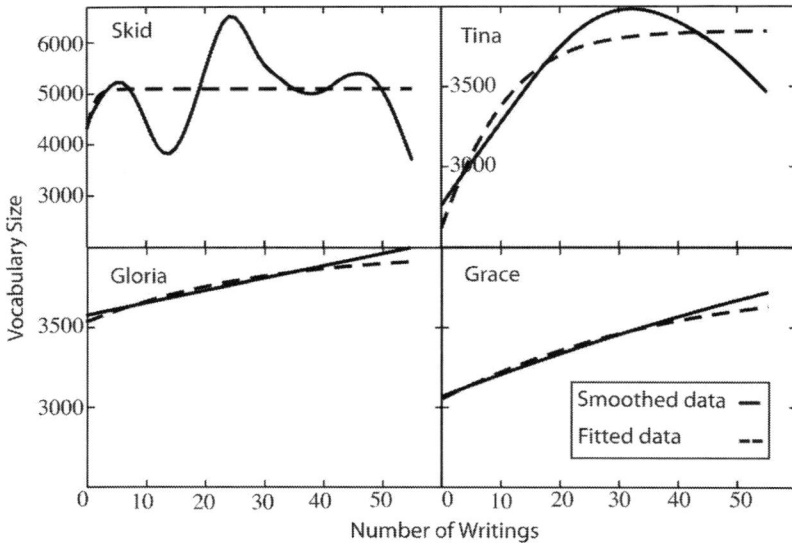

Figure 3: Smoothed and fitted data of V-size of the four learners

has fewer fluctuations, indicating that their writing performance was more stable than Skid's. However, the trajectories of the data did not give us a clear picture of the development of V-size due to the high variability and the scale. We obtained the smoothed data, leaving out some variability, to gain a clearer idea of how to explore the trend of the development.

5.2 Developmental trajectory of smoothed data

The trajectory of smoothed data is depicted in Figure 3 in the form of solid lines. Skid's smoothed data is still more variable than the other three participants'; Tina's data shows an s-curve pattern in the logistic model; Gloria's and Grace's data is identical, showing as an increasing line. We could conclude that the four learners in our study, judging from their writing productions, had increased their V-size values over the five-month period.

5.3 Parameter values of the model fitting

By fitting the smoothed data with the logistic model, we were able to obtain the values of the three variables determining the development of V-size. We first had to ascertain whether the fitting was good enough to interpret the data. The trajectory of the fitted data (dashed line) is depicted in Figure 3 together with the smoothed data (solid line). As can be seen, the logistic model did not capture the entirety of Skid's developmental pattern. There is great disparity between the trajectory of the smoothed data and that of the fitted data (the model). However, the logistic model fits well with the smoothed data of the other three participants.

The values of the three variables (initial value, learning rate, and carrying capacity) generated from the model fitting are displayed in Table 1. Since the smoothed data from Tina, Grace, and Gloria demonstrated a good fit with the model, we were able to use the logistic model to describe their lexical sophistication in terms of V-size. Tina had a lower initial value of V-size; she had a value of 2732 words to produce. However, she had a higher learning rate (0.119), and was therefore able to produce almost the same number of words (3846) as Gloria and Grace (3973 and 3778 words). Tina's V-size increased when receiving increasing amounts of input outside the classroom (data point 1 to 17) but started to stagnate in episode 38, which was about the moment that the input outside the classroom became much less than in previous periods. We could conclude that since Tina's V-size increased with the higher degree of English input, but also decreased with the lower degree of English input, Tina was sensitive to the volume of input she was exposed to.

Table 1: Values of the three variables for the four learners

Learner's name	Initial value	Learning rate	Carrying capacity
Skid	4307	1	5094
Tina	2732	0.119	3846
Gloria	3531	0.03	3973
Grace	3070	0.03	3778

Gloria had a V-Size value of 3531 words at the beginning of the experiment. These values increased with a lower learning rate (0.03) but steadily reached 3973 after the increasing exposure to input outside the classroom. Grace had a V-size value of 3070 words at the beginning. Her V-size grew with the same learning rate as Gloria's (0.03) and ended up as 3778 with the increasing volume of English input. We can conclude that Gloria and Grace were less sensitive to the volume of input outside the classroom than Tina.

Skid's model showed a relatively poor fitting, as it did not fit well with the smoothed data. As can be observed from Figure 3, the logistic model was able to describe the initial value accurately but failed to capture the learning rate and the carrying capacity, since the development pattern of the data in the middle and the final stage largely deviated from the expected pattern of the logistic model. A very high learning rate was generated from the model fitting and the carrying capacity reached its final value at a very early stage. In other words, the logistic model generally did not reflect the reality in Skid's data set. Therefore, we can only state that Skid had a level of 4307 V-size at the beginning of the experiment.

5.4 Mean of V-size in each input stage

We show the mean of V-size in each input stage along with the timeline in Table 2 and 3. Skid's V-size, even during the period of low input, still increased through reflection and practice of the words, which he originally knew receptively but started to produce in his writing. Skid was highly motivated by the input from movies, where his V-size grew by about 1469 words in size. However, Skid was less motivated by the input from online articles and his V-size decreased by 979 words.

Table 2: Mean of V-size in each input stage of Skid

Stage	1	2	3
Writing number	1–19	20–38	39–56
Input volume	Low	Intermediate movie	Intermediate reading
Mean of V-size	4415	5884	4905

Table 3: Mean of V-Size in each input stage of Tina, Gloria, and Grace

Stage	1	2	3	4
Writing number	1–10	11–20	21–37	38–56
Input volume	Low	Intermediate Reading	High	Intermediate movie
Mean of V-size (Tina)	3060	3270	4111	3652
Mean of V-size (Gloria)	3620	3570	3958	3842
Mean of V-size (Grace)	3030	3120	3600	3621

During the low input period, Tina's V-size did not grow, but it increased by 210 words when receiving intermediate input from reading online news and by 841 words when receiving high input. When receiving less input in the last period, her V-size reduced by 459 words. Tina showed that she was sensitive to the volume of input, i.e. the more she was exposed to English input, the more her V-size increased. From her writings, we found that she liked to use new words gained from chats with friends in her writing, especially the more native-like chunks. Her writings reflected her preferred way of saying things while interacting with other people in English, because she liked to sound and speak like a native speaker.

During the low input and the intermediate input period, Gloria's V-size did not grow, but it increased by 388 words in the high input stage. Her V-size reduced by 116 words in the last intermediate input stage when she received less input than during the previous stage. Gloria only showed a slight growth in the high input period; she was less sensitive to the volume of input, showed a stable learning curve, and carefully used new words gained from reading online news, especially words of low frequency.

Grace's V-size, even during the low input period, gradually increased, but her growth slowed down during the following intermediate input period. Her V-size increased by 480 when receiving high input, and she was able to retain her words in the following intermediate input period with a difference of only 21 words. On the other hand, the data suggested that Grace had a delayed effect from the exposure to input. Her V-size tended to grow, to stabilize, to grow again, and to stabilize again. From her writing productions, we found that she usually only used the words she already knew very well and only started to use new words when she was completely confident in how to use them correctly. This pattern may explain the delayed effect of the exposure to the input on V-size.

5.5 Summary of results

The first research question asked whether learners of English developed their writing in terms of lexical sophistication (represented by the measure of V-size) with more exposure to input outside of the classroom. The increase of lexical sophistication was determined by the difference between the carrying capacity (the final vocabulary size learners reached) and the initial value (the beginning vocabulary size learners held). Their V-size values increased by about five-hundred words in a period of five months with extra incidental English input, mostly from movies and reading. Since the learning conditions for these learners were otherwise very similar, it is unlikely that this effect was caused by external intervening variables.

The second research question asked whether the learners of English decreased their lexical sophistication with less exposure to input outside the classroom. The decrease of lexical sophistication was determined by the difference between the mean of lexical sophistication in the earlier stage (high input stage) and the mean in the later stage (low input stage). Tina, sensitive to the volume of input, demonstrated an immediate decrease in her lexical sophistication.

Grace's and Gloria's lexical sophistication did not decrease immediately, as there may have been a delayed learning effect from the input on their writings.

The third research question asked whether the logistic model could meaningfully interpret the development of lexical sophistication for these four learners. We found that the model fitting was ideal in Tina's, Gloria's, and Grace's data. The values of the three variables of initial value, learning rate, and carrying capacity, were sufficiently meaningful to describe the lexical development of these three learners. Skid's data, however, did not demonstrate a trajectory similar to the logistic model. We were only able to use the initial value to describe Skid's beginning state of the lexical development.

6 Discussion

The objective of this study was to find out in what way input outside the classroom influences the quality of writing productions, which was operationalized in terms of lexical sophistication. The logistic model analysis showed that three of the participants in our study (Tina, Gloria, and Grace) developed their lexical sophistication with input outside the classroom. They did not have equivalent initial values of lexical sophistication but reached approximately the same degree of lexical sophistication by the end of the experiment due to different learning rates. We could argue that the differences in sensitivity to the volume of English input between the three different learners were determined by the learning rate. Tina's vocabulary development demonstrated a higher learning rate; apparently, she was more sensitive to input outside the classroom than Grace and Gloria, whose learning rates were lower. Skid's lexical development did not progress in the same way as the other three participants'. His vocabulary development showed considerable variability. In fact, his smoothed data indicated that there might be three overlapping logistic models. A single logistic model could not capture all of the characteristics of his lexical development.

The logistic model successfully quantified the development of lexical sophistication for Tina, Gloria, and Grace with the three variables, i.e, initial value, learning rate, and carrying capacity. The values of these three variables enabled us to make explicit observations of how input outside the classroom influences lexical development. However, this preliminary model of L2 lexical development was not able to represent Skid's data. We should consider at least two more variables in the equation of the logistic model: the quantity of input and the quality of input. When the quantity of the input is lowered to a certain level, the lexicon not only ceases to grow but also begins to decrease. Additionally, the quality of the input, determined by the absolute value of the difficulty of input and the level of learners' vocabulary size, could influence the lexical development. These two concepts have not yet been included in our current logistic model.

The variability of the data is relatively large within each individual. One factor that may have contributed to this variability may be found in the nature of the V-size measure in combination with a change of the individual's writing over time. For instance, Skid had the tendency to often use low frequency words that he had incidentally acquired receptively. Since V-size is very sensitive to words in low frequency bands, these fluctuations rather strongly affect the variability in Skid's data. For all learners, the length of the writing samples generally decreased over time, which may also have influenced the amount of variability in the data.

The other factor that may have led to the high variability is the topic of the writing tasks. Although all topics were general and did not require much specific vocabulary, the performance of the writings on different types of topics may depend on personal experience and preferences. This is an inherent challenge for all studies that use longitudinal approaches to investigating writings in a natural environment. Our study looked at the beginning learners of English, who have a limited number of lexical items, with only the focus on the topics related to their life experience. The effect of writing topic cannot be avoided, and we have tried to minimize it by giving rather simple types of writing topics.

The lexical sophistication increased by about 500 in V-size value through incidental English input over five months. The time window of the observation may not have been long enough for learners to show a larger growth in lexical sophistication, especially when looking at productive lexical sophistication. Learners may receptively know some words partially and then may have a more thorough understanding of the words through input or may activate the words through input. However, learners may also acquire some new words, yet may not be able to use them productively in a text. The time window of this study may not have been long enough to allow for incidental learning by simply watching movies and reading online news. We will continue to collect the writings of these participants to extend the time scale of the observations.

7 Conclusions

This study has investigated how the development of L2 lexical sophistication interacts with input outside the classroom. We have used the logistic model to account for the lexical development. This model quantifies the important components determining lexical development, which are the initial value, the learning rate, and the carrying capacity. Though the preliminary logistic model was not able to describe the vocabulary development of one participant, the trajectory of this participant indicated two possible variables to be added in the equation of the logistic model, the quantitative input, i.e. the total amount of input exposure, and the qualitative input, i.e. the degree to which learners absorb the vocabulary from the exposure.

Learners with input outside the classroom kept themselves in an English context, and benefited from having more opportunities for using English than without the additional input. With pure incidental English input in the form of movies and online reading, the increase of lexical sophistication was approximately 500 words in five months. Although this longitudinal study has collected data on a relatively short-term time scale, it has explored the microscopic level of understanding the actual lexical development. Our study attempts to complement earlier vocabulary learning studies by going beyond a static means of looking at the data to an understanding of the dynamics of the vocabulary learning process as it develops over time.

References

Bulté, Bram & Alex Housen. 2012. Defining and operationalising L2 complexity. In Alex Housen, Folkert Kuiken & Ineke Vedder (eds.), *Dimensions of L2 performance and proficiency*, 21–46. Amsterdam/Philadelphia: John Benjamins.

Caspi, Tal. 2010. *A dynamic perspective on second language development*. Netherlands, Groningen: University of Groningen dissertation.

Chan, HuiPing. 2010. *Testing the effectiveness of computer assisted language learning website: WordChamp*. Netherlands, Groningen: University of Groningen MA thesis.

de Bot, Kees, Petey de Quay-Peeters & Riet Evers. 2004. *English proficiency in lower secondary education: A cross-national comparison. Final report*. Netherlands, Nijmegen: Department of Applied Linguistics, University of Nijmegen. Retrieved from http://books.google.ch/books?id=X8aAGwAACAAJ (Accessed 15 April 2014).

de Bot, Kees & Diane Larsen-Freeman. 2011. A dynamic approach to second language development: Methods and techniques. In Marjolijn Verspoor, Wander Lowie & Kees de Bot (eds.), *Researching second language development from a dynamic systems theory perspective*, 5–24. Amsterdam/Philadelphia: John Benjamins.

Ellis, Nick C. 2002. Frequency effects in language processing. *Studies in Second Language Acquisition* 24(2). 143–188. doi:http://dx.doi.org/10.1017/S0272263102002024

Elman, Jeffrey L. 2004. An alternative view of the mental lexicon. *Trends in Cognitive Sciences* 8(7). 301–306. doi:http://dx.doi.org/10.1016/j.tics.2004.05.003

Green, Peter J. & Bernard W. Silverman. 1994. *Nonparametric regression and generalized linear models: A roughness penalty approach*. London: Chapman and Hall.

Hulstijn, Jan & Batia Laufer. 2001. Some empirical evidence for the involvement load hypothesis in vocabulary acquisition. *Language Learning* 51(3). 539–558. doi:10.1111/00238333.00164

Knight, Susan. 1994. Dictionary use while reading: The effects on comprehension and vocabulary acquisition for students of different verbal abilities. *The Modern Language Journal* 78(3). 285–299. doi:http://dx.doi.org/10.2307/330108

Larsen-Freeman, Diane & Lynne Cameron. 2008. *Complex systems and applied linguistics.* Oxford: Oxford University Press.

Larsen-Freeman, Diane. 2002. Making sense of frequency. *Studies in Second Language Acquisition* 24(2). 275–285. doi:http://dx.doi.org/10.1017/S0272263102002127

Larsen-Freeman, Diane. 2006. The emergence of complexity, fluency, and accuracy in the oral and written production of five Chinese learners of English. *Applied Linguistics* 27(4). 590–619. doi:10.1093/applin/aml029

Laufer, Batia. 1989. What percentage of text-lexis is essential for comprehension? In Christer Laurén & Marianne Nordman (eds.), *Special language: From humans thinking to thinking machines,* 316–323. Clevendon/Philadelphia: Multilingual Matters.

Levelt, Willem J. M. 1989. *Speaking: From intention to articulation.* Cambridge, MA: Bradford Books.

Meara, Paul. 2005. Lexical frequency profiles: A Monte Carlo analysis. *Applied Linguistics* 26(1). 32–47. doi:http://dx.doi.org/10.1093/applin/amh037

Meara, Paul & Irma Miralpeix. 2004. *V_size.* Retrieved from http://www.lognostics.co.uk (Accessed 15 April 2014).

Nation, I. S. P. 2006. How large a vocabulary is needed for reading and listening? *Canadian Modern Language Review* 63(1). 59–82. doi:http://dx.doi.org/10.3138/cmlr.63.1.59

Press, William H., Saul A. Teukolsky, William T. Vetterling & Brian P. Flannery. 1986. *Numerical recipes: The art of scientific computing.* New York: Cambridge University Press.

Schmitt, Norbert. 2008. Review article: Instructed second language vocabulary learning. *Language Teaching Research* 12(3). 329–363. doi:10.1177/1362168808089921

Smith, Bryan. 2004. Computer-mediated negotiated interaction and lexical acquisition. *Studies in Second Language Acquisition* 26(3). 365–398. doi:http://dx.doi.org/10.1017/S027226310426301X

Spivey, Michael J. 2007. *The continuity of mind.* Oxford University Press.

Van Geert, Paul & Henderien Steenbeek. 2005. Explaining after by before: Basic aspects of a dynamic systems approach to the study of development. *Developmental Review* 25(3–4). 408–442. doi:http://dx.doi.org/10.1016/j.dr.2005.10.003

Verhulst, Pierre F. 1845. Recherches mathématiques sur la loi d'accroissement de la population. *Mémoires De L'Académie Royale Des Sciences Et Des Belles-Lettres De Bruxelles* 18(1). 1–45.

Walters, JoDee & Neval Bozkurt. 2009. The effect of keeping vocabulary notebooks on vocabulary acquisition. *Language Teaching Research* 13(4). 403–423. doi:http://dx.doi.org/10.1177/1362168809341509

Wu, Jessica R. W. 2012. GEPT and English language teaching and testing in Taiwan. *Language Assessment Quarterly* 9(1). 11–25. doi:10.1080/15434303.2011.553251

Xu, Xiaoyan. 2010. *English language attrition and retention in Chinese and Dutch university students.* Netherlands, Groningen: University of Groningen Dissertation.

Zipf, George K. 1935. *The psycho-biology of language.* Boston: Houghton Mifflin.

V Concluding remarks

Pieter Muysken
Fine tuning cross-linguistic interaction: The nuts and bolts

Abstract: The complexity of bilingual language use has led to the development of a range of empirical frameworks that are currently used by scholars. Interestingly, even scholars working within similar bilingual research traditions allow for a degree of variation in their terminological practice. My contribution addresses this phenomenon in the context of research presented in the current volume.

Keywords: linguistic terminology, bilingualism, diversity of approaches

1 Introduction

This very interesting book illustrates the diversity and range of approaches and themes found in the literature on multilingualism. It contains six contributions. On the one hand, there are studies on L2 development, i.e. István Kecskés' reflections on bilingual pragmatic competence and HuiPing Chan's (with Wander Lowie and Kees de Bot) dynamic perspective on the relation between input outside the classroom and vocabulary development. On the other hand, a second cluster is concerned with bilingual children. Antje Endesfelder Quick's study (with Elena Lieven and Michael Tomasello) of mixed NPs in German-English and German-Russian bilingual children, and Catrin Bellay's analysis of how French-English bilingual children use phrases from nursery rhymes, songs, stories, and children's television. The third cluster focuses on adult code-mixing and contains Nikolay Hakimov's insightful and sophisticated analysis of effects of frequency and word repetition on switch-placement in Russian-German code-mixing, and an exploration of viewing code-mixing from the perspective of Construction Grammar by Philipp Wasserscheidt. Reflecting the primarily European background (with one exception) of the authors, the language pairs involved are French-English, Russian-German, German-English, and English as L2 for Chinese learners in Taiwan.

As such, this book reflects the state of the discipline, which is characterized by a high degree of diversity in topics, subject groups, and approaches both during conferences and in collective volumes. I think many researchers in this area are attracted by this diversity. This certainly holds true for me. Is this diversity a good or a bad thing?

It is good in that the phenomenon of multilingualism is multi-faceted and requires a variety of perspectives – sociological, psychological, and linguistic (Muysken 1984). There are different kinds of multilingual populations, speaking a host of different languages, and showing many different types of contact phenomena. Also, policy implications involve anything from educational and legal to political and health issues.

However, this very diversity may also lead to a certain terminological imprecision, which may in turn lead to conceptual vagueness and insufficient integration of different perspectives. To give but a few examples:

–   The terms *language mixing, code-switching*, and *code-mixing* are sometimes used with identical, sometimes with different, meanings. Within this broad category, we find terms like *extra-sentential switching, tag-switching*, and *emblematic switching* sometimes used interchangeably, and sometimes used with different nuances.

–   A similar case involves *transfer, cross-linguistic influence, convergence, advergence* and similar terms. Sometimes these terms imply uni- or bi-directionality, sometimes they do not.

–   Yet a third example concerns the terms *host language, recipient language*, or *matrix language* versus *donor language, source language*, or *embedded language*.

–   The terms *system morpheme, functional category, function word*, and *functional element* are sometimes used interchangeably. Exactly what falls under the notion and whether it refers to concrete morphemes or more abstract entities is often left unspecified.

–   Finally, the word *cognate* refers to words in different languages having the same sound shape or orthography in psycholinguistics, and to historical reflexes in two languages of a common ancestral root in historical linguistics.

It is evident that researchers may be using the same term, but with slightly different denotations, or different terms with the same denotations. We would want a set of terms which (a) avoids redundancies, i.e. two words for the same concept, as much as possible; (b) clearly distinguishes the relevant separate empirical phenomena; and (c) has no overlaps. I do not pretend to solve this problem here on the spot, but would like to approach the six very interesting studies from this perspective, focusing on the terminology used, and where possible, the conceptual structure behind it.

I would like to make a final point before going on. I do not think we would want to sweep issues of substantial disagreement under the rug of terminological standardization. Notice I have not mentioned the issues regarding 'nonce borrowing' versus insertional code-mixing in the above list. There we have a conceptual issue at the very least, possibly with empirical implications.

By and large, the papers in this volume adopt what is generally referred to as a usage-based perspective. It would be interesting to see to what extent this paradigmatic perspective will require further terminological elaboration.

2 Terminology and conceptual structure

In this section I present the 16–20 key terms (somewhat subjectively harvested from the texts) found in each article, as a way of studying the terminology and conceptual structure of the materials.

Kecskés

In his analysis of adult L2 pragmatic competence (the focus of his paper), Kecskés uses quite a few terms, naturally, from the domain of pragmatics and L2 development. These terms are:

adult sequential bilinguals
appropriateness
bidirectional influence
bilingual pragmatic competence
conceptual socialization
consciousness
cross-linguistic influence
figurative language
formulaic language
individual control

individual will
legitimate peripheral participation
metalinguistic awareness
non-native speakers
pragmalinguistic transfer
pragmatic transfer
situation-bound utterances
sociopragmatic factors
sociopragmatic transfer
subjectivity

Central to Kecskés' account is the notion that adult second language learners show a kind of reflectivity and 'consciousness' (notice also the terms *individual control, individual will, metalinguistic awareness,* and *subjectivity*) absent in child learners. It would be interesting to develop the mostly anecdotal evidence for this presented in Kecskés' account into some experimental paradigm.

Chan, Lowie & de Bot

These authors apply dynamic systems theory to test whether input outside the classroom helps stimulate vocabulary development (it does) and use the following terms.

dynamic systems theory	*quantitative input*
input	*reading ability*
language modeling	*speaking ability*
learning rate	*variability*
lexical sophistication	*vocabulary development*
listening ability	*vocabulary learning*
non-authentic context	*writing ability*
proficiency	*writing production*

Endesfelder Quick, Lieven & Tomasello

In this paper a psycholinguistic perspective is adopted, and a comparative paradigm is put forward involving two language pairs that differ in their structural similarity. The authors use the following terms:

Accommodation Hypothesis	*function words*
balanced competence	*home mixers*
code-mixing	*Grammatical feature spell-out hypothesis*
communicative strategy	*language strategy*
comprehension	*lexical access*
content words	*matrix language*
cross-linguistic priming	*production*
cross-linguistic transfer	*shared representation*
dominance	*structural similarity*
frequency	*underlying syntactic representation*

Structural similarity appears to play a role, the data in this paper suggest, supporting much other research. It is also possible that the practice or 'language strategy' of mixing at home favours mixing in an experimental setting as well.

Bellay

This multiple case study involving a single family (the author's own) shows the advantage of detailed ethnographic knowledge to answer an otherwise almost intractable question: do specific phrases picked up from nursery rhymes, songs, stories, and children's television shows influence children's bilingual speech? Bellay uses the following terms.

adapted reuse	*One-Person-One-Language strategy*
convergence	*oral narrative translation*
crosslinguistic influence	*rhyme*
dual cultural knowledge	*rhythm*
formulaic language	*scripted dialogue*
grammatical parallelism	*situation-bound utterances*
input	*verbatim borrowing*
linguistic repertoire	*verbatim quote*
mental corpus theory	*verbatim repetition*

Bellay uses the term *convergence* in a special way: 'The notion of *convergence*, the idea that children imitate members of the surrounding speech community, motivated by a desire to sound like them and be recognised as belonging to that community [...]'. Typically, a term such as *accommodation* has been used in such cases. There is a link to Kecskés' paper in that formulaic language plays an important role in the argument.

Wasserscheidt

Here, a broad framework is sketched in which several of the constraints proposed in the code-switching literature are argued to follow from more general principles of construction grammar. Wasserscheidt uses the following terms:

Bilingual Production Model	*language tags*
calque	*loan translation*
composite structure	*matrix language discussion*
construction grammar	*Matrix Language Frame Model*
Dual Language Model	*schematicity*
grammatical constraints	*standard language bias*
Inhibitory Control Model	*transference*
language marking	*usage*

As such this approach is very similar to what we find in the generative literature, where numerous attempts have been made to formulate 'null' theories of constraints on code-mixing (MacSwan 1999). The great advantage of Wasserscheidt's approach is that the schematicity and 'unit' character of many (although by no means all) code-mixes is neatly accounted for in such a model. Wasserscheidt struggles, as do other authors, with the problem of language distance and similarity, which will need to find a natural operationalization in his framework.

Hakimov

Hakimov studies whether frequency and word repetition can predict the placement of switches in adpositional structures in Russian-German code-mixing. To some extent, his work is in the same line as Wasserscheidt's, and supports it with quantitative results from a large corpus. The author employs the following terminology:

alternation	*lexicogrammatical pattern*
code-mixing	*Linear Fusion Hypothesis*
code-switching	*matrix*
cognates	*mental lexicon*
congruence	*nonce character*
conventionalisation	*online language production*
co-occurrence	*priming*
frequency	*probabilistic information*
holistic unit	*switch placement*
insertion	*word repetition*

Hakimov studies the lexical items the bilingual speaker was exposed to in the prior discourse, the general frequency of the words used, and which word combinations occur. All these factors help determine where an actual switch takes place.

3 Perspectives

What the papers share, in spite of the different topics and speaker populations covered, is a general commitment to usage- and unit-based, rather than rule- and formal grammar-based, approaches. This is in line with the general orientation of Cognitive Linguistics. Terminology from this framework includes the following terms in these papers, at first glance from the lists above:

(co-occurrence) frequency	*lexicogrammatical pattern*
conventionalization	*probabilistic information*
formulaic language	*schematicity*
holistic unit	*situation-bound utterances*
language strategy	

What is further needed, then, is a fairly standard vocabulary for the broad field of language contact. Particular attention would need to be paid, I think, to terms for talking about language distance and about the precise forms that convergence may take.

References

MacSwan, Jeff. 1999. *A minimalist approach to intrasentential code switching*. New York: Routledge.
Muysken, Pieter. 1984. Linguistic dimensions of language contact: The state of the art in interlinguistics. *Revue Québecoise de Linguistique* 14(1). 49–76.

Index

Printed in Great Britain
by Amazon